CONTENTS

CONTENTS

PREFACE

STUDY TEXT

The study text is written in a practical and interactive style:

- key terms and concepts are clearly defined
- all topics are illustrated with practical examples with clearly worked solutions
- frequent practice activities throughout the chapters ensure that what you have learnt is regularly reinforced

WORKBOOK

The workbook comprises three main elements:

A question bank of key techniques to give additional practice and reinforce the work covered in each chapter. The questions are divided into their relevant chapters and students may either attempt these questions as they work through the study text, or leave some or all of these until they have completed the study text as a sort of final revision of what they have studied.

A mock simulation to give you practice at tackling this part of your assessment.

Two mock examinations which closely reflect the type of examination students may expect.

STANDARDS OF COMPETENCE

Unit commentary

This unit is concerned with how organisations record, analyse and report current and future costs and revenue data for use within the organisation. You will need to know that organisations build up costs and revenues in different ways. The way costs are recorded vary with the type of industry as well as the measurement rules chosen by the organisation. You have to understand the meaning and consequence of these different ways of recording costs and revenues and be able to apply them in relevant circumstances.

There are three elements. The first element focuses on direct costs and revenues, the second on overheads. You will need to apply both types of cost to the reporting of the organisation's expenses. In addition, you will need to apply both types of costing to the recording and analysing of unit and departmental costs. The third element is concerned with using cost and revenue information to help organisations make decisions. You will need to know about cost behaviour and apply it appropriately to managerial decisions for both short- and long-term planning purposes.

Elements contained within this unit are:

Element 6.1

Record and analyse information relating to direct costs and revenues

Element 6.2

Record and analyse information relating to the allocation, apportionment and absorption of overhead costs

Element 6.3

Prepare and evaluate estimates of costs and revenues

Knowledge and understanding

To perform this unit effectively you will need to know and understand

		Chapter
	The business environment	
1	The nature and purpose of internal reporting (Elements 6.1, 6.2 & 6.3)	1
2	Management information requirements (Elements 6.1, 6.2 & 6.3)	1
3	Maintaining an appropriate cost accounting system (Elements 6.1 & 6.2)	1
	Accounting techniques	
4	Recording of cost and revenue data in the accounting records (Elements 6.1 & 6.2)	2, 8
5	Methods of stock control and valuation including First In First Out, Last In First Out and Weighted Average Cost (Element 6.1)control (Element 4.1)	2
6	Methods for and calculation of payments for labour (Element 6.1)	3
7	Procedures and documentation relating to expenses (Elements 6.1 & 6.2)4.1)	4
8	Bases of allocating and apportioning indirect costs to responsibility centres: direct and step down methods (Element 6.2)	5
9	Marginal versus absorption costing for costing and reporting purposes (Elements 6.1 & 6.2)(Element 4.2)	9
10	The arbitrary nature of overhead apportionments (Element 6.2)	5
11	Bases of absorption (Element 6.2)	5
12	Calculation of product and service cost (Elements 6.1, 6.2 & 6.3)	1, 6, 7, 9
13	Analysis of the effect of changing activity levels on unit costs (Elements 6.1, 6.2 & 6.3)	1, 5, 10
14	Methods of presenting information in written reports (Element 6.3)	Throughout
15	The identification of fixed, variable and semi-variable costs and their use in cost recording, cost reporting and cost analysis (Elements 6.1, 6.2 & 6.3)	1, 10
16	Cost-volume-profit analysis (Element 6.3)	10
17	The identification of limiting factors (Element 6.3)	10
18	Methods of project appraisal: payback and discounted cash flow methods (NPV and IRR) (Element 6.3)	11
	Accounting principles and theory	
19	Relationship between the materials costing system and the stock control system (Element 6.1)	2, 8
20	Relationship between the labour costing system and the payroll accounting system (Element 6.2)	3, 8
21	Relationship between the accounting system and the expenses costing system (Elements 6.1 & 6.2)	4, 8
22	Marginal costing (Elements 6.1 & 6.3)	9
23	Absorption costing (Elements 6.2 & 6.3)	9

		Chapter
24	Cost behaviour (Element 6.3)	1
25	The principles of discounted cash flow (Element 6.3)	11

The organisation

26	Costing systems appropriate to the organisation: job, batch, unit and process costing systems (Elements 6.1, 6.2 & 6.3)	6, 7
27	The sources of information for revenue and costing data (Elements 6.1, 6.2 & 6.3)	2, 3, 4, 5, 8

Element 6.1 Record and analyse information relating to direct costs and revenues

Performance criteria

In order to perform this element successfully you need to:

		Chapter
A	Identify **direct costs** in accordance with the organisation's costing procedures	1, 2, 3, 4, 6, 7
B	Record and analyse information relating to direct costs	1, 2, 3, 4, 6, 7, 8
C	Calculate direct costs in accordance with the organisation's policies and procedures	2, 3, 4, 6, 7
D	Check cost information for **stocks** against usage and stock control practices	2
E	Resolve or refer queries to the appropriate person	Throughout

Range statement

Performance in this element relates to the following contexts

Direct costs

- Materials
- Direct labour costs

Stocks

- Raw materials
- Part-finished goods
- Finished goods

Element 6.2 Record and analyse information relating to the allocation, apportionment and absorption of overhead costs

Performance criteria

In order to perform this element successfully you need to:

		Chapter
A	Identify **overhead costs** in accordance with the organisation's procedures	4
B	Attribute overhead costs to production and service cost centres in accordance with agreed **bases of allocation and apportionment**	5
C	Calculate overhead absorption rates in accordance with agreed **bases of absorption**	5
D	Record and analyse information relating to overhead costs in accordance with the organisation's procedures	4, 5, 6, 7, 8
E	Make adjustments for under and over recovered overhead costs in accordance with established procedures	5
F	Review methods of allocation, apportionment and absorption at regular intervals in discussions with senior staff and ensure agreed changes to methods are implemented	5
G	Consult staff working in operational departments to resolve any queries in overhead cost data	Throughout

Range statement

Performance in this element relates to the following contexts

Direct costs

- Fixed
- Variable
- Semi-variable

Bases of allocation and apportionment

- Direct methods
- Step down methods

Bases of absorption

- Labour hour methods
- Machine hour methods

Element 6.3 Prepare and evaluate estimates of costs and revenues

Performance criteria

In order to perform this element successfully you need to:

		Chapter
A	Identify information relevant to estimating current and future revenues and costs	10
B	Prepare **estimates** of future income and costs	10, 11
C	Calculate the effects of variations in capacity on product costs	10
D	Analyse critical factors affecting costs and revenues using appropriate accounting techniques and draw clear conclusions from the analysis	10
E	State any assumptions used when evaluating future costs and revenues	10, 11
F	Identify and evaluate options and solutions for their contribution to organisational goals	10, 11
G	**Present** recommendations to appropriate people in a clear and concise way and supported by a clear rationale	10

Range statement

Performance in this element relates to the following contexts

Estimates

- Short-term decisions
  - Break-even analysis
  - Margin of safety
  - Target profit
  - Profit volume ratio
  - Limiting factors
- Long-term decisions
  - Project appraisal using payback and discounted cash flow methods

Methods of presentation

- Verbal presentation
- Written reports

Present value factor = $\frac{1}{(r+r)^n}$

Where r = discount rate
n = number of periods until payment

PRESENT VALUE TABLES

Discount rate (r)

Periods (n)	1%	2%	3%	4%	5%	6%	7%	8%	9%	10%	
1	0.990	0.980	0.971	0.962	0.952	0.943	0.935	0.926	0.917	0.909	1
2	0.980	0.961	0.943	0.925	0.907	0.890	0.873	0.857	0.842	0.826	2
3	0.971	0.942	0.915	0.889	0.864	0.840	0.816	0.794	0.772	0.751	3
4	0.961	0.924	0.888	0.855	0.823	0.792	0.763	0.735	0.708	0.683	4
5	0.951	0.906	0.863	0.822	0.784	0.747	0.713	0.681	0.650	0.621	5
6	0.942	0.888	0.837	0.790	0.746	0.705	0.666	0.630	0.596	0.564	6
7	0.933	0.871	0.813	0.760	0.711	0.665	0.623	0.583	0.547	0.513	7
8	0.923	0.853	0.789	0.731	0.677	0.627	0.582	0.540	0.502	0.467	8
9	0.914	0.837	0.766	0.703	0.645	0.592	0.544	0.500	0.460	0.424	9
10	0.905	0.820	0.744	0.676	0.614	0.558	0.508	0.463	0.422	0.386	10
11	0.896	0.804	0.722	0.650	0.585	0.527	0.475	0.429	0.388	0.350	11
12	0.887	0.788	0.701	0.625	0.557	0.497	0.444	0.397	0.356	0.319	12
13	0.879	0.773	0.681	0.601	0.530	0.469	0.415	0.368	0.326	0.290	13
14	0.870	0.758	0.661	0.577	0.505	0.442	0.388	0.340	0.299	0.263	14
15	0.861	0.743	0.642	0.555	0.481	0.417	0.362	0.315	0.275	0.239	15

(n)	11%	12%	13%	14%	15%	16%	17%	18%	19%	20%	
1	0.901	0.893	0.885	0.877	0.870	0.862	0.855	0.847	0.840	0.833	1
2	0.812	0.797	0.783	0.769	0.756	0.743	0.731	0.718	0.706	0.694	2
3	0.731	0.712	0.693	0.675	0.658	0.641	0.624	0.609	0.593	0.579	3
4	0.659	0.636	0.613	0.592	0.572	0.552	0.534	0.516	0.499	0.482	4
5	0.593	0.567	0.543	0.519	0.497	0.476	0.456	0.437	0.419	0.402	5
6	0.535	0.507	0.480	0.456	0.432	0.410	0.390	0.370	0.352	0.335	6
7	0.482	0.452	0.425	0.400	0.376	0.354	0.333	0.314	0.296	0.279	7
8	0.434	0.404	0.376	0.351	0.327	0.305	0.285	0.266	0.249	0.233	8
9	0.391	0.361	0.333	0.308	0.284	0.263	0.243	0.225	0.209	0.194	9
10	0.352	0.322	0.295	0.270	0.247	0.227	0.208	0.191	0.176	0.162	10
11	0.317	0.287	0.261	0.237	0.215	0.195	0.178	0.162	0.148	0.135	11
12	0.286	0.257	0.231	0.208	0.187	0.168	0.152	0.137	0.124	0.112	12
13	0.258	0.229	0.204	0.182	0.163	0.145	0.130	0.116	0.104	0.093	13
14	0.232	0.205	0.181	0.160	0.141	0.125	0.111	0.099	0.088	0.078	14
15	0.209	0.183	0.160	0.140	0.123	0.108	0.095	0.084	0.074	0.065	15

1

PRINCIPLES OF COST ACCOUNTING

INTRODUCTION

The main aim of this chapter is to introduce you to Unit 6 Recording and Evaluating Costs and Revenues. Management accounting and management information are at the heart of this unit and we will be introducing these topics to you in this chapter. In order to find out how much something costs it is important that you are able to calculate a cost per unit. The cost of a unit of product is usually made up of materials, labour and overhead. These costs can be further analysed as direct, indirect, fixed, variable, semi-variable or stepped costs, that is to say that they are analysed according to how they behave or how they are classified. Cost classification and cost behaviour are very important topics and it is essential that you understand these concepts clearly. Much of what we are covering here is fundamental to this unit and you are likely to come across the ideas and techniques used as you progress through your Unit 6 studies – so pay careful attention!

KNOWLEDGE & UNDERSTANDING

- The nature and purpose of internal reporting (Elements 6.1, 6.2 and 6.3)
- Management information requirements (Elements 6.1, 6.2 and 6.3)
- Maintaining an appropriate cost accounting system (Elements 6.1 and 6.2)
- Calculation of product and service cost (Elements 6.1, 6.2 and 6.3)
- Analysis of the effect of changing activity levels on unit costs (Elements 6.1, 6.2 and 6.3)
- The identification of fixed, variable and semi-variable costs and their use in cost recording, cost reporting and cost analysis (Elements 6.1, 6.2 and 6.3)
- Cost behaviour (Element 6.3)

CONTENTS

PERFORMANCE CRITERIA

- Identify direct costs in accordance with the organisation's costing procedures (Element 6.1)
- Record and analyse information relating to direct costs (Element 6.1)

1 Financial accounting, management accounting and cost accounting

1.1 Introduction

Most business entities, whether large or small, generate large numbers of **different types of transaction**. To make sense of those transactions, they need to be **recorded, summarised and analysed**. In all businesses, it is the **accounts department** that performs these tasks.

From the raw data of the business's transactions, accountants provide **information for a wide range of interested parties**. Each party requires, however, slightly different information, dependent upon their interest in the business.

1.2 Financial accounting

Accountants provide information to **external groups**, such as the owners of the business and HM Revenue and Customs. This information tends to be presented as financial accounts. Financial accounts are a historic record of transactions which are presented in a standard format laid down in law. Such accounts are normally only produced once or twice a year.

Financial accounting could be described in simple terms as **keeping score**. Financial accounting is not, however, the only type of accounting. The other main type is management accounting, of which cost accounting is a major part.

1.3 Management accounting

The management accounting function of a business normally provides accounting information for **internal users**, such as the managers of the business. **Management accounting** compares actual results with predicted results and tries to use information to make further predictions about the future. It also provides information which managers can use to make decisions.

Management accounts can be produced in any format that is useful to the business and tend to be produced frequently, for instance every month. The important point about management accounts is that they contain the information that management require to run the business.

1.4 The aim of management accounting

The aim of management accounting is to assist management in the following areas.

- **Planning**
  Primarily through the preparation of annual budgets (short-term planning), but also through long-range strategic planning.

- **Co-ordinating**
  Planning enables all departments to be co-ordinated and to work together for the benefit of the entity. This avoids lack of goal congruence, i.e. individual managers who want good results for their department at the expense of the organisation as a whole.

- **Controlling**
  The comparison of actual results with the budget helps to identify areas where operations are not running according to plan. Investigating the causes, and acting on the results of that investigation, help to control the activities of the business.

- **Communicating**
  Preparing budgets that are distributed to department managers helps to communicate the aims of the entity to those managers.

- **Motivating**
  A tight but attainable budget communicated effectively should motivate managers (and staff) and improve their performance. If the target is too difficult, however, it is likely to demotivate and it is unlikely to be achieved (see later in this textbook).

1.5 What is useful management information?

For **management information** to be of use to a particular group of managers, it must have the following attributes:

- **Relevance to their responsibilities**. For example, a production manager will be primarily concerned with information about stocks, production levels, production performance and machine loads within his particular department. He is not concerned with the problems of other departments unless they specifically affect his department.
- **Relevance to any particular decision**. Management must have the relevant information to be able to identify areas where decisions must be made, upon which to base those decisions.
- **Timely production**. Information has to be up-to-date to be of any value.
- **Value.** There is no benefit in producing information if it is not of value to the enterprise. If information is produced which has no effect on the decisions made by management, then it has no value to the business and should not be produced.

1.6 Cost accounting

Cost accounting is usually a large part of management accounting. As its name suggests, it is concerned with **establishing costs**. It developed within manufacturing businesses where costs are most difficult to isolate and analyse.

Financial accounts give totals of costs and revenues. They do not show, for example:

(a) the amount of costs and profit on each unit of product or service provided

(b) the amount of cost and/or revenue attributable to each manager.

A **cost accounting system** will provide sufficiently detailed information concerning both historic and projected costs and revenues to enable analyses such as these to be carried out.

1.7 The aim of cost accounting

Cost accounting is primarily directed at providing the **required information for management**, whether on a routine basis, or on an ad hoc basis to enable management to perform the functions of **planning, control** and **decision making.** To that end, cost accounting is concerned with:

(a) determining costs and profits during a control period

(b) valuing stocks of raw materials, work in progress and finished goods, and controlling stock levels

(c) preparing budgets, forecasts and other control data for a forthcoming control period

(d) creating a reporting system which enables managers to take corrective action where necessary to control costs

(e) providing information for decision-making.

Items (a) and (b) are traditional **cost accounting roles**; (c) to (e) extend into management accounting.

Cost accounting is not confined to the environment of manufacturing, although it is in this area that it is most fully developed. **Service industries, central and local government, and even accountancy and legal practices** make profitable use of cost accounting information. Furthermore, it is not restricted purely to manufacturing and operating costs, but also to administration, selling and distribution and research and development.

Be prepared for non-manufacturing scenarios in the central assessments.

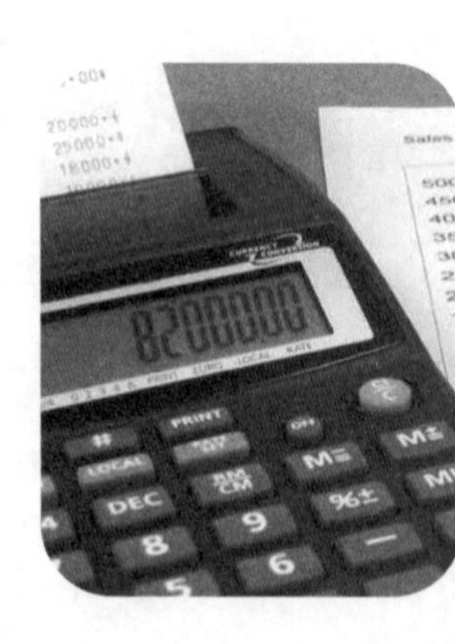

2 Calculating a cost per unit

2.1 Why we need to calculate a cost per unit

As mentioned above, cost accounting is important for a variety of reasons. In Unit 6 it is vital that you can calculate the cost per unit of a business' output. This can be used for the following purposes:

(a) decision making – e.g. pricing products, whether to accept an order

(b) control – e.g. to see if costs are higher than expected

(c) financial reporting – e.g. stock valuation

(d) planning – e.g. budgeting future costs.

2.2 Cost units

The idea of a cost unit will mean different things to different businesses but always looks at what the business produces.

- A car manufacturer will want to determine the cost of each car and probably different components as well.
- In a printing firm, the cost unit would be the specific customer order.
- For a paint manufacturer, the unit would be a litre (or a thousand litres) of paint.
- An accountancy firm will want to know the costs incurred for each client. To help with this it is common to calculate the cost per hour of chargeable time spent by staff.
- A hospital might wish to calculate the cost per patient treated, the cost of providing a bed for each day, the cost of an operation and so on.

2.3 Cost centres

A **cost centre** is a small part of a business in respect of which costs may be determined and then related to cost units.

Terminology varies from organisation to organisation, but the small part of a business could be a whole department or merely a sub-division of a department. A number of departments together would comprise a function. Thus a cost centre could be a location, function or item of equipment or a group or combination of any of these.

It is important to recognise that cost centre costs are necessary for control purposes, as well as for relating costs to cost units.

▷ ACTIVITY 1 

Suggest **ONE** suitable cost unit and **TWO** cost centres for a college of further education.

[Answer on p. 18]

3 Cost classification

3.1 Types of cost classification

Costs can be **classified** (collected into logical groups) in many ways. The particular classification selected will depend upon the purpose for which the resulting analysed data will be used, for example:

Purpose	Classification
Cost control	By type – materials, labour, other costs (overheads)
Cost accounts	By relationship to cost units – direct/indirect costs
Budgeting, decision making	By behaviour – fixed/variable costs

The first classification will be considered in detail in later chapters. The latter two types are now considered in more detail.

3.2 Direct costs

DEFINITION

Direct costs are those which can be related directly to a cost unit.

Examples of direct costs might be:

- **Business**: furniture manufacturer

  Cost unit: chair

  Direct costs = cost of wood and screws used (direct material cost), cost of manufacturing labour hours per chair (direct labour costs), royalty payable as a result of using the particular chair design (direct expense)

- **Business**: hotel

  Cost unit: guest-night

  Direct costs: cost of meals served, room-cleaning costs, laundry costs, costs of other services provided directly to the guest.

3.3 Indirect costs

DEFINITION

Indirect costs cannot be identified directly with a cost unit and are often referred to as **'overheads'**.

Examples of indirect costs might be:

- **Business**: furniture manufacturer

  If the chair legs are turned on a lathe, the oil used to lubricate the machine would be a production overhead because the oil cannot be traced directly to a specific cost unit.

  The salaries of the salesmen who promote and sell the chairs to retail outlets would be a non-production selling overhead.

- **Business**: hotel

  The costs of reception and other general staff together with the maintenance of the hotel would be overheads of this service business, as they are not incurred specifically for an individual guest-night.

3.4 Production and non-production indirect costs

A distinction needs to be made between indirect costs (overheads) incurred in the production process (production costs) and indirect costs (overheads) incurred outside the production process (non-production costs).

□ DEFINITION

Production indirect costs (production overheads) are indirect costs that are involved in the production process.

An example would be the salary of the production supervisor. His salary is an indirect cost because it cannot be related to a specific cost unit. But it is a production cost because it is related to the production process.

□ DEFINITION 

Non-production indirect costs (non-production overheads) are indirect costs involved in converting finished goods into revenue. They include:

(a) administrative overheads (e.g. executive salaries and office costs)
(b) marketing, selling and distribution overheads.

3.5 Direct and indirect costs

The basic classification of costs may be illustrated as follows:

	£
Direct costs	
Direct materials	250,000
Direct labour	120,000
Direct expenses (e.g. royalty payable per unit produced)	10,000
Prime cost (= Total of direct costs)	380,000
Indirect production cost (production overhead)	
(e.g. production supervisor's salary; machine oil)	25,000
Production cost	405,000
Indirect non-production cost	
(e.g. administration overhead; selling overhead)	45,000
Total cost	450,000

Note that the **prime cost** of production is the total of direct materials, direct labour and direct expenses.

ACTIVITY 2

(a) Explain briefly the difference between a direct cost and an indirect cost, giving an example of each.

(b) For each of the following items, state whether they are direct or indirect costs:

(i) sheet steel for a motor-car manufacturer

(ii) machine operators' wages for a golf-ball manufacturer

(iii) supervisors' wages for a golf-ball manufacturer

(iv) chargeable time in an accountancy practice

(v) factory rates for an oven manufacturer

(vi) production royalties for a mining company

(vii) electricity for a brewery

(viii) hire plant for a building contractor in a long-term contract

(ix) the audit fee of an oil company

(x) glue for a furniture-maker.

[Answer on p. 18]

4 Cost behaviour

4.1 Introduction

For budgeting purposes, management needs to be able to predict **how costs will vary with differing levels of activity** (usually measured by the number of cost units arising in the period). For example, if a furniture manufacturer expected to produce 1,000 chairs in a particular month, what should he budget for the costs of wood and screws, manufacturing labour, oil, selling costs, factory heat and light, manager's salaries, etc? How would these costs differ (if at all) if he expected to produce 2,000 chairs?

Similarly, the manager of a hotel will want to know how the budgets for costs of meals, cleaning costs, staff costs, hotel running costs, etc will depend upon guest-nights sold during a particular period.

Managers need to determine the **behaviour of the differing costs involved**. There are four basic patterns of behaviour by which costs (both indirect and direct) can be classified: variable costs, fixed costs, stepped costs and semi-variable (or mixed) costs.

4.2 Variable costs

DEFINITION

Variable costs are those that vary (usually assumed in direct proportion) with changes in level of activity of the cost centre to which they relate (e.g. output volume).

Therefore, if activity levels increase, the variable cost increases in proportion.

EXAMPLE

Material X is used in a product. If 1,000 units of the product are made then £5,000 of Material X is used. If 2,000 units of the product are made, what is the cost of Material X used?

Solution

2,000 units x £5 = £10,000

The variable cost per unit **may not remain constant over a wide range**. It may be possible in the above example to obtain discounts for large purchases of material, reducing the cost per unit.

Note that variable costs can be direct (e.g. materials) or indirect (e.g. cost of electricity used in making the product).

4.3 Fixed costs

DEFINITION

Fixed costs accrue with the passage of time and are not affected by changes in activity level. They are also known as **period costs.**

EXAMPLE

A hotel pays rent of £10,000 per week. What is the rental cost for 1,000 guests and 2,000 guests?

Solution

Guests	Hotel rent
1,000	£10,000
2,000	£10,000

As with variable costs, fixed costs may be direct (e.g. direct labour would be fixed if production workers are salaried) or indirect (e.g. factory rent). Direct costs are usually assumed to be variable unless otherwise specified.

▷ ACTIVITY 3

Which of the following best describes a 'pure' fixed cost?

A cost which:

A represents a fixed proportion of total costs
B remains at the same level up to a particular level of output
C has a direct relationship with output
D remains at the same level when output changes.

[Answer on p. 18]

4.4 Stepped costs

Stepped costs are costs that remain fixed up to a particular level of activity, but which rise to a higher (fixed) level if activity goes beyond that range.

For example, a firm may pay £10,000 per year to rent a factory in which they can produce up to 1 million units of product per year. However, if demand increases to more than 1 million units a second factory may be required, in which case the cost of factory rent may step up to, say, £20,000 per year.

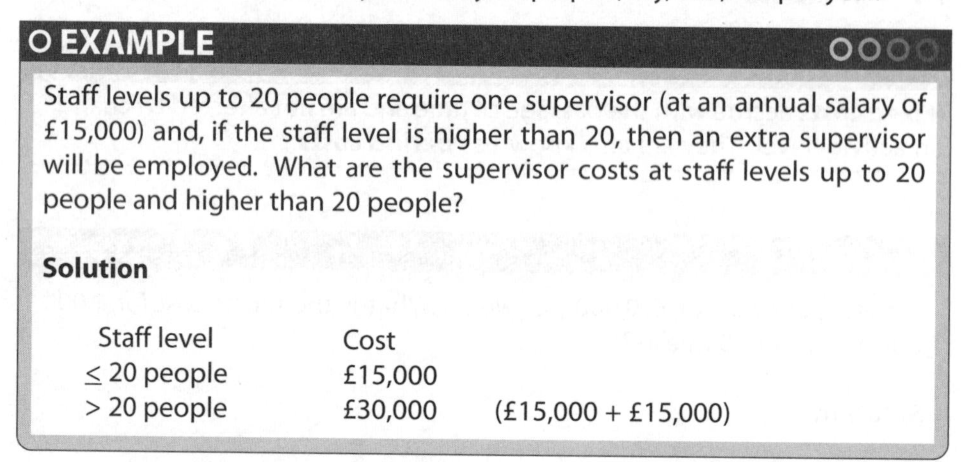

O EXAMPLE

Staff levels up to 20 people require one supervisor (at an annual salary of £15,000) and, if the staff level is higher than 20, then an extra supervisor will be employed. What are the supervisor costs at staff levels up to 20 people and higher than 20 people?

Solution

Staff level	Cost	
≤ 20 people	£15,000	
> 20 people	£30,000	(£15,000 + £15,000)

4.5 Semi-variable (or mixed) costs

□ DEFINITION

Semi-variable (or mixed) costs contain both a fixed and a variable element.

When output is nil, costs are still incurred, like fixed costs: but they also increase, like variable costs, as output increases.

O EXAMPLE

For **telephone charges**, the fixed element is the quarterly rental and the variable element is the charge for the calls made. The quarterly rental is £80 and calls are charged at 50p each. What is the quarterly telephone bill for no calls, 500 calls and 1,000 calls?

Solution

Number of calls made	Telephone bill
0	£80
500	£330 (£80 + 500 x 50p)
1,000	£580 (£80 + 1,000 x 50p)

4.6 Graphical representation of cost behaviour

The four different types of cost behaviour are illustrated below.

Variable costs

Examples: **Direct materials, direct labour costs**

Fixed costs

Examples: **Managerial salaries**

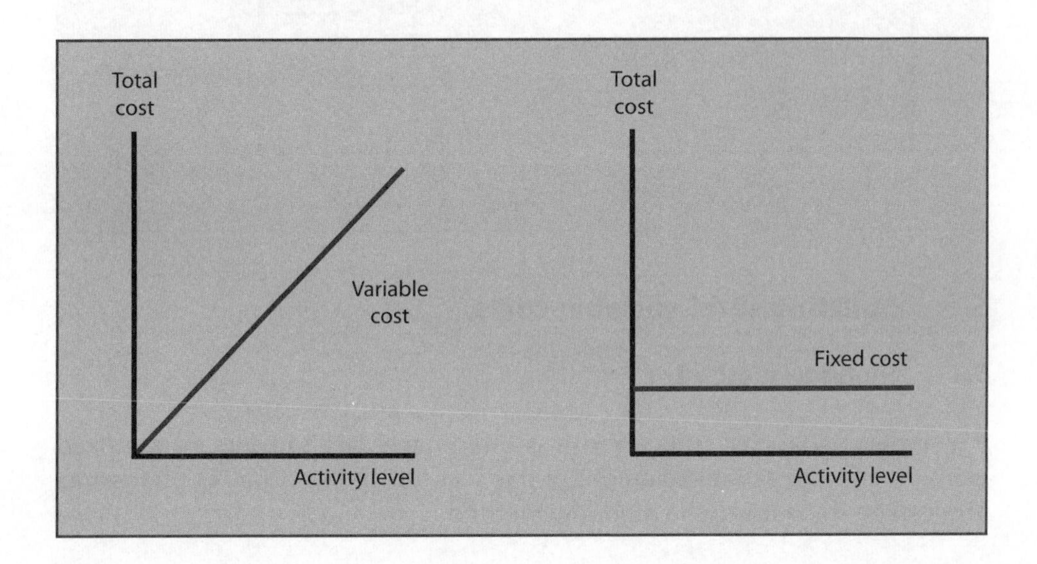

Semi-variable costs		**Stepped costs**	
Examples:	**Power costs** (electricity, gas, etc)	Examples:	**Stock storage costs** (extra warehouses required as output increases)
	Salesmen's salaries (basic + bonus based on selling activity level)		**Hospital staff costs** (need to hire agency nurses)

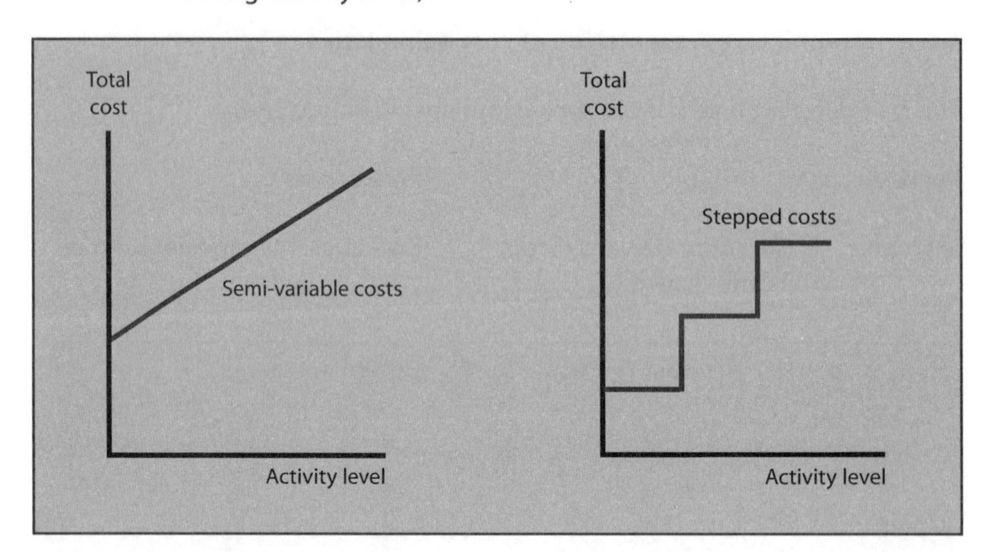

5 Splitting semi-variable costs

5.1 High/low method

If a semi-variable cost is incurred, it is often necessary to estimate the fixed element and the variable element of the cost for the purposes of budgeting. This can be done using the high/low method.

O EXAMPLE

A factory has incurred the following power costs in the last six months with different levels of production in each month:

Month	*Production in units*	*Power cost*
		£
January	20,000	18,000
February	16,000	16,500
March	18,000	17,200
April	24,000	20,500
May	22,000	19,400
June	19,000	17,600

(i) What are the fixed and variable elements of the power cost?

(ii) If production of 30,000 units is anticipated next month, what is the expected power cost?

Solution

Step 1

Find the highest and lowest levels of production and their related power costs.

		Units	Cost
			£
High	April	24,000	20,500
Low	February	16,000	16,500

Step 2

Find the variable cost element by determining the increased power cost per unit between highest and lowest production levels.

		Units	Cost
			£
High	April	24,000	20,500
Low	February	16,000	16,500
		8,000	4,000

The power cost has increased by £4,000 for an increase of 8,000 units of production. The variable power cost is therefore:

$$\frac{£4,000}{8,000} = 50 \text{ pence per unit}$$

Step 3

Using either the highest or the lowest production level find the fixed cost element by deducting the variable cost from the total cost.

		£
April	Total cost	20,500
	Variable cost 24,000 x 0.5	12,000
Fixed cost		8,500
February	Total cost	16,500
	Variable cost 16,000 x 0.5	8,000
Fixed cost		8,500

Step 4

Use the fixed cost and variable cost figures to estimate the total power cost if production were 30,000 units.

	£
Variable cost 30,000 x 0.5	15,000
Fixed cost	8,500
Total cost	23,500

When calculating the variable and fixed elements, make sure that you pick the highest and lowest **production levels** and not the highest and lowest **costs**, which will not necessarily be the same.

▷ ACTIVITY 4

The total production cost for making 10,000 units was £12,000 and the total production cost for making 25,000 was £21,000. What is the full production cost for making 40,000 units?

[Answer on p. 18]

6 Changing activity levels

6.1 Introduction

The behavioural characteristics of the various costs of producing cost units can be used to plan the activities of a business. In particular the distinction between fixed, variable, stepped and semi-variable costs can be used to determine the total cost of production and cost per unit at various activity levels.

O EXAMPLE

A manufacturing business has variable production costs of £3 per unit and fixed costs of £60,000. A further cost is the salary of the factory supervisor of £18,000 per annum. If more than 100,000 units of the product are made then an additional factory supervisor must be employed at the same salary.

What is the total cost of production and the cost per unit at the following production levels:

(i) 60,000 units

(ii) 90,000 units

(iii) 120,000 units?

Solution

		Production level	
	60,000 units	*90,000 units*	*120,000 units*
	£	£	£
Variable production costs			
60,000 x £3	180,000		
90,000 x £3		270,000	
120,000 x £3			360,000
Fixed costs	60,000	60,000	60,000
Supervisor's salary	18,000	18,000	36,000
Total production cost	258,000	348,000	456,000
Cost per unit	£4.30	£3.87	£3.80

As some of the costs are fixed then the cost per unit falls as the production quantity increases, as the fixed costs are spread over a higher number of units of production.

Note the tabular layout of the solution – use this whenever you have to do repeated computations for different activity levels, products etc.

▷ ACTIVITY 5

A manufacturing business has variable production costs of £3 per unit and fixed costs of £50,000. Theses include rent of £18,000 per annum. If more than 50,000 units of the product are made, then additional floor space must be rented at a cost of £20,000 per annum.

What is the total cost of production and the cost per unit at the following production levels:
(i) 40,000 units
(ii) 50,000 units
(iii) 60,000 units?

[Answer on p. 19]

7 Cost coding

7.1 Introduction

Cost accounting involves the **detailed analysis of costs** – between cost centres and cost units and between the various types of direct and indirect costs (labour, materials, production overheads, selling, administration, etc).

To facilitate this analysis, a system of **cost coding** is likely to be devised by the organisation. As costs are incurred and recorded within the cost accounts, they will be allocated a code according to the system set out in the costing system manual. For example, the purchases clerk enters the appropriate code on an invoice received for materials before passing it to the data processing department for input. Similarly, timesheets and other documentation used for the initial recording of labour time will generally have a space for coding.

Thus the costs are **analysed accurately and unambiguously at source**, allowing easy production of cost centre and product cost information.

7.2 The structure of cost codes

The simplest form of code structure would be **sequential** where cost, stock and other types of items to be coded are listed and codes allocated in numerical sequence. This is not very useful for sorting and analysis purposes and therefore most coding systems will have some degree of connection between the code and the item it represents.

7.3 Hierarchical systems

The most common structure of cost codes is hierarchical with the detail of the classification of the cost built up from left to right by the individual digits within the code.

For example, the code for the cost of a manager's time spent on a particular client's work in a firm of solicitors may be recorded under a code built up as follows:

4	=	Conveyancing department
42	=	Direct cost (within the conveyancing department, etc)
421	=	Chargeable employee time
4212	=	Managerial time
42123	=	Correspondence with client
42123ROB15	=	Client

This will allow **analysis of costs** to any level of detail required – by cost centre (using the first digit), by chargeable/non-chargeable time (using the third digit) through to analysis to client (using the last five digits/characters).

Note that the above coding system has used a **mix of numbers and alphabetical characters**. Often codes will be entirely numerical, as these are processed more efficiently on a computer.

7.4 Other code structures

Some items may not form part of a hierarchical structure, but may still have certain characteristics by which they may be grouped (e.g. stock items). An example is a faceted code where each digit or group of digits represents a different characteristic of an item.

EXAMPLE

An extract from a business's coding manual shows the following:

Factory cost centre	02
Administration cost centre	05
Direct materials	01
Direct labour	04

What is the cost code for:

(i) direct materials used in the factory?

(ii) direct labour in the administration department?

Solution

(i) 0201

(ii) 0504

7.5 Desirable qualities of a coding system

- **Simple to understand and use** – a sophisticated structure will be of little use if used inaccurately.
- **Flexible** – this allows the addition of extra items within the structure or minor changes of classification, etc.
- **Unique and comprehensive** – every item must have one, unique code.
- **Self-checking** – all numerical codes can have a 'check digit' at the end which will be related to the position and size of the digits in the rest of the code by some mathematical formula. This allows the computer to check the accuracy of the code.

If codes have some alphabetical element and if this relates directly to the item being coded, errors may be more easily **spotted by eye**; the solicitor's coding system included the first three letters of the client's name. If this was not compatible with the name written in full on the timesheet, for example, it could easily be spotted.

8 Test your knowledge

1 Define the terms:
- cost unit
- cost centre

and give examples from a business with which you are familiar.

2 Give an example of a cost unit for each of the following businesses:
- limestone quarry
- accountant's office (in practice)
- train service
- restaurant.

3 Planning, controlling and decision-making are features in which branch of accounting?

4 For cost accounting purposes costs are classified into which groups?

5 Give three examples of indirect costs or overheads that would be classed as fixed overheads.

[Answers on p. 19]

9 Summary

In this introductory chapter we looked at some of the basic principles and terminology used in cost and management accounting. Costs can be classified in a variety of different ways for different purposes. The basic classification is into materials, labour and expenses, each of which will be dealt with in detail in the following chapters. A further method of classification of costs is between direct and indirect costs. You need to be aware of the difference between cost units (individual units of a product or service for which costs can be separately ascertained) and cost centres (locations or functions in respect of which costs are accumulated).

For decision-making and budgeting purposes, it is often useful to distinguish costs according to their behaviour as production levels change. The basic classifications according to behaviour are fixed and variable costs although there are also stepped costs and semi-variable costs. The fixed and variable elements of semi-variable costs can be isolated using the high/low method. This is a very important technique – make sure that you have mastered it fully.

Finally, make sure that you can code costs according to the system of coding in operation – coding costs is a very common Unit 6 examination task.

Answers to chapter activities & 'test your knowledge' questions

ACTIVITY 1

Student hours	=	Cost unit
Computer room and library	=	Cost centres

ACTIVITY 2

(a) A **direct cost** is an item of cost that is traceable directly to a cost unit. A good example would be the cost of a bought-in component (e.g. an engine) for a motor car.

An **indirect cost** is a cost that either cannot be identified with any one finished unit, or is not traced to individual cost units because of the insignificance of the cost. Examples of indirect costs are rent and nails (the cost of which are too insignificant).

(b) (i) Direct
(ii) Direct
(iii) Indirect
(iv) Direct
(v) Indirect
(vi) Direct
(vii) Indirect
(viii) Direct
(ix) Indirect
(x) Indirect

ACTIVITY 3

D – Pure fixed costs remain exactly the same in total regardless of the activity level.

ACTIVITY 4

	£
Cost of 25,000 units	21,000
Less cost of 10,000 units	12,000
Difference = variable cost of 15,000 units	9,000

Variable cost per unit = $\frac{£9,000}{15,000}$ = 60p each

Fixed costs = total cost – variable costs
Fixed costs = £21,000 – £(25,000 x 0.6) = £6,000

Therefore total cost for 40,000

	£
Variable (40,000 x 0.6)	24,000
Fixed	6,000
	30,000

ACTIVITY 5

	Production level		
	40,000 units	*50,000 units*	*60,000 units*
	£	£	£
Variable production costs			
40,000 x £3	120,000		
50,000 x £3		150,000	
60,000 x £3			180,000
Fixed costs	50,000	50,000	50,000
Additional rentals	–	–	20,000
Total production cost	170,000	200,000	250,000
Cost per unit	£4.25	£4.00	£4.17

Test your knowledge

1 (a) **Cost unit**
A quantitative unit of product or service to which cost can be ascertained.

(b) **Cost centre**
A location, function activity or items of equipment to which costs can be allocated or apportioned.

2
- Per tonne.
- Per chargeable hour.
- Per passenger mile.
- Per meal or cover.

3 Management accounting.

4 Direct and indirect.

5
- Rent.
- Depreciation.
- Insurance.

MATERIAL COSTS

INTRODUCTION

One of the main elements of cost included in the total cost of a product is materials. In this chapter we are going to look at the different ways in which materials are valued when they are issued from stock to production and how these issues are recorded on a stores record card. We are also going to look at the procedures and documentation involved in the purchasing process before we go on to look at one of the most important aspects of the topic of materials, that of stock control. It is essential that organisations have the right quantity of stock available at the right time – we will be looking at a number of formulae that will help this to be achieved. There is a lot to take in as you work through this chapter, so if it takes you a long time or you feel you need to read through it again, don't worry. It is vital that you have a clear understanding of this topic as it will almost certainly be tested in the examination and assessment you will be facing.

KNOWLEDGE & UNDERSTANDING

- Recording of cost and revenue data in the accounting records (Elements 6.1 and 6.2)
- Methods of stock control and valuation including First In First Out, Last In First Out, and Weighted Average Cost (Element 6.1)
- Relationship between the materials costing system and the stock control system (Element 6.1)
- The sources of information for revenue and costing data (Elements 6.1, 6.2 and 6.3)

CONTENTS

PERFORMANCE CRITERIA

- Identify direct costs in accordance with the organisation's costing procedures (Element 6.1)
- Record and analyse information relating to direct costs (Element 6.1)
- Calculate direct costs in accordance with the organisation's policies and procedures (Element 6.1)
- Check cost information for stocks against usage and stock control practices (Element 6.1)

1 Calculating a cost per unit

As mentioned in Chapter 1, a key aspect of this unit is the need to be able to calculate a cost per unit for a product. A typical cost per unit could be written as follows:

	Cost / unit
	£
Direct labour cost	1.50
Direct material cost	3.20
Prime cost	4.70
Production overheads	4.30
Total cost per unit	9.00

This chapter looks first at how to calculate the direct material cost figure. The practicalities of managing materials are also covered.

2 Pricing issues of raw materials

2.1 Introduction

The cost of materials purchased will normally be derived from suppliers' invoices but, where many purchases have been made at differing prices, a decision has to be taken as to which cost is used when stock is issued to the user department (cost centre).

2.2 Methods of pricing

Various methods exist including:

(a) FIFO (first in, first out)
(b) LIFO (last in, first out)
(c) Weighed average (AVCO)
(d) Standard cost.

The choice of method will not only affect the charge to the user department for which the material is required, but also the value of the stock left in stores.

2.3 FIFO and LIFO methods

These systems attempt to reflect the movements of individual units in and out of stock under different assumptions:

DEFINITIONS

FIFO assumes that issues will be made from the oldest stock available, leaving the latest purchases in stock.

LIFO assumes that issues will be made from the newest stock available, leaving the earliest purchases in stock.

EXAMPLE

Sid makes the following purchases of Component X.

		Quantity	Unit price	
			£	£
Purchases:	10 January	50	1.00	50
	20 January	60	1.10	66
	30 January	40	1.25	50
		150		166

On 31 January Sid issues 60 units for use in production. No stock was held at the beginning of the month.

Calculate the value of closing stock and the cost of stock issued to production using:

(a) a FIFO basis, and

(b) a LIFO basis for January.

Solution

(a) Cost of issue FIFO

Under a FIFO (first in, first out) basis, the 60 units issued will comprise:

	£
50 units purchased 10 January @ £1.00	50
Balance of 10 units purchased 20 January @ £1.10	11
Cost of stock issued to production	61

Therefore closing stock on 31 January will comprise:

	£
Balance of 50 units purchased 20 January @ £1.10	55
40 units purchased 30 January @ £1.25	50
Closing stock FIFO	105

(b) Cost of issue LIFO

Under a LIFO (last in, first out) basis, the 60 units sold will comprise:

	£
40 units purchased 30 January @ £1.25	50
Balance of 20 units purchased 20 January @ £1.10	22
Cost of stock issued to production	72

Therefore the value of closing stock on 31 January will comprise:

	£
Balance of 40 units purchased 20 January @ £1.10	44
50 units purchased 10 January @ £1.00	50
Closing stock LIFO	94

This example illustrates the importance of stock valuation techniques in determining profit. The fact that closing stock is valued at £105 under FIFO and only £94 under LIFO means that Sid's reported profit will be £11 higher if he uses FIFO than if he uses LIFO.

Take care with FIFO not to issue stock before it is bought – for example if Sid had issued his 60 units to production on 25 January, the latest price paid up to that date was £1.10, at which the issue would be costed. The 40 units bought on 30 January would thus remain in stock at the end of January.

▷ ACTIVITY 1

A company is thinking of moving to an alternative basis of material costing and stock valuation. Projected movements in Material Y for August are as follows:

		Kilos	£
1 August	Opening stock	700	2,730
6 August	Receipt	600	2,280
9 August	Issue	1,000	
20 August	Receipt	300	1,320
25 August	Issue	400	

Required

Cost the issues of Material Y for August:

(a) on a LIFO basis

(b) on a FIFO basis

and determine closing stock values under each method.

(c) Using your results from (a) and (b), explain the difference in costings and stock values between the FIFO and LIFO methods.

[Answer on p. 51]

2.4 Comparison of FIFO and LIFO

FIFO is fairly easy to understand but it has the following disadvantages:

- In times of rapidly increasing prices, material may be charged out at an early and unrealistic price, resulting in the particular job showing an unusually large profit.
- Two jobs started on the same day may show a different cost for the same quantity of the same material.

Again, **LIFO** is simple to follow. The justification claimed for the LIFO method is that, by using the latest price for costing materials for jobs, the figure obtained is more likely to be in line with other costs and with selling prices.

As with FIFO, LIFO is a method whereby, in time, the total cost to jobs equals the total of purchases. These pricing methods relate to the cost office accounting only. So do not think that these methods influence the actual stock movements.

There are also disadvantages of LIFO:

- As for FIFO, two jobs started on the same day may show a different cost for the same quantity of the same material.
- Closing stocks will be shown at the earliest prices which means that in times of rapidly increasing or decreasing prices, the stock figure bears little resemblance to the current cost of replacement.

▷ ACTIVITY 2

(a) If raw material prices are subject to inflation, which method of valuing stocks will give the lowest profit?

(b) Explain the potential problem of using out of date prices under the FIFO method of stock valuation.

[Answer on p. 52]

2.5 Weighted average cost (AVCO) method

A weighted average cost takes account of the relative quantities purchased at different prices in the cost per unit. The weighted average cost is the total cost of the items in stock divided by the number of items in stock.

○ EXAMPLE ○○○○

A business made the following purchases of stock HJ during March:

5 March	100 units @ £2.40
12 March	120 units @ £2.50
28 March	80 units @ £2.80

There were 50 units of HJ in stock at the start of March valued at a cost of £2.20 per unit.

Two issues of HJ were made during the month of March:
10 March 100 units
20 March 110 units

Calculate the cost of the issues and the value of the closing stock units using the weighted average cost method.

Solution

Step 1

Find the value of the opening stock of HJ.

		Units	*Average price*	*Total*
			£	£
1 March	Opening stock	50	2.20	110

Step 2

Find the value of the purchase on 5 March. Total the value of all of the stocks then held and divide by the number of units to give the weighted average price.

		Units	*Average price*	*Total*
			£	£
1 March	Opening stock	50	2.20	110
5 March	Purchase	100	2.40	240
		150	2.33	350

The weighted average price is £350/150 units = £2.33.

Step 3

Price the issue on 10 March at the weighted average price of £2.33 per unit.

		Units	*Average price*	*Total*
			£	£
1 March	Opening stock	50	2.20	110
5 March	Purchase	100	2.40	240
		150	2.33	350
10 March	Issue	(100)	2.33	(233)
		50	2.33*	117

* Note that the average price is now actually £117/50 = £2.34. This change from £2.33 is due to rounding, and it is best to ignore it – it is the total units and £ value that will determine the average price for future issues.

Step 4

Find the cost of the purchase on 12 March and calculate the new weighted average price.

		Units	Average price	Total
			£	£
1 March	Opening stock	50	2.20	110
5 March	Purchase	100	2.40	240
		150	2.33	350
10 March	Issue	(100)	2.33	(233)
		50	2.33	117
12 March	Purchase	120	2.50	300
		170	2.45	417

Step 5

Price the issue on 20 March at the new weighted average price of £2.45 per unit.

		Units	Average price	Total
			£	£
1 March	Opening stock	50	2.20	110
5 March	Purchase	100	2.40	240
		150	2.33	350
10 March	Issue	(100)	2.33	(233)
		50	2.33	117
12 March	Purchase	120	2.50	300
		170	2.45	417
20 March	Issue	(110)	2.45	(270)
		60	2.45	147

Step 6

Find the total price of the purchase on 28 March and calculate the new weighted average price which is used to value the closing stock at the end of March.

		Units	Average price	Total
			£	£
1 March	Opening stock	50	2.20	110
5 March	Purchase	100	2.40	240
		150	2.33	350
10 March	Issue	(100)	2.33	(233)
		50	2.33	117
12 March	Purchase	120	2.50	300
		170	2.45	417

20 March	Issue	(110)	2.45	(270)
		60	2.45	147
28 March	Purchase	80	2.80	224
		140	2.65	371

The closing stock of 140 units is therefore valued at the new weighted average cost of £2.65 per unit giving a total value of £371.

You only need to calculate the weighted average cost after each purchase. This weighted average price is then used for each issue until a new purchase is made.

▷ ACTIVITY 3

(a) Define the FIFO and LIFO methods of pricing issues of materials to production.

(b) From the data given below, compute the costs of issues, and closing stock value, for Material No 1234, using the weighted average method of pricing issues.

September 1	Stock on hand	100 litres, valuation £100
September 18	Issue	60 litres
September 30	Receipt	40 litres, cost £1.20 per litre
October 12	Issue	60 litres
October 31	Receipt	80 litres, cost £1.30 per litre
November 4	Receipt	20 litres, cost £1.50 per litre
November 19	Issue	70 litres

[Answer on p. 52]

2.6 The stores record card

It is usual to record quantities of a stock item (and often stock values as well) on a **stores record card** (also called a **stores ledger card**). One such card is maintained for each different stock item, showing receipts of new stock from suppliers, issues of stock to production, and balance of stock remaining on hand.

Using the previous example of Sid, the stores record card might appear as follows for the month of January for the FIFO method.

EXAMPLE

FIFO basis

Stores Record Card

Material description: Component X

Code: X100

Date	Receipts			Issues			Balance		
	Qty	Unit price £	Total £	Qty	Unit price £	Total £	Qty	Unit price £	Total £
10 Jan	50	1.00	50.00				50	1.00	50.00
20 Jan	60	1.10	66.00				50	1.00	50.00
							60	1.10	66.00
							110		116.00
30 Jan	40	1.25	50.00				50	1.00	50.00
							60	1.10	66.00
							40	1.25	50.00
							150		166.00
31 Jan				50	1.00	50.00	50	1.10	55.00
				10	1.10	11.00	40	1.25	50.00
				60		61.00	90		105.00

ACTIVITY 4

Amp plc is a printing company specialising in producing accounting manuals. There is no formal stores accounting system in operation at present.

(a) You are asked, as a step towards improving this situation, to write up the following information on the stores record card given below using weighted average prices to value the issues.

Material: Paper – Code 1564A

Opening stock: 10,000 sheets – value £3,000

Purchases			Issues	
3 May	4,000 sheets	£1,600	6 May	7,000 sheets
12 May	10,000 sheets	£3,100	15 May	6,000 sheets
25 May	10,000 sheets	£3,200	22 May	7,200 sheets

(Calculations: weighted average to two decimal places of a £; value of issues to the nearest £.)

Stores Record Card
Material : Paper
Code: 1564A

Date	Details	Receipts		Issues			Stock		
		Sheets	£	Sheets	Price	£	Sheets	Price	£

(b) Amp has always held large quantities of paper in stock in case it should become difficult to obtain. Suggest TWO problems that this could create.

[Answer on p. 53]

3 The stores department

3.1 Function of the stores department

The stores or stock department is responsible for the receipt, storage, issue and recording of the raw materials used in the production process.

3.2 Receipt of goods

When raw materials are received from suppliers they will normally be delivered to the stores department. The stores personnel must check that the goods delivered are the ones that have been ordered, in the correct quantity, of the correct quality and in good condition.

3.3 Storage of materials

Once the materials have been received they must be stored until required by the production departments.

Storage of materials must be appropriate to their type. For example, foodstuffs must be stored at the correct temperature and wood must be stored in dry conditions. Storage should also be laid in such a manner that the correct materials can be accessed easily either manually or by machinery.

3.4 Issue of materials

When the production departments require raw materials for production, it is essential that the stores department can provide the correct quantity and quality of materials at the time they are required. This will require careful attention to stock control policies to ensure that the most efficient levels of stocks of raw materials are kept.

3.5 Recording of receipts and issues

In many organisations the stores department is also responsible for the recording of the quantities of raw materials that are received from suppliers and issued to the production departments. This normally takes place on the bin cards.

4 The materials control cycle

4.1 Introduction

Materials can often form the largest single item of cost for a business so it is essential that the material purchased is the most suitable for the intended purpose.

4.2 Control of purchasing

When goods are purchased they must be ordered, received by the stores department, recorded, issued to the manufacturing department that requires them and eventually paid for. This process needs a great deal of paperwork and strict internal controls.

Internal control consists of full documentation and appropriate authorisation of all transactions, movements of materials and of all requisitions, orders, receipts and payments.

If control is to be maintained over purchasing, it is necessary to ensure that:

- only necessary items are purchased
- orders are placed with the most appropriate supplier after considering price and delivery details
- the goods that are actually received are the goods that were ordered and in the correct quantity
- the price paid for the goods is correct (i.e. what was agreed when the order was placed).

To ensure that all of this takes place requires a reliable system of checking and control.

4.3 Overview of procedures

It is useful to have an overview of the purchasing process.

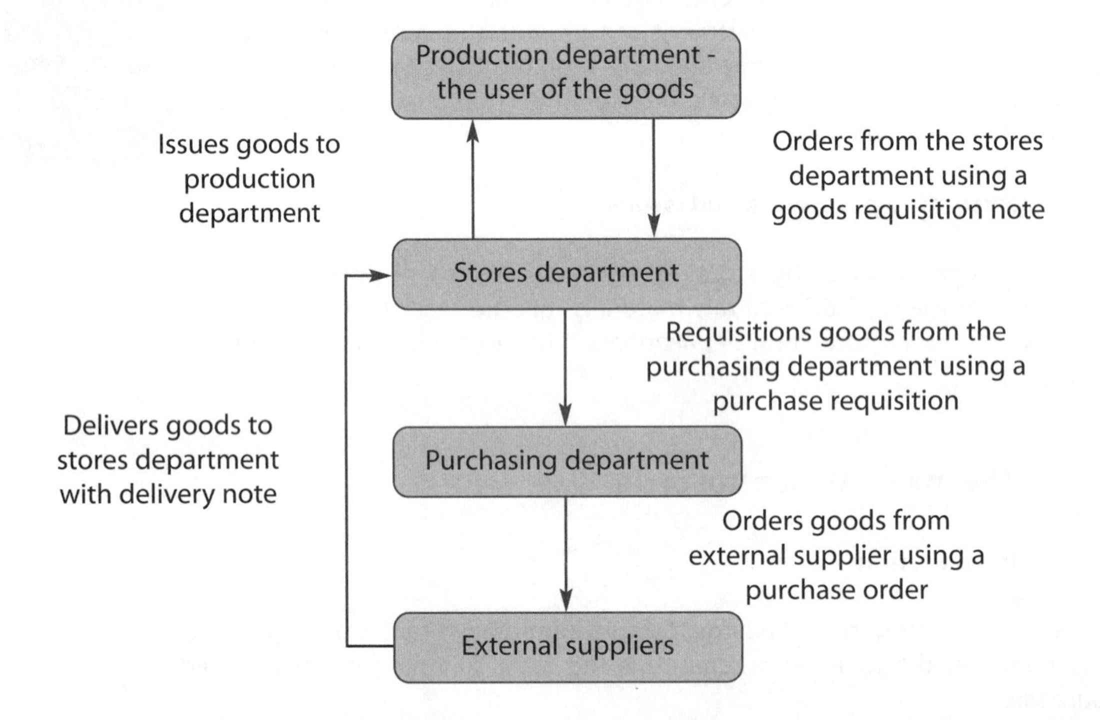

There are many variations of the above system in practice, but it is a fairly typical system and does provide good control over the purchasing and issuing process.

▷ ACTIVITY 5 (no feedback) 

Your organisation may have a slightly different process to this. See if you can draw a similar diagram illustrating the way your organisation's (or a familiar organisation's) purchasing process works.

We shall now study in detail the various key elements of the above procedures.

5 Materials documentation

5.1 Goods requisition note (also called 'materials requisition')

The user department (e.g. a production department) will notify the stores department that it requires certain goods using a 'goods requisition note'. This note will be authorised by the production manager.

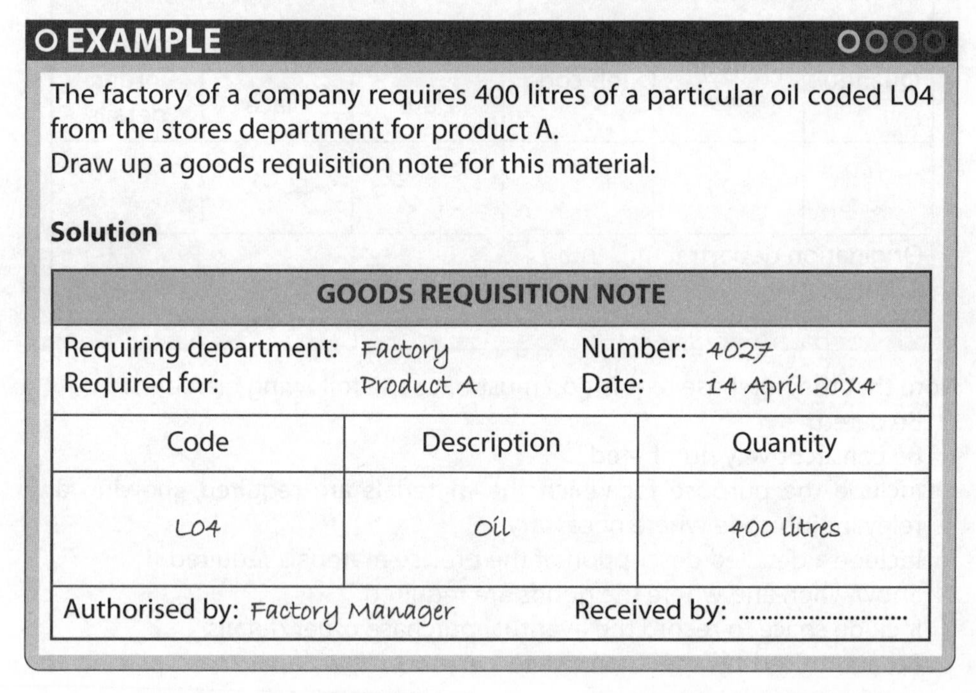

EXAMPLE

The factory of a company requires 400 litres of a particular oil coded L04 from the stores department for product A.
Draw up a goods requisition note for this material.

Solution

GOODS REQUISITION NOTE		
Requiring department: Factory Required for: Product A		Number: 4027 Date: 14 April 20X4
Code	Description	Quantity
L04	Oil	400 litres
Authorised by: Factory Manager		Received by: ....

5.2 Purchase requisition

It is important that an organisation controls the goods that are ordered from suppliers. Only goods that are genuinely necessary should be ordered. Therefore, before any order for goods is placed, a purchase requisition must be completed.

Each purchase requisition must be authorised by the appropriate person. This will usually be the storekeeper or store manager.

When the purchase requisition has been completed it is sent to the purchasing department so that the purchase order is prepared.

EXAMPLE

On 15 April the storekeeper of an organisation wishes to order 400 more litres of oil for the machinery. The code for the type of oil that is to be purchased is L04. Delivery is to be made directly to the stores department by 2 May.

Draw up the purchase requisition.

Solution

PURCHASE REQUISITION					
Date: 15 April 20X4				Number: 6843	
Purpose: General machinery maintenance Goods requisition note (if any): 4027					
Quantity	Material code	Job code	Delivery details		Purchase order details
			Date	Place	
400 litres	L04	-	2 May 20X4	Stores	
Origination department: Stores Authorisation: Storekeeper					

Note that the purchase requisition must have the following elements:

- Be dated.
- Be consecutively numbered.
- Include the purpose for which the materials are required, showing any relevant job code where necessary.
- Include a detailed description of the precise materials required.
- Show when and where the goods are required.
- Include space to record the eventual purchase order details.
- Be authorised by the appropriate person in the department placing the purchase requisition.

5.3 Purchase order

Purchase orders will be placed with suppliers by the purchasing department. The choice of supplier will depend upon the price, delivery promise, quality of goods and past performance.

The person placing the order must first check that the purchase requisition has been authorised by the appropriate person in the organisation.

Once the supplier of the goods has been chosen, the purchase price of the goods must be determined. This will either be from the price list of the supplier or from a special quotation of the price by that supplier. The price agreed will be entered on the purchase order together with details of the goods being ordered.

The purchase order must then be authorised by the appropriate person in the organisation before being dispatched to the supplier.

A copy of the purchase order is sent to the stores department as confirmation of expected delivery. The stores department therefore know that goods are due and can alert appropriate management if they are not received. A copy is also sent to the accounts department to be matched to the supplier's invoice. An example purchase order is shown below.

EXAMPLE

The purchase requisition for 400 litres of oil L04 has been received by the purchasing department.

PURCHASE REQUISITION					
Date: 15 April 20X4				Number: 6843	
Purpose: General machinery maintenance					
Quantity	Material code	Job code	Delivery details		Purchase order details
			Date	Place	
400 litres	L04	–	2 May 20X4	Stores	
Origination department: Stores					
Authorisation: Storekeeper					

From looking at the various possible suppliers' price lists Rowson Supplies Ltd has been chosen. They agree to deliver the oil at a price of £1.50 per litre.

Complete the purchase order in the proforma below.

PURCHASE ORDER				
To:	Number: 81742 Date: Purchase requisition number:			
Please supply in accordance with attached conditions of purchase.				
Quantity	Description/code	Delivery date	Price £	Per
Your quotation: Authorisation:				

Solution

PURCHASE ORDER				
To:	Number: 81742 Date: 15 April 20X4 Purchase requisition number: 6843			
Please supply in accordance with attached conditions of purchase.				
Quantity	Description/code	Delivery date	Price £	Per
400 litres	L04	2 May 20X4	1.50	Litre
Your quotation: £600 (400 litres x £1.50) Authorisation: Purchasing Manager				

5.4 Delivery note

A delivery note is sent by the supplier to the stores with the goods being delivered. This must include full details of the goods being delivered. The delivery note is signed by the person receiving the goods as evidence that the goods arrived.

EXAMPLE

Rowson Supplies Ltd is delivering 400 litres of oil, code L04, to French Productions Ltd. The delivery takes place on 2 May 20X4 and is in response to a purchase order from French Productions number 81742.

Draw up the delivery note.

Solution

ROWSON SUPPLIES LTD – DELIVERY NOTE		
Delivery to: French Productions Ltd Date: 2 May 20X4 Purchase order no: 81742 Delivery note no: D6582		
Please supply in accordance with attached conditions of purchase.		
Quantity	Description	Code
400 litres	Oil	L04
Signed: Storeman		

5.5 Goods received note

When goods are received by the organisation they will be taken to the stores department rather than being delivered directly to the part of the organisation that will use the goods. This enables the receipt of goods to be controlled. When the goods are received, the stores department will check:

(a) that the goods that arrive agree in **all** detail to those ordered on the purchase order
(b) that the details of the delivery note agree with the actual goods delivered.

When the stores department are satisfied with all of the details of the delivery, the details are recorded on a goods received note (GRN).

Any concerns about the goods being delivered (for example, too few, too many, the wrong colour, the wrong size) should be referred immediately to the appropriate manager before accepting the goods.

The GRN is evidence that the goods that were ordered have been received and therefore should be, and can be, paid for. The GRN will, therefore, be sent to the accounts department to be matched with the supplier's invoice.

As evidence of the actual receipt of the goods the GRN is also used for entering receipts of materials in the stores records.

5.6 Illustration

FRENCH PRODUCTIONS LTD
GOODS RECEIVED NOTE

No: GRN 272

SUPPLIER: Rowson Supplies Ltd | DATE: 2 May 20X4
PURCHASE ORDER NO: 81742

Description	Code	Qty	No of packages
Oil	LO4	400 litres	1

Received by: STORES – FINISHING AREA
Required by: FACTORY
Accepted by: STORES SUPERVISOR

QUALITY ASSURANCE
Inspected by: SIG: ....
Qty passed: 400 Qty rejected: Nil

5.7 Issues to the user department (production department)

The circle is completed when the stores issues the goods to the production department. The goods must agree with the original goods requisition note.

5.8 Purchase invoice

The purchase invoice for goods details the amount that the receiver of the goods must pay for them and the date that payment is due. The purchase invoice might be included when the goods themselves are delivered, or might be sent after delivery.

The person responsible for payment must check that the details of the purchase invoice agree to the goods received note, the delivery note and the purchase order. This is to ensure that:

- what was ordered was received
- what was received is what is being paid for
- the price changed is that agreed.

Once it is certain that the purchase invoice agrees with the goods that were actually received then the invoice can be authorised for payment by the appropriate person in the organisation.

5.9 Illustration

ROWSON SUPPLIES LTD – PURCHASE INVOICE	
To: French Productions Ltd Purchase order no: 81742 Invoice no: I6582	Date: 2 May 20X4
	£
For supply and delivery of: 400 litres of oil L04 @ £1.50 per litre	600.00
Payment due in 30 days	

5.10 Goods returned note

If goods are damaged or are not as ordered, they will be returned to the supplier. A goods returned note will be used, authorised by the stores manager.

If goods have been returned to the supplier, or there is some fault with the invoice (e.g. incorrect price or discount), a credit note will be requested from the supplier.

5.11 User department

When unused materials are returned from user departments to the stores, the transaction will be recorded on a document similar to the materials requisition but usually printed in a different colour. This will be a goods returned note. It will be completed by the user department that is returning the goods and signed by the storekeeper as evidence that the goods were returned to stores. These returns must also be recorded in the bin card and stock ledger account.

When the goods are returned the details on the goods returned note must be checked to the actual goods themselves.

6 The stores record card

6.1 Introduction

When materials are received by the stores department, as we have seen, they will be immediately checked to ensure that the correct quantity and quality have been delivered. Once this has been done using the GRN then the details of the receipt must be entered into the stores accounting records.

6.2 Stores record card (bin card)

Every line of stock, e.g. component X and material Y, will have a record card showing precisely how much of this item is in stock. Therefore each time a receipt of a material arrives from a supplier then the stores record card must be updated.

A typical stores record card might look like this:

EXAMPLE

Material description: Component X
Code: X100

Date	Receipts			Issues			Balance		
	Qty	Unit price £	Total £	Qty	Unit price £	Total £	Qty	Unit price £	Total £

6.3 Quantity and price

In many management accounting systems only the quantity of the materials is entered by the stores department as that is the only information that they have. Therefore the copy of the stores record card that is held in the stores department will be for quantities only as this is the only information that is truly relevant to the stores department.

6.4 Accounts department

Once the stores record card reaches the accounts department then the correct price of the materials, taken from the purchase invoice will be entered.

The stores record card is an important document that helps to control the movement of materials and assess the stock levels of that material.

6.5 Stock ledger account

The accounting for material is dealt with through a stores ledger account (or a stock ledger account). This is maintained by the accounting unit, the physical stock shown on these accounts is reconciled with the bin card.

DEFINITION

A **stock ledger account** records the quantity and value of receipts, issues and the current balance of each item of stock.

EXAMPLE

Vibrant Ltd has recently placed an order for 5,000 adhesive strips, showing the company logo, which are used on the company's range of products. It currently had 100 units in stock at a value of £25. The invoice from the supplier, Slough Labels Ltd shows:

Slough Labels Ltd
Station Unit Slough SL1 3EJ
Tel: 01947 825431
Fax: 01947 825429
e-mail: Sloughlab@virgin.net

VAT No: 7243716923
Tax point: 30 June 04
Invoice No: 72936

INVOICE

To:
Vibrant Ltd
10 Royal Crescent
Whitby YO21 3EA

Order No: 7921

QTY	Description	Unit price	Value £
5,000	Ad Label TS 12	£0.25 each	1,250.00
		VAT 17.5%	218.75
		Total due	£1,468.75

Terms: Net 30 days

The Goods Received Note would be completed on receipt of the goods:

VIBRANT LTD
GOODS RECEIVED NOTE

No: GRN 272

SUPPLIER: Slough Labels DATE: 25/6/X3
PURCHASE ORDER NO: TS 7921

Description	Code	Qty	No of packages
AD Lables	TS 12	5,000	1

Received by: STORES – FINISHING AREA
Required by: FINISHING COST CENTRE 121
Accepted by: STORES SUPERVISOR

QUALITY ASSURANCE
Inspected by: SIG: ....
Qty passed: 5,000 Qty rejected: Nil

The stock ledger card would be completed as follows:

STORES LEDGER ACCOUNT

Material Chipboard
Code D35

Receipts					Issues				Balance		
Date	GRN Ref	Qty	Price per unit £	Amount £	Issue Ref	Qty per unit	Price £	Amount £	Qty per unit	Price £	Value £
									100	0.25	25.00
25/6	272	5,000	0.25	1,250.00					5,100	0.25	1,275.00

▷ ACTIVITY 6 

In connection with a materials control system, describe the functions of the following documents, stating clearly the essential information each should provide:

(a) purchase requisition
(b) materials requisition
(c) goods received note.

[Answer on p. 53]

7 Costs of holding stock

7.1 Introduction

Most businesses, whatever their size, will be concerned with the problem of which items to have in stock and how much of each item should be kept.

7.2 Functions of stock

The principal reasons why a business needs to hold stock are as follows:

(a) It acts as a buffer in times when there is an unusually high rate of consumption.

(b) It enables the business to take advantage of quantity discounts by buying in bulk.

(c) The business can take advantage of seasonal and other price fluctuations (e.g. buying coal in the summer when it is cheaper).

(d) Any delay in production caused by lack of parts is kept to a minimum, so production processes will flow smoothly and efficiently.

(e) It may be necessary to hold stock for a technical reason: for example, whisky must be matured.

7.3 Stock control

DEFINITION

Stock control is 'the method of ensuring that the **right quantity** of the **right quality** of the relevant stock (or **inventory**) is available at the **right time** and in the **right place**'.

This chapter concerns three of the four 'right' attributes included in the definition, namely:

(a) **Quantity**

(b) **Time**

(c) **Place**

7.4 Costs of holding stock

Irrespective of the nature of the business, a certain amount of **stock** will always need to be held.

However, **holding stock costs money** and the principal 'trade-off' in a stockholding situation is between the costs of acquiring and storing stocks on the one hand and the level of service that the company wishes to provide on the other.

The **total cost of holding stock** consists of the following:

(a) **Purchase price** (as affected by discounts).

(b) **Holding costs**:

  (i) the opportunity cost of capital tied up

  (ii) insurance

  (iii) deterioration

(iv) obsolescence
(v) damage and pilferage
(vi) warehouse upkeep
(vii) stores labour and administration costs.

(c) **Re-order costs**:
(i) clerical and administrative expenses
(ii) transport costs.
Note, if goods are produced internally, the set-up costs for each production run are equivalent to the re-order costs.

(d) **Shortage costs**:
(i) loss of sales, therefore lost contribution
(ii) long-term damage to the business through loss of goodwill
(iii) production stoppages caused by 'stock-outs' of raw materials
(iv) extra costs caused by the need for emergency orders.

(e) **Stock recording systems costs.**

7.5 Terminology

The following terms will be used in this section:

Lead time	The time between an order for goods being placed and the receipt of that order.
Usage	The quantity of items required for sale (in the case of goods for resale) or production (in the case of components or raw materials) in a given period.
Stock-outs	Occasions when one or more items of stock are needed but there are none in stock.
Re-order level	The quantity of stock in hand at the time when a new order is placed.
Re-order quantity	The quantity of stock ordered. (Be careful to distinguish between re-order level and re-order quantity.)
Economic order quantity (EOQ) **Economic batch quantity** (EBQ)	The quantity to be ordered/produced to minimise the total of the inventory costs.
Buffer stock	Stock held to cover variations in: – lead time, and – demand during the lead time. Sometimes defined as 'stock held in excess of average units demanded in average lead time'.

7.6 Choosing an optimum stock level

The aim of a stock control system is to maintain the quantities of stocks held by a company at a level which optimises some predetermined management criterion (e.g. minimising costs incurred by the business). There are obviously disadvantages in holding either too much or too little stock, and the problem is to balance these disadvantages against the benefits obtained.

In setting an optimum stock level and re-order quantity, we will assume that management's aim is to minimise the costs of holding stock.

7.7 Disadvantages of low stock levels

- Customer demand cannot always be satisfied; this may lead to loss of business if customers become dissatisfied.
- In order to fulfil commitments to important customers, costly emergency procedures (e.g. special production runs) may become necessary in an attempt to maintain customer goodwill.
- It will be necessary to place replenishment orders more frequently than if higher stocks were held, in order to maintain a reasonable service. This will result in higher re-order costs being incurred.

7.8 Disadvantages of high stock levels

- Storage or holding costs are very high; such costs will usually include rates, rent, labour, heating, deterioration, etc.
- The cost of the capital tied up in stocks can become prohibitive.
- If the stored product becomes obsolete, a large stockholding of that item could, at worst, represent a large capital investment in an unsaleable product whose cash value is only that of scrap.
- If a great deal of capital is invested in stocks, there will be proportionately less money available for other requirements such as improvement of existing production facilities, or the introduction of new products.
- When a high stock level of a raw material is held, a sudden drop in the market price of that material represents a cash loss to the business for having bought at the higher price. It follows that it would seem sensible to hold higher stocks during an inflationary period and lower stocks during a period of deflation.

7.9 Stock control levels

Many stock control systems will incorporate some or all of four stock control levels that assist in keeping costs of stockholding and ordering down, whilst minimising the chances of stock-outs. The four control levels are:

- re-order level
- economic order quantity (EOQ)
- maximum stock level
- minimum stock level.

7.10 Re-order level

DEFINITION

The **re-order level** is the level to which the stock will be allowed to fall before a replenishment order is placed.

This level will be determined with reference to the time it will take to receive the order (the lead time) and the possible stock requirements during that time.

If it is possible to estimate the **maximum possible lead time** and the **maximum usage rate**, then a 'safe' re-order level, that will almost certainly avoid stock-outs, will be given by:

Re-order level = Maximum usage x Maximum lead time

7.11 Economic order quantity (EOQ)

Once the re-order level is reached, an order will be placed. The size of the order will affect:

(a) average stock levels (the larger the order, the higher the stock levels will be throughout the year)

(b) frequency of orders placed in the year (the larger the order, the longer it will take for stocks to fall to the re-order level, and thus the fewer the orders placed in the year).

Increasing the order size will have two conflicting effects on costs: increased holding costs through higher stock levels and decreased re-ordering costs due to fewer orders placed in the year.

Under certain 'ideal' conditions (including constant rates of usage and constant lead times) a mathematical model can be used to determine the optimum (economic) order quantity (EOQ) that will minimise the total of these two costs. This is often shown as:

$$EOQ = \sqrt{\frac{2 \times C \times D}{h}}$$

where C = cost of placing each order (note this is not the cost of the materials purchased but the administrative cost of placing the order).

D = annual demand/usage in units

h = cost of holding one unit of stock for one year

7.12 Maximum and minimum stock levels

Many stock systems will also incorporate maximum and minimum stock 'warning' levels, above or below which (respectively) stock should not be allowed to rise/fall.

In practice, the maximum stock level is fixed by taking into account:

(a) rate of consumption of the material

(b) time needed to obtain new supplies

(c) financial considerations due to high stocks tying up capital
(d) storage space with regard to the provision of space and maintenance costs
(e) extent to which price fluctuates
(f) risks of changing specifications
(g) possibility of loss by evaporation, deterioration, etc
(h) seasonal considerations as to both price and availability
(i) economic order quantities.

The minimum stock level is fixed by taking into account:
(a) rate of consumption
(b) time needed to obtain delivery of supplies
(c) the costs and other consequences of stock-outs.

A simplified method of determining these control levels is by reference to the re-order level, re-order quantity and estimates of possible lead times and usage rates, as follows:

Minimum level = Re-order level – (Average usage x Average lead time)
Maximum level = Re-order level + Re-order quantity – (Minimum usage x Minimum lead time)

If at any time stocks **fall below the minimum level** (which can only happen whilst waiting for an order to come in, as by definition this will be lower than the re-order level), this is a warning **that usage or lead time are above average**. Thus the storekeeper will need to keep an eye on stock levels and be prepared to place an emergency order if stocks get too low.

If stocks **rise above the maximum level** (often when an order has just been received), then **usage or lead time have actually been lower** than the expected minimum. If it is usage, this may indicate a general decline in the demand for the stock and the order quantity (and possibly the re-order level) should be reviewed to avoid holding excess stock with associated holding costs.

EXAMPLE

The demand for a particular product is expected to vary between 10 and 50 per day, with an average of 25. Lead time is, on average, 5 days, although it has been as short as 3 days and as long as 10 days.

Each time an order is placed, administrative costs of £15 are incurred and one unit of stock held for one year incurs £0.10 of holding costs.

The company operates a 300-day year.

Calculate the four control levels.

Solution

Re-order level = Maximum usage x Maximum lead time
= 50 per day x 10 days = 500 units

EOQ = $\sqrt{\dfrac{2 \times C \times D}{h}}$

Order quantity = $\sqrt{\dfrac{[2 \times £15 \times 7{,}500 \text{ (W)}]}{£0.10}}$ = 1,500 units

Minimum level = Re-order level – (Average usage x Average lead time)
= 500 – (25 per day x 5 days) = 375 units

Maximum level = Re-order level + EOQ – (Minimum usage x Minimum lead time)
= 500 + 1,500 – (10 per day x 3 days) = 1,970 units

Working

Annual demand D = 300 x 25 = 7,500

▷ ACTIVITY 7

Given below is information about one stock line that a business holds:

	Lowest	Average	Highest
Daily usage (units)	15	20	25
Lead time	2	5	8

The business operates for 250 days a year.

The cost of placing each order is £20 and it costs £0.20 to hold an item of stock for one year.

Calculate:

(i) the re-order level

(ii) the economic order quantity

(iii) the maximum stock level

(iv) the minimum stock level.

[Answer on p. 54]

8 Systems of stock control

8.1 Introduction

There are three main types of stock control systems:

(a) the re-order level (two-bin) system

(b) the periodic (cyclical) review system

(c) just-in-time systems.

8.2 Re-order level system

In a **re-order level system**, a replenishment order of fixed size (Q) is placed when the stock level falls to the fixed re-order level (R). Thus a **fixed quantity** is ordered at **variable intervals of time**. This is the most common system used and was assumed in the discussion of control levels above.

The most common practical implementation of the basic re-order level system is the two-bin system. Here, two bins of the stock item are used and a replenishment order is placed when the first bin becomes empty; stock is then drawn from the second bin until the order is received. When the order arrives, the second bin is filled up to its original level and the remainder goes into the first (empty) bin. Thus the amount of stock held in the second bin gives the re-order level.

8.3 Periodic review system

☐ DEFINITION

In a **periodic review system**, the stock levels are reviewed at fixed points in time, when the quantity to be ordered is decided.

By this method **variable quantities** are ordered at **fixed time intervals**.

Although this may increase the chances of a stock-out (between review times), it has the advantage of being easier to plan the scheduling of stock-counts and orders in advance.

8.4 Just-in-time (JIT) systems

☐ DEFINITION

JIT may be defined as 'production of the smallest possible quantity at the latest possible time using a minimum of resources and elimination of waste in manufacturing processes'.

JIT management is a philosophy rather than merely a production control technique. Finished goods are produced just in time for sale, component parts just in time to make the finished goods and materials purchased just in time to become the component parts.

The **JIT philosophy** is based on the reduction, as far as possible, of:

(a) work-in-progress levels
(b) raw material stocks
(c) scrap reworking
(d) finished goods stocks
(e) material handling costs.

8.5 Materials usage in production

Materials can often represent a **significant direct cost of production** and the levels of usage should be carefully monitored to ensure there is not excessive or needless waste. Such controls can be implemented by the following procedures:

- Adequate quality control and inspection checks at appropriate stages in the production cycle. This will minimise the use of materials on partly completed products which are faulty and which should have been scrapped before the additional material was added.

- A system of re-working of faulty goods. This will reduce overall material losses by converting faulty units into a saleable state.
- Proper storage and security of work in progress in order to minimise damage or loss occurring while the work in progress awaits the next stage in the production cycle.
- Adequate training and supervision of the workforce in order to minimise losses due to faulty production units.
- A properly planned maintenance programme for production machinery to help reduce the level of scrap or faulty goods produced.
- Proper recording of the incidence of material losses in order that the points of incidence may be monitored and corrective action implemented where necessary.
- Control of scrap material to ensure that it is either sold or re-used in later batches where possible. Any necessary disposal of material should be at least cost to the business.

8.6 Causes of wastage of materials

In addition to material losses due to faulty production, as discussed above, raw materials may be lost or wasted through:

- poor storage: inadequate protection from damp, theft, rats, etc
- fire, flood, etc
- human error in preparing the material for production: inaccurate measurement, etc
- inferior quality: materials with flaws or of inadequate strength or heat resistance, etc
- deterioration or obsolescence.

8.7 Accounting for materials wastage

The classification and recording of the cost of materials wasted (net of any scrap proceeds) will depend upon the stage at which the material was lost and the nature of the loss.

- If it is lost prior to input into production, it will be treated as a non-production overhead.
- If it is lost during production as part of the normal or expected level of loss/wastage (off-cuts, trimmings, evaporation, etc) it will be treated as a production overhead (i.e. an indirect cost) that will be absorbed into all production.
- If it is lost during production due to a one-off event (machine breakdown, human error, etc) it will again be treated effectively as a non-production overhead, in that it will not be allowed to affect the stock valuation of production but will be written off in the period in which it was incurred.

In most production processes there will be some level of wastage known as the normal loss or wastage. However, any additional losses or wastage should be kept to a minimum.

9 Test your knowledge

1 Material cost is classified as either direct or indirect. Give two examples of each for a shoe manufacturer.

2 Explain the purpose of a purchase requisition.

3 Define the terms:
- FIFO
- LIFO.

4 Which method of stock valuation would normally value stock at current cost?

5 What costs are incurred in holding stock and are termed 'holding costs'?

6 What is the formula for calculating the EOQ?

[Answers on p. 54]

10 Summary

Pricing issues of raw materials and valuing stocks are two of the most important techniques that you need to know about in the topic of materials. We have looked at three main methods of pricing issues and valuing stocks: FIFO, LIFO, and Weighted Average Cost. A common examination task is to ask you to record receipts and issues of materials onto a stores ledger card using one of these methods.

We have also looked at the documents involved in the process of purchasing materials and the different stock control systems (re-order level (two-bin) system, periodic review system and the just-in-time system).

Another important part of the topic of materials is that of stock control levels – these assist in keeping the costs of stockholding and stock ordering at a minimum, whilst minimising stock-outs at the same time. Make sure that you can calculate the re-order level, the EOQ, the maximum stock level and the minimum stock level.

Answers to chapter activities & 'test your knowledge' questions

ACTIVITY 1

(a) **LIFO**

Date		*Issues*			*Receipts*		*Balance*	
		No	*£*		*No*	*£*	*No*	*£*
1/8	Balance					700	2,730	
6/8	Receipts				600	2,280	1,300	5,010
9/8	Issues	1,000	3,840	(W1)			300	1,170
20/8	Receipts				300	1,320	600	2,490
25/8	Issues	400	1,710	(W2)			200	780
		1,400	5,550					

(W1) 2,280 + (400/700 x 2,730)
(W2) 1,320 + (1/7 x 2,730)

(b) **FIFO**

Date		*Issues*			*Receipts*		*Balance*	
		No	*£*		*No*	*£*	*No*	*£*
1/8	Balance						700	2,730
6/8	Receipts				600	2,280	1,300	5,010
9/8	Issues	1,000	3,870	(W1)			300	1,140
20/8	Receipts				300	1,320	600	2,460
25/8	Issues	400	1,580	(W2)			200	880
		1,400	5,450					

(W1) 2,730 + (300/600 x 2,280)
(W2) (3/6 x 2,280) + (1/3 x 1,320)

(c) The results of (a) and (b) can be summarised as:

	LIFO	FIFO	Difference
Cost of issues (£)	5,550	5,450	£100
Closing stock (£)	780	880	(£100)

Under LIFO, issues are costed at the latest purchase price (usually higher) leaving earlier purchases (usually lower price) in stock. In this example, the 200 units of closing stock are priced at the b/f stock cost under LIFO (£3.90) and at the 20/8 receipt cost under FIFO (£4.40). The difference in stock value is thus 50p x 200 = £100, which is also reflected in the cost of issues.

ACTIVITY 2

(a) When raw material prices are subject to inflation, the LIFO method of valuation will give the lowest profits as the cost of sales will be charged at the latest (highest) prices.

(b) The argument for using an up to date price for issues from stock is to ensure that materials usage is being charged at a realistic price representing the cost of replacing the materials. FIFO can result in out of date (usually lower) prices being used resulting in higher profits being taken now, possibly at the risk of having insufficient funds to replace stocks for later use.

ACTIVITY 3

(a) Under the FIFO method, issues to production are priced at the cost price of the oldest material order taken into stock until those units originally taken into stock have been exhausted, then the next oldest price is used and so on.

Under LIFO, the issue price is the cost price of the material most recently taken into stock from which the issue could have been drawn until those units are exhausted, then the next most recent price is used and so on.

(b) Weighted average pricing

Date	*Receipts*			*Issues*			*Balance*		
	Qty	*Per unit*	*Value*	*Qty*	*Per unit*	*Value*	*Qty*	*Per unit*	*Value*
	£	£		£	£		£	£	
01 Sep							100	1.00	100
18 Sep				60	1.00	60	40	1.00	40
30 Sep	40	1.20	48				80 (a)	1.10	88
12 Oct				60	1.10	66	20	1.10	22
31 Oct	80	1.30	104				100 (b)	1.26	126
04 Nov	20	1.50	30				120 (c)	1.30	156
19 Nov				70	1.30	91	50	1.30	65

Calculation of weighted average prices:

(a)	40	in hand at £1.00	£40		
	40	received at £1.20	£48		
	80		£88	therefore average	£1.10
(b)	20	in hand at £1.10	£22		
	80	received at £1.30	£104		
	100		£126	therefore average	£1.26
(c)	100	in hand at £1.26	£126		
	20	received at £1.50	£30		
	120		£156	therefore average	£1.30

ACTIVITY 4

(a)

Stores Record Card
Material description: Paper
Code: 1564 A

Date	Details	Receipts		Issues			Stock		
		Sheets	£	Sheets	Price	£	Sheets	Price	£
1.5	Opening stock						10,000		3,000
3.5	Receipt	4,000	1,600				14,000	0.33	4,600
6.5	Issue			7,000	0.33	2,310	7,000		2,290
12.5	Receipt	10,000	3,100				17,000	0.32	5,390
15.5	Issue			6,000	0.32	1,920	11,000		3,470
22.5	Issue			7,200	0.32	2,304	3,800		1,166
25.5	Receipt	10,000	3,200				13,800	0.32	4,366

(b) Tie-up of capital; reduction in space available for production.

ACTIVITY 6

(a) A **purchase requisition** is a document used to initiate the materials purchasing procedure in an organisation. It represents a request to the buying department to purchase the materials specified on the form. The essential information which should be provided on a purchase requisition includes a serial number, the date of issue, the quantity, description and code of the material, the date by which delivery is required and the signature of the official who has authorised the requisition. In some cases it may be essential to state on the requisition the name of the supplier.

(b) A **materials requisition** is a document used as authority for the issue of materials from stores. It represents a request to the stores department to issue to the person presenting the requisition the materials specified on the form.

The essential information which should be provided on a materials requisition includes a serial number, the date of issue, the quantity, description and code of each material required, the cost centre or cost unit to which the material is to be charged and the signature of the official who has authorised the requisition. Subsequently the price of the material and the charge to the cost centre or cost unit will need to be entered on the accounting department's copy of the form.

(c) A **goods received note** is a document used to record the physical receipt of goods. The use of the goods received note helps to ensure that control is exercised upon delivery of goods and initial data capture is effected reliably. The form notifies the buying and accounting departments of receipt of the goods so that the buying records and stores ledger accounts can be updated. The goods received note acts as a documentary reference for the stores department.

The essential information which should be provided on a goods received note includes a serial number, the date of receipt, the supplier, carrier and advice note number, the purchase order number, the quantity, description and code of the material, and the reports of the receiving clerk and inspector (with their signatures).

ACTIVITY 7

(i) Re-order level = Maximum usage x Maximum lead time
= 25 units x 8 days
= 200 units

(ii) EOQ $= \sqrt{\dfrac{2 \times C \times D}{h}}$

$= \sqrt{\dfrac{2 \times £20 \times 20 \times 250)}{0.2}}$

= 1,000 units

(iii) Maximum stock level = Re-order level + EOQ – (Minimum usage x Minimum lead time)
= 200 + 1,000 – (15 x 2)
= 1,170 units

(iv) Minimum stock level = Re-order level – (Average usage x Average lead time)
= 200 – (20 x 5)
= 100 units

Test your knowledge

1 Direct material:
- Leather
- Eyelets for laces

Indirect material:
- Maintenance materials
- Oils and greases, consumables

2 A purchase requisition is an internal document informing the purchasing department that an amount of stock needs to be ordered.

3 FIFO and LIFO are methods of pricing stores issues and valuing stock.

FIFO prices issues at the earliest price for purchases recorded. LIFO prices issues at the latest price for purchases recorded.

4 FIFO

5
- Insurance
- Storage
- Labour and admin cost
- Interest on capital
- Effect of deterioration and or obsolescence

6 $$EOQ = \sqrt{\frac{2 \times C \times D}{h}}$$

C = Cost of placing an order
D = Annual demand in units
h = Cost of holding one unit of stock for one year

LABOUR COSTS

INTRODUCTION

Labour is another major cost for many organisations. The cost of labour will depend on the remuneration system employed by an organisation (for example, annual salary, hourly rates and overtime or piecework payments). One of the most important calculations in this topic is the analysis of labour costs into direct and indirect costs. We will also be looking at employee records including the records held by organisations which detail the hours worked by employees.

KNOWLEDGE & UNDERSTANDING

- Methods for and calculation of payment for labour (Element 6.1)
- Relationship between the labour costing system and the payroll accounting system (Element 6.2)
- The sources of information for revenue and costing data (Elements 6.1, 6.2 and 6.3)

CONTENTS

PERFORMANCE CRITERIA

- Identify direct costs in accordance with the organisation's costing procedures (Element 6.1)
- Record and analyse information relating to direct costs (Element 6.1)
- Calculate direct costs in accordance with the organisation's policies and procedures (Element 6.1)

1 Calculating a cost per unit

An understanding of labour costs should be seen in the context of calculating a cost per unit for a product:

	Cost / unit
	£
Direct labour cost	1.50
Direct material cost	3.20
Prime cost	4.70
Production overheads	4.30
Total cost per unit	9.00

This chapter looks first at how to calculate the labour cost figures. The practicalities of accounting for labour costs are also covered.

2 Remuneration systems

2.1 Introduction

All employees in a business will be remunerated or paid for the work that they do. There are a variety of different ways in which this payment is calculated. The main systems of remuneration are:

- annual salaries
- hourly rates of pay and overtime payments
- piecework payments
- bonus schemes.

Different types of employees within a business may well be paid according to different systems depending upon which is the most appropriate for the type of work that they perform.

2.2 Annual salaries

Annual salaries tend to be paid to management and non-production staff such as administrators, secretaries, accounts staff, etc. The annual salary is simply divided by the 12 months in the year and that is the amount of gross pay for that employee for the month.

EXAMPLE

The sales manager of a business has an annual salary of £30,000. What is the gross amount of his pay each month?

Solution

Monthly gross pay = £30,000/12
= £2,500

2.3 Hourly rates and overtime payments

Many production and manual workers will be paid for every hour that they work (the recording of these hours is considered later in the chapter). Normally hourly paid workers will have a standard number of hours that they work each week. If they work for more than this number of hours then they will receive an overtime payment, which will usually be more than the basic hourly rate.

O EXAMPLE

An employee works for a standard week of 40 hours at an hourly rate of pay of £8.20. Any overtime hours are paid at time and a half.

In one week he works for 45 hours.

(i) What is his gross pay?
(ii) What is his overtime payment?
(iii) What is his overtime premium?

Solution

(i)		£
	Basic hours 40 x £8.20	328.00
	Overtime 5 x (£8.20 x 1.5)	61.50
	Gross pay	389.50
(ii)	Overtime payment	£61.50

(iii) Overtime premium = amount paid over the basic hourly rate for the overtime hours
5 x (£8.20 x 0.5) = £20.50

The **overtime premium** is the extra element of payment over and above the basic hourly rate for the additional hours. It is this overtime premium that is normally important for costing purposes rather than the total overtime payment (see later in the chapter).

▷ ACTIVITY 1

Give two reasons why the majority of production employees are paid on the basis of time (e.g. hourly rates of pay), rather than on the basis of work done.

[Answer on p. 72]

▷ ACTIVITY 2

An employee's basic week is 40 hours at a rate of pay of £5 per hour. Overtime is paid at 'time and a half'. This means that the payment for the hours of overtime is one and a half times the basic hourly rate.
What is the wage cost of this employee if he works for 45 hours in a week?

[Answer on p. 72]

2.4 Piecework payments

DEFINITION

Piecework rates occur where a fixed constant amount is paid per unit of output.

The fixed rate will often be based upon the standard (expected) time per unit. This method is an example of 'payment by results'.

EXAMPLE

Graeme MacHue works in the Scottish Highlands producing carved wooden animals for a small company supplying the tourist market. In week 26 his production was:

	Standard time allowed/unit
6 Stags	2.0 hours
5 Otters	1.5 hours
12 Owls	1.0 hour
6 Golden Eagles	2.0 hours

He is paid £5 per standard hour of production (irrespective of actual time worked).

What are his earnings for week 26?

Solution

			£
Stags	6 x 2	x £5	60.00
Otters	5 x 1.5	x £5	37.50
Owls	12 x 1	x £5	60.00
Golden Eagles	6 x 2	x £5	60.00
			217.50

2.5 Advantages of the piecework system

- It produces a **constant labour cost per unit**.
- It **encourages efficient work** – an employee taking more than the standard time per unit will only be paid for the standard time. In order for this to be motivational, the standard time must be accepted as fair by the employee.

To increase motivation, a **differential piecework system** may be implemented, whereby the piece rate is increased for higher output levels.

2.6 Disadvantages of the piecework system

- Employees **lack security of income**, which may become demotivating.

- The employee can be **penalised** for low levels of production due to factors that are outside his/her control (e.g. machine breakdown or faulty materials).

2.7 Guaranteed minimum payment

To overcome these disadvantages, the **straight piecework rate** may be accompanied by **a guaranteed minimum payment** (weekly or daily).

EXAMPLE

Standard rate per hour = £4.50
Guaranteed minimum per week = 35 hours

Actual production: 10 units @ 3 hours per unit. Calculate the weekly pay.

Solution

Standard hours = 10 x 3 = 30 hours
Pay = 30 x £4.50 = £135
Subject to guaranteed minimum pay = 35 x £4.50 = £157.50

Therefore weekly pay = £157.50

ACTIVITY 3

List two advantages of paying employees by the results achieved.

[Answer on p. 72]

ACTIVITY 4

A company operates a piecework system of remuneration. Employees must work for a minimum of 40 hours per week. Joe produces the following output for a particular week:

Product	Quantity	Standard time per item (hours)	Total actual time (hours)
Gaskets	50	0.2	9
Drive belts	200	0.06	14
Sprockets	100	0.1	12
Gears	10	0.7	6
			41

He is paid £6.20 per standard hour worked. What are his earnings for the week?

[Answer on p. 72]

▷ ACTIVITY 5

Jones is paid £3.00 for every unit that he produces but he has a guaranteed wage of £28.00 per eight-hour day. In a particular week he produces the following number of units:

Monday	12 units
Tuesday	14 units
Wednesday	9 units
Thursday	14 units
Friday	8 units

Calculate Jones's wages for this week.

[Answer on p. 72]

▷ ACTIVITY 6

Continuing with the example of Jones above, what would be his weekly wage if the guarantee were for £140 per week rather than £28 per day?

[Answer on p. 73]

2.8 Bonus schemes

Bonus schemes are a compromise between a day rate and a piecework system. Earnings will comprise:

(a) a day rate amount, based on hours worked, and

(b) a bonus based on quantity produced (usually above a certain standard) or on time saved in relation to standard time allowance for the output achieved.

O EXAMPLE

On a particular day, Fred worked for 8.5 hours, producing 15 units. The standard time allowance for each unit is 40 minutes. Fred's basic hourly rate is £4.50 and he is paid a bonus for time saved from standard at 60% of his basic hourly rate.

Calculate Fred's pay for the day.

Solution

			£
Day rate = 8.5 x £4.50			38.25
Bonus			
Standard time 15 x 40/60	10	hours	
Actual time	8.5	hours	
Time saved	1.5	hours	
Bonus = 1.5 x £4.50 x 60%			4.05
Total			42.30

Note that the **benefit of time saved is shared between the employer and the employee**, in this case in the ratio 40/60. This method partially safeguards both the employee and the employer against badly set standards; it also safeguards cases where it is difficult to set accurate standards because of the nature of the work.

2.9 Group bonus schemes

In the case of, for example, an assembly line, where it is impossible for an individual worker on the line to increase productivity without the others also doing so, a group bonus scheme may be used. The bonus is calculated by reference to the output of the group and split between the members of the group (often equally).

▷ ACTIVITY 7

Ten employees work as a group. The standard output for the group is 200 units per hour and when this is exceeded each employee in the group is paid a bonus in addition to the hourly wage.

The bonus percentage is calculated as follows:

$$50\% \times \frac{\text{Excess units}}{\text{Standard units}}$$

Each employee in the group is then paid as a bonus this percentage of an hourly wage rate of £7.20 no matter what the individual's hourly wage rate is:

The following is one week's record of production by the group:

	Hours worked	Production units
Monday	90	24,500
Tuesday	88	20,600
Wednesday	90	24,200
Thursday	84	20,100
Friday	88	20,400
Saturday	40	10,200
	480	120,000

(a) What is the rate of the bonus per hour and what is the total bonus to be split between group members?

(b) If Jones worked for 42 hours and was paid £6.00 per hour as a basic rate what would be his total pay for this week?

[Answer on p. 73]

2.10 Holiday pay

As well as the normal payments of wages and salaries, there are other labour costs which include holiday pay and training time.

Holiday pay is non-productive, but it is nevertheless charged to the cost of production by allocating the full year's holiday pay to overhead and charging it to production for the whole year.

Alternatively, wages may be allocated at **labour rates inflated to include holiday pay** and other non-productive time costs.

2.11 Training time and supervisors' wages

Wages paid during a period of **training** may be charged partly to the job and partly to production overhead. The fact that learners work more slowly than trained employees is offset by the learners' lower rate of pay. Apprentices' remuneration will be charged to a separate account.

Normally, **supervisors' wages** are treated as part of department overhead unless only a particular job is concerned. Where instruction is being given, the remuneration of instructors and supervisors may be included in training time.

2.12 Summary

Different types of employee in an organisation will be paid in different ways. For example, management are normally paid by salary, production workers will be either hourly paid or paid on a piecework basis and the sales team may well be paid according to a bonus scheme.

3 Direct and indirect labour costs

3.1 Introduction

We have seen that there are a variety of different methods of remunerating employees and a number of different elements to this remuneration. For costing purposes the total labour costs must be split between the direct labour costs, which can be charged to the units of production and any indirect labour costs, which are charged as overheads to the relevant cost centre.

3.2 Production workers

The wages that are paid to the production workers will on the whole be direct labour costs. This will include piecework payments and bonus payments. The direct labour cost will also include the basic rate for any overtime hours but the overtime premium may be treated as an indirect cost.

3.3 Overtime premium

Whether the overtime premium is treated as a direct or indirect labour cost will depend upon the reasons for the overtime:

- If the overtime were worked due to a customer's specific instruction, then the overtime premium will be treated as a direct labour cost.
- If the overtime were due to general pressure of work, then the premium is treated as an indirect labour cost.

3.4 Holiday pay

Holiday pay is normally treated as an indirect labour cost.

3.5 Training time

The hours paid for the labour force to train are treated as an indirect labour cost.

3.6 Idle time

Controllable idle time is treated as an indirect labour cost. Uncontrollable idle time is treated as an expense in the costing profit and loss account.

DEFINITION

Idle time is made up of non-productive hours that are nevertheless paid for.

It should obviously be prevented as far as possible. It is important to analyse the causes of idle time so that necessary corrective action can be taken. There are three groups of causes of idle time:

(a) Productive causes (e.g. machine breakdown, power failure or time spent waiting for work, tools, materials or instructions).

(b) Administrative causes (e.g. surplus capacity, policy changes, unforeseen drop in demand).

(c) Economic causes (e.g. seasonal fluctuations in demand, cyclical fluctuations in demand, changes in demand because of tax changes).

Some of these causes are **controllable** (and therefore **'normal'**), while others are **uncontrollable** (and regarded as **'abnormal'**). Controllable idle time is shown under a separate account and charged as an overhead, although it may be charged to a department if it arose through the fault of that department. Uncontrollable idle time is charged directly to the costing profit and loss account.

3.7 Management and supervisor's salaries

Management salaries and supervisor's salaries are all labour costs which are not related to actual production of the cost units, therefore they are all treated as indirect labour costs.

ACTIVITY 8

(a) Calculate the gross wages earned for each of the following employees for Week 32. The normal week is 38 hours and an individual production bonus of 10p per 100 sheets produced is paid.

	Singh	Smith
Basic rate per hour	£6.50	£6.00
Total hours worked	39½	41
Overtime hours paid:		
at time plus a third	1½	1
at time plus a half		2
Output (sheets)	10,500	10,900

(Calculations to two decimal places of a £.)

(b) There has been some pressure from the employees for a piecework system to be introduced.

What would the piecework price per 100 sheets have to be, to at least equal the gross wages earned by Singh in (a) above, assuming the same output level of 10,500 sheets?

(Calculations to two decimal places of a £.)

(c) The overtime premium paid to Singh and Smith could be analysed to direct wages or to departmental overheads. Detail the circumstances which would give rise to these differing treatments.

[Answer on p. 73]

4 Employee records

4.1 Personnel record details

When an employee joins an organisation it is necessary to record a number of details about him and the details of his job and pay. This is done by the personnel department in the individual employee's personnel record.

The type of details that might be kept about an employee are as follows:

- Full name, address and date of birth.
- Personal details such as marital status and emergency contact name and address.
- National Insurance number.
- Previous employment history.
- Educational details.
- Professional qualifications.
- Date of joining organisation.
- Employee number or code.
- Clock number issued.
- Job title and department.
- Rate of pay agreed.
- Holiday details agreed.
- Bank details if salary is to be paid directly into bank account.
- Amendments to any of the details above (such as increases in agreed rates of pay).
- Date of termination of employment (when this takes place) and reasons for leaving.

EXAMPLE

Jonathan Minor started to be employed by your organisation on 1 July 2001 as an engineer in the maintenance department of the organisation. He was born on 22 January 1983 and this is his first job after training at college for an HND in engineering.

His employee code and clock number are M36084 and his agreed rate of pay is £375.60 per week. He is to be paid in cash.

Complete the employee personnel record for Jonathan.

Solution

PERSONNEL RECORD CARD

PERSONAL DETAILS			EMPLOYMENT DETAILS
Surname: MINOR Other names: JONATHAN	Address: 24 Hill St Reading	Emergency contact: Jane MINOR 24 Hill St Reading	**Previous Employment History**
Date of birth: 22/1/83	Nationality: British	Sex: M	Employer: Date:
Marital status: Single		Dependents: None	(1)
National Insurance Number: WE 22 41 79 J9			(2)
			(3)
			(4)

EDUCATIONAL DETAILS				TRAINING DETAILS
Degree: -		Btec/HND: Engineering		
A Levels: 2	O levels: 0	GCSE: 7	CSEs: 0	Course attended: Date:
University attended: - College attended: Reading Schools attended (with dates): Reading High (1994 – 1999) Reading Junior (1987 – 1994)				

JOB DETAILS			OTHER DETAILS
Date of joining: 1/7/01	Clock number:	M36084	Bank account:
Job title: Engineer	Department:	Maintenance	
Rate of pay:	Overtime:	1½ times basic	Date of termination:
Date £	Holiday:	15 days	
1/7/01 375.60 pw	Pension Scheme: Joined:	1/7/01	Reason for leaving:

4.2 Holiday records

An employee will usually have an agreed number of days holiday per year. This will usually be paid holiday for salaried employees but may well be unpaid for employees paid by results or on time rates.

It is important for the employer to keep a record of the days of holiday taken by the employee to ensure that the agreed number of days per year are not exceeded.

4.3 Sickness records

The organisation will have its own policies regarding payment for sick leave as well as legal requirements for statutory sick pay. Therefore, it will be necessary to keep a record of the number of days of sick leave each year for each employee.

4.4 Other periods of absence

A record will need to be kept of any other periods of absence by an employee. These might be perfectly genuine such as jury service or training courses or alternatively unexplained periods of absence that must be investigated.

4.5 Source of information

This information about an employee's attendance will come from various sources such as clock cards, time sheets and cost cards. These will all be examined in more detail later in the chapter.

▷ ACTIVITY 9

In the first three months of the year the time records of an organisation show that Thomas Yung (employee number Y4791) had the following days off work:

January	2 days sick leave
	5 days holiday
February	4 days holiday
	3 days training
March	2 days sick leave

The total working days in these three months were 21, 18 and 21 respectively.

Record these details in Thomas's attendance record.

[Answer on p. 74]

4.6 Attendance records

In most businesses, **records** are needed of the time spent by each employee in the workplace (attendance time) and time spent on the operations, processes, products or services whilst there (job time). Such timekeeping provides basic data for statutory records, payroll preparation, ascertainment and control of labour costs of an operation or product, overhead distribution (where based on wages or labour hours) and statistical analysis of labour records for determining productivity.

Attendance may be recorded by using a **register**, in which employees note their times of arrival and departure, or by means of a **time recording clock** which stamps the times on a card inserted by each employee. Alternatively, employees may be required to submit periodic **timesheets** showing the amounts of normal and overtime work; these may also include job times as described below.

4.7 Clock cards

DEFINITION

A **clock card** is a document on which is recorded the starting and finishing time of an employee for ascertaining total actual attendance time.

A clock card is usually some form of electronic or computerised recording system whereby when the employee's clock card is entered into the machine the time is recorded. This will give the starting and finishing time for the day and also in some systems break times taken as well.

Clock cards are used as a source document in the calculation of the employee's earnings.

EXAMPLE

Example of a clock card

Works number:			**Name:**		
		Lunch			
Week ending	In	Out	In	Out	Hours
Monday					
Tuesday					
Wednesday					
Thursday					
Friday					
Saturday					
Sunday					
FOREMAN'S SIGNATURE:.................................					

4.8 Daily timesheets

One of these sheets is filled in by each employee (to indicate the time spent by them on each job) and passed to the cost office each day. The total time on the timesheet should correspond to the time shown on the attendance record. Because times are recorded daily, there is less risk of times being forgotten or manipulated, but these timesheets create a considerable volume of paperwork.

Below is an illustration of a daily timesheet.

O EXAMPLE

Name:		Frank Smith		**Date:**		11/6/X5
Clock number:		3		**Week number:**		31
Job order number	Description	Time		Hours worked	Rate	£
		Start	Finish			
349	Servicing Ford Ka Y625 AAB	9.00	11.05	2.05		
372	Repair to Range Rover TC03 XYZ	11.05	16.30	4.25		
Signed: F Smith		**Certified:** A Foreman			**Office ref:**	

4.9 Weekly timesheets

These are similar to daily timesheets but they are passed to the cost office at the end of the week instead of every day (although entries should be made daily in order to avoid error). Weekly timesheets are particularly suitable where there are few job changes in the course of a week.

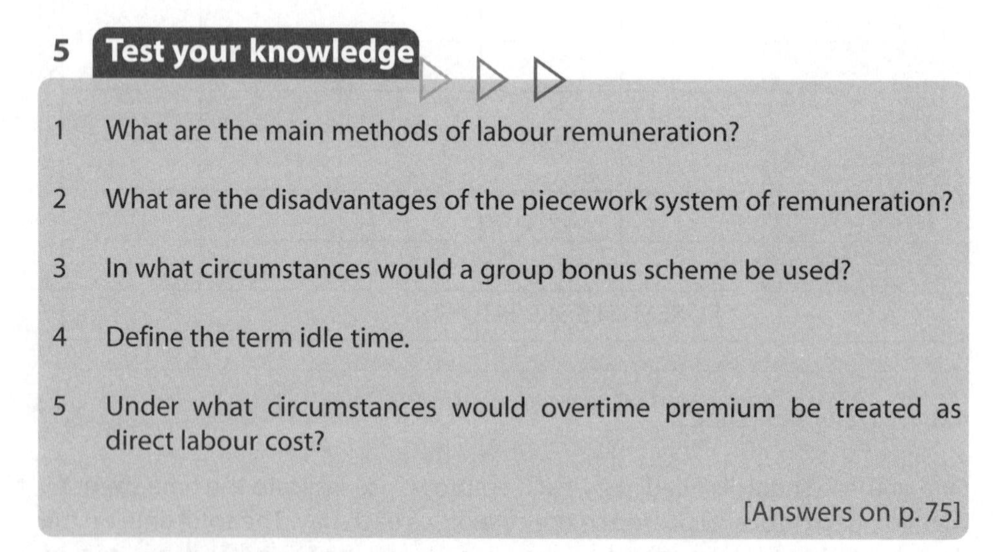

5 Test your knowledge

1 What are the main methods of labour remuneration?

2 What are the disadvantages of the piecework system of remuneration?

3 In what circumstances would a group bonus scheme be used?

4 Define the term idle time.

5 Under what circumstances would overtime premium be treated as direct labour cost?

[Answers on p. 75]

6 Summary

This chapter started by considering the methods of payment of labour that may be used by organisations. These may be annual salaries, hourly rates of pay, performance related pay (piecework) and profit related pay (bonus schemes). In order to pay the correct amount to employees there must be detailed recording of the time spent at work by each employee on time sheets or by a time clock and clock cards.

The distribution between direct and indirect labour costs is an important one.

Direct labour costs including the following:

- production workers' wages (excluding overtime premiums)
- bonus payments for production workers
- overtime premiums where overtime was worked at the specific request of the customer.

Indirect labour costs include the following:

- holiday pay
- training time
- idle time
- supervisors' salaries
- management salaries
- overtime premiums where overtime was due to the general pressure of work.
- production supervisor's wages that cannot be allocated to specific cost units.

Answers to chapter activities & 'test your knowledge' questions

ACTIVITY 1

(a) Difficulty in measuring work.

(b) Need to maintain quality, etc.

ACTIVITY 2

	£
Basic pay (40 x £5)	200.00
Overtime (5 hours x (£5 x 1.5))	37.50
Weekly wage cost	237.50

Alternatively this could be shown as:

	£
Basic pay (45 x £5)	225.00
Overtime premium (5 hours x (£5 x 0.5))	12.50
	237.50

Conclusion

This second method is the only one that shows the overtime premium separately. The premium is the additional amount over the basic rate that is paid for the overtime hours rather than the total payment. This method is preferred because it provides the information needed for costing products.

ACTIVITY 3

(a) Employee can earn higher wages.

(b) Employer achieves higher output.

ACTIVITY 4

		Hours
50 x 0.2	=	10
200 x 0.06	=	12
100 x 0.1	=	10
10 x 0.7	=	7
		39 x £6.20 = £241.80 earnings

ACTIVITY 5

Total weekly wage:

	£
Monday (12 x £3)	36
Tuesday (14 x £3)	42
Wednesday (guarantee)	28
Thursday (14 x £3)	42
Friday (guarantee)	28
	176

△ ACTIVITY 6

Total weekly wage:

	£
Monday (12 x £3)	36
Tuesday (14 x £3)	42
Wednesday (9 x £3)	27
Thursday (14 x £3)	42
Friday (8 x £3)	24
	171

As the weekly earnings are above £140, the guaranteed amount is not relevant to the calculations in this instance.

Conclusion

The payment of any guaranteed amount is not a bonus for good work but simply an additional payment required if the amount of production is below a certain level.

△ ACTIVITY 7

(a) Actual production for the week — 120,000 units

Standard production for the week
480 hours x 200 units — 96,000 units

Excess production — 24,000 units

Bonus percentage $= \frac{24,000}{96,000} \times 50\%$

$= 12.5\%$

Bonus rate $= 12.5\% \times £7.20$

$= £0.90$ per hour

The total bonus to split between the group is therefore:
480 hours x £0.90 = £432

(b) Total pay for Jones:

		£
Basic pay	42 hours x £6.00	252.00
Bonus	42 hours x £0.90	37.80
		289.80

△ ACTIVITY 8

(a)

		Singh		Smith
Normal rate	39½ x £6.50	£256.75	41 x £6	£246.00
Overtime premium	1½ ÷ 3 x £6.50	3.25	[(1 ÷ 3) + (2 x ½)] x £6	8.00
		260.00		254.00
Bonus	10,500/100 x £0.10	10.50	10,900/100 x £0.10	10.90
Gross earnings		270.50		264.90

(b) Gross earnings £270.50 ÷ 10,500 x 100 = £2.58 per 100 sheets.

(c) If the overtime was analysed to direct wages, it would be either because the work was done at the customer's request or because the overtime is normally worked at this level.

If analysed to overheads, it would be because overtime is not normally worked or, if it is, it varies.

ACTIVITY 9

ATTENDANCE RECORD

Name: Thomas Yung
Employee number: Y4791

Month	Work	Sick leave	Holiday	Training	Unpaid leave	Other	
January	14	2	5				21
February	11		4	3			18
March	19	2					21
April							
May							
June							
July							
August							
September							
November							
December							

Reasons for 'other' leave:

Test your knowledge

1
- Annual salary
- Hourly rate
- Piecemeal payments
- Bonus

2
- Employees lack security of guaranteed income.
- Employees can be penalised for low levels of production due to factors out of their control – e.g. poor quality material.
- May adversely affect quality of output.

3 On an assembly line or process where it is impossible for an individual person to increase productivity without the others doing so. In such circumstances it is not possible to measure individual output.

4 Idle time is made up of non-productive hours of direct labour which still has to be paid for.

5 Overtime premium is treated as direct labour when the overtime is worked to a customer's specific request.

4

EXPENSES

INTRODUCTION

We have now looked at two of the main cost items included in the cost of a product. All other costs that are not material or labour related are known as expenses. Expenses can be either direct or indirect. Indirect expenses are also known as overheads and we will be studying overheads in some detail in the next chapter. This chapter looks at the distinction between different types of expense, how expenses are recorded and capital and revenue expenditure.

KNOWLEDGE & UNDERSTANDING

- Procedures and documentation relating to expenses (Elements 6.1, 6.2)
- Relationship between the accounting system and the expenses costing system (Elements 6.1 and 6.2)
- The sources of information for revenue and costing data (Elements 6.1, 6.2 and 6.3)

CONTENTS

PERFORMANCE CRITERIA

- Identify direct costs in accordance with the organisation's costing procedures (Element 6.1)
- Record and analyse information relating to direct costs (Element 6.1)
- Calculate direct costs in accordance with the organisation's policies and procedures (Element 6.1)
- Identify overhead costs in accordance with the organisation's procedures (Element 6.2)
- Record and analyse information relating to overhead costs in accordance with the organisation's procedures (Element 6.2)

1 Categorisation of expenses

1.1 Introduction

We have already seen in earlier chapters how both materials and labour costs are categorised as either direct or indirect. Therefore the categorisation of costs that we have so far are:

Direct materials	–	materials actually used in making the product or providing the service.
Indirect materials	–	other materials such as those used by the maintenance department, stationery, etc.
Direct labour	–	labour costs of the employees working on the cost units.
Indirect labour	–	Other labour costs such as management and supervisory salaries.

1.2 Expenses

All of the other costs incurred by a business are known as expenses. In just the same way as with materials and labour, these expenses must be categorised as either direct expenses or indirect expenses (overheads).

1.3 Types of expense

Expenses of a business can cover a wide variety of areas. They might include:

- rent and rates
- electricity and power costs
- hire of machinery
- royalties
- patent costs
- sub-contractors costs
- insurance
- food for the canteen
- petrol for the delivery vans.

The list could go on and we will consider many of these later in this chapter and in the next chapter.

▷ ACTIVITY 1 

Give two significant overhead costs likely to be incurred by an international firm of management consultants.

[Answer on p. 88]

2 Direct and indirect expenses

2.1 Introduction

Remember that direct costs are those that can be related directly to a **cost unit**, whilst indirect costs (overheads) cannot be specifically traced to individual units.

It is worthwhile reminding yourself of the way these costs are dealt with in building up the total cost of a product. The following analysis is repeated for convenience from Chapter 1.

The **basic classification of costs** may be illustrated as follows:

	£
Direct costs	
Direct materials	250,000
Direct labour	120,000
Direct expenses (e.g. royalty payable per unit produced)	10,000
Prime cost (= Total of direct costs)	380,000
Indirect production cost (production overhead)	
(e.g. production supervisor's salary; machine oil)	25,000
Total production cost	405,000
Indirect non-production cost	
(e.g. administration overhead; selling overhead)	45,000
Total cost	450,000

2.2 Direct expenses

Expenses are far more likely to be indirect; however, some examples of direct expenses are given below. Note that direct expenses are production costs.

- **Royalty or patent costs** payable for use of a particular component, technique, trade name, etc in the production or service.
- **Sub-contracted charges**: if the business hires another company or a self-employed person to perform a particular function directly related to the product or service provided, this will be treated as a direct expense.

  Note that payments to a sub-contractor are not treated as labour costs but as a direct expense.

  For example, a building contractor will very often use sub-contractors to carry out electrical and plumbing work on a particular contract. The charge invoiced to the builder for this work (which will include both labour and materials) will be analysed as a direct expense of the contract.
- Expenses associated with **machinery or equipment** used for a particular job: hire charges, maintenance, power, etc.

2.3 Indirect expenses (overheads)

Indirect expenses are far more common and can be categorised in various ways, depending upon the organisational structure of the business and the level of detail required in the cost accounts.

Depending upon their nature, indirect expenses may be:
- production costs (production overheads); or
- non-production costs (non-production overheads).

2.4 Production overheads

We saw earlier that production overheads (although an indirect cost) are included in the total production cost of the product. They will include factory rent, rates, insurance, light, heat, power and other factory running costs; plant and machinery depreciation (see later in the chapter) and production service centres (works canteen, maintenance department, etc).

For a **service business**, it is more difficult to make a clear distinction between production and non-production overheads. For example, there is rarely a building that is devoted entirely to the provision of the service itself (i.e. equivalent to a factory) that does not also house the administrative, financial, selling and other functions of the business. Thus it is common to include most, if not all, of a service business's expenses under the other functional headings described below.

2.5 Non-production overheads

(a) **Administrative costs**

These are usually: non-productive buildings running costs; staff and other expenses for the accounts, secretarial, data processing, general maintenance and other support service departments; management salaries and motor vehicle expenses; training costs.

(b) **Selling and distribution costs**

These are usually: sales persons' salaries, commissions, etc; running costs of sales showrooms and offices; delivery vehicle expenses; packaging costs; advertising and promotional costs.

(c) **Finance costs**

These are usually: loan and overdraft interest payable; bank charges; lease interest element; cost of bad debts.

(d) **Legal and professional charges**

These are usually: auditors', accountants', solicitors', financial advisors' fees; professional subscriptions; professional indemnity insurance; licence costs.

These headings are, of course, only one possible way to analyse expenses (by function). One of the alternatives could be by **nature** (i.e. staff costs, buildings costs, fixtures, fittings and equipment costs).

It is in the area of expenses that your understanding of the distinction between direct/indirect and production/non-production costs is most severely tested – make sure you have this very clear in your mind.

▷ ACTIVITY 2

RFB plc makes wheels for a variety of uses: wheelbarrows, carts, toys, etc.

Complete the following form by analysing the cost items into the appropriate columns and agreeing the balances.

	Total £	Prime cost £	Production expense £	Admin expense £	Selling and distribution expense £
Wages of assembly employees	6,750				
Wages of stores employees	3,250				
Tyres for toy wheels	1,420				
Safety goggles for operators	810				
Job advert for new employees	84				
Depreciation of salesmen's cars	125				
Depreciation of production machines	264				
Cost of trade exhibition	1,200				
Computer stationery	130				
Course fee for AAT training	295				
Royalty for the design of Wheel 1477	240				
	14,568				

[Answer on p. 88]

3 Recording expenses

3.1 Allocation to cost centres

For control purposes, all costs eventually need to be **allocated to cost centres and/or cost units.** For materials and labour costs, this may be achieved by use of coded materials requisitions or analysed timesheets. The same principle will apply to expenses, although the allocation of indirect expenses may be done in stages

The general approach to expense recording and allocation will be as follows.

3.2 Direct expenses

When the invoice arrives (e.g. from a sub-contractor), the relevant product/job/client will be identified and the invoice **coded** accordingly before being passed to the data processing department for recording in the ledgers.

3.3 Indirect expenses

These, by definition, will not be directly identifiable with a particular cost unit and will therefore initially be charged to an **appropriate cost centre**.

Some expenses will relate solely to **one cost centre**. For example, advertising invoices will be allocated to the marketing/selling department and petrol bills for delivery vehicles will be charged to distribution. The invoices can therefore be coded to the appropriate centre.

Many expenses will, however, relate to **more than one cost centre** – for example, rent, rates and other buildings costs, where the building is shared by several cost centres.

Ultimately, these costs will need to be **shared between the appropriate cost centres** using some agreed basis (e.g. floor area occupied). The topic of such overhead apportionment is covered in detail in the next chapter.

Initially, however, the invoiced expense will generally be coded to a '**collecting**' cost centre for such costs – for example, building costs may be defined as a cost centre in itself. The subsequent apportionment will then be made as a set of transfers from this centre to the appropriate organisational cost centres.

3.4 Documentation

Most expenses will be documented by way of a **supplier's invoice or bill**. The authorisation for payment, codings for posting to the appropriate ledger accounts/cost centres and other internally added information may be attached by way of a standard **ink stamp** with appropriate boxes for manual completion

As with materials and labour, expense invoices will also be coded to indicate whether they are direct expenses or to which cost centre they are to be allocated if they are indirect expenses.

4 Capital and revenue expenditure

4.1 Introduction

One particular distinction in expenditure classification is between capital expenditure and revenue expenditure. This distinction is important when we consider a particular type of expense, depreciation, in the next section.

4.2 Capital expenditure

DEFINITION

Capital expenditure is expenditure incurred in:

(a) the acquisition of fixed assets required for use in the business and not for resale

(b) the alteration or improvement of fixed assets for the purpose of increasing their revenue-earning capacity.

4.3 Revenue expenditure

DEFINITION

Revenue expenditure is expenditure incurred in:

(a) the acquisition of assets acquired for conversion into cash (e.g. goods for resale)

(b) the manufacturing, selling and distribution of goods and the day-to-day administration of the business

(c) the **maintenance** of the revenue-earning capacity of the fixed assets (i.e. repairs, etc).

In practice, there can be some **difficulty** in clearly distinguishing between alteration/improvement of fixed assets (capital) and their maintenance (revenue). For example, is the installation of a modern heating system to replace an old inefficient system an improvement or maintenance? However, you should not need to make such decisions in your assessments.

4.4 The accounting treatments

Capital expenditure is initially shown in the balance sheet as fixed assets. It is then charged to profit and loss over a number of periods, via the depreciation charge.

Revenue expenditure is generally charged to the profit and loss account for the period in which the expenditure was incurred.

4.5 The relevance of the distinction to cost accounting

Cost accounting is mainly directed towards gathering and analysing cost information to assist management in planning, control and decision-making. In particular:

(a) the determination of **actual and budgeted costs** and profits for a period and for individual cost centres and cost units

(b) the valuation of **stocks** (raw materials, finished goods, etc).

Thus **revenue expenditure** is of far greater relevance than capital expenditure. The main impact of capital expenditure on the above will be the depreciation charges that arise and that may be charged as a direct product/service cost (as in the depreciation of machinery or equipment used in production or provision of a service) or as an overhead (depreciation of buildings, motor vehicles, etc).

5 Depreciation

5.1 Introduction

One of the major expenses of a business is the internally generated expense of depreciation and for Unit 6 you need to understand its purpose in outline and some simple calculations.

5.2 Purpose of depreciation

When a fixed asset is bought, it is usually expected to be **kept and used within the business for a number of years.** At the end of this period, it will be disposed of – either scrapped or sold at a price usually below the original price.

The asset will have been used to the business's benefit over several years and thus the cost of its use should be **spread over the same period.**

Thus the purpose of depreciation is to provide a **systematic method** of spreading the '**depreciable amount**' (cost less estimated disposal proceeds) over the '**useful life**' of the asset (how long the business intends to use it for).

Note that, in historic cost accounting, it is **not** the intention of depreciation to reflect the change in actual market value of the asset over its life.

5.3 Methods of depreciation

Depreciation can be calculated in a variety of different ways but there are two main methods for calculating the amount of depreciation to be charged in each year of the asset's useful life: **straight-line method** and **reducing balance method.**

5.4 Straight-line depreciation

This method provides for an **equal amount to be charged each year**; the annual charge would be calculated as:

$$\frac{\text{Cost} - \text{estimated disposal proceeds}}{\text{Years of expected useful life}}$$

5.5 Reducing balance depreciation

A **percentage** is applied to the asset's net book value or NBV.

DEFINITION

NBV is the original cost of the asset less the cumulative total of depreciation charged over its life to date.

The percentage to be used will be given in an assessment.

The depreciation rate is expressed as a percentage and the annual charge under this method is calculated as:

Net book value at the start of the year x depreciation rate

Note you do **not** adjust the NBV by the disposal proceeds – the rate will have been calculated so as to reduce the NBV down to the disposal proceeds over the useful life.

EXAMPLE

A delivery van is purchased for £6,000 cash. It is expected to be used within the business for four years, at the end of which it will be sold in part-exchange for a new one, with an expected trade-in value of £800.

Calculate the annual depreciation charges over the next four years using (i) the straight-line method and (ii) the reducing-balance method at a rate of 40%.

Solution

(i) The annual charge under the straight-line method will be:

$$\frac{£6,000 - £800}{4} = £1,300$$

(ii) Under the reducing balance method:

	£
Cost	6,000.00
Year 1 depreciation 6,000 x 40%	2,400.00
NBV at end of year 1	3,600.00
Year 2 depreciation 3,600 x 40%	1,440.00
NBV at end of year 2	2,160.00
Year 3 depreciation 2,160 x 40%	864.00
NBV at end of year 3	1,296.00
Year 4 depreciation 1,296 x 40%	518.40
NBV at end of year 4	777.60

The net book value at the end of year 4 should equate to the estimated disposal proceeds of £800 – the difference is due to rounding in the calculation of the 40% rate.

Year		*Straight line*		*Reducing balance*	
		NBV	*Charge*	*NBV*	*Charge*
		£	£	£	£
1	(start)	6,000		6,000.00	
		(1,300)	1,300	(2,400.00)	2,400.00
	(end)	4,700		3,600.00	
2		(1,300)	1,300	(1,440.00)	1,440.00
		3,400		2,160.00	
3		(1,300)	1,300	(864.00)	864.00
		2,100		1,296.00	
4		(1,300)	1,300	(518.40)	518.40
		800		777.60	

The **straight line method**, as its name suggests, leads to **equal depreciation charges** each year. The reducing balance method leads to **high charges in early years** (when NBV is high) and lower charges later on (when NBV is lower).

5.6 Choice of depreciation method

Management may choose whichever depreciation method they think most appropriate for each type of asset.

5.7 Disposal of fixed assets

If the estimates of the useful life and disposal proceeds (if any) incorporated into the calculation of the annual depreciation charges are accurate, the fixed asset will be standing at a book value equal to the proceeds (or nil) at the time of disposal. Thus there will be no adjustment to make on disposal.

Nearly always, though, things do not work out quite so neatly and there will be an adjustment to the depreciation charge in the year of disposal; this is the financial accounting '**profit or loss on disposal**'.

The **adjustment** will be calculated as:

Disposal proceeds – Net book value at date of disposal

and will be credited or charged (if negative) to the cost profit and loss account.

5.8 Recording depreciation

As depreciation is an internal calculation within a business, there will be no invoice or bill for the amount. Therefore the depreciation charges are normally recorded in the journal for inclusion in the accounting records.

▷ ACTIVITY 3

A PC costing £3,000 was expected to last for four years and to have a resale value of £200. The company policy is to depreciate assets using the straight-line method of depreciation.

(a) What is the annual depreciation charge to the administration cost centre?

(b) The computer was replaced after three years with no resale value. Calculate the obsolescence charge and state where this charge should be shown in the cost accounts.

[Answer on p. 88]

6 Test your knowledge

1 Indirect expenses are termed overheads. Make a list of six items of overhead expenditure incurred by a transport company.

2 Selling and distribution, admin and finance costs are considered overhead costs. Give one example of each for this classification.

3 Define the term capital expenditure.

4 Define the term depreciation.

[Answers on p. 89]

7 Summary

We have now seen how expenses cover all expenditure that is not related to materials or labour. It is important that you are able to distinguish between direct and indirect expenses. Direct expenses are any expenses that can be related specifically to a cost unit. Indirect expenses are far more common and are known as overheads.

The distinction between capital and revenue expenditure is also important as one of the major expenses of an organisation is the expense of depreciation. You must be able to decide whether an expense is capital or revenue in nature. Revenue expenditure is written off to the profit and loss account in the period in which it is incurred, whilst capital expenditure is written off to the profit and loss account over a number of accounting periods, via a depreciation charge (straight-line or reducing balance method).

Answers to chapter activities & 'test your knowledge' questions

ACTIVITY 1

Rent of premises, travelling expenses, etc.

ACTIVITY 2

	Total £	Prime cost £	Production expense £	Admin expense £	Selling and distribution expense £
Wages of assembly employees	6,750	6,750			
Wages of stores employees	3,250		3,250		
Tyres for toy wheels	1,420	1,420			
Safety goggles for operators	810		810		
Job advert for new employees	84			84	
Depreciation of salesmen's cars	125				125
Depreciation of production machines	264		264		
Cost of trade exhibition	1,200				1,200
Computer stationery	130			130	
Course fee for AAT training	295			295	
Royalty for the design of Wheel 1477	240	240			
	14,568	8,410	4,324	509	1,325

ACTIVITY 3

(a) $\frac{£3,000 - £200}{4}$ = £700 per annum

(b) Obsolescence is £(3,000 – 2,100) = £900. This should be written off to the cost profit and loss account.

Test your knowledge

1
- Rent and rates
- Insurance
- Telephone and postage
- Cleaning of vehicles
- Depreciation
- Road fund licence

2
- Salesmens' commission
- Computer stationery
- Interest on loans

3 Capital expenditure is that incurred on the acquisition or alteration and improvement of fixed assets used by the business to increase its revenue-earning capacity.

4 Depreciation is the reduction in the intrinsic value of an asset owing to wear and tear and/or the lapse of time.

ACCOUNTING FOR OVERHEADS

INTRODUCTION

We saw in the previous chapter how expenses are allocated to cost centres. However, when the benefit of an item of cost is shared by a number of different cost centres, the overhead will be apportioned (shared out) over a number of different cost centres in a process known as overhead apportionment. This chapter looks at how overheads are shared out (apportioned) between cost centres and how overheads are then absorbed into the cost of a product via an overhead absorption rate.

KNOWLEDGE & UNDERSTANDING

- Bases of allocation and apportioning indirect costs to responsibility centres: direct and step down methods (Element 6.2)
- The arbitrary nature of overhead apportionments (Element 6.2)
- Bases of absorption (Element 6.2)
- Analysis of the effect of changing activity levels on unit costs (Elements 6.1, 6.2 and 6.3)
- The sources of information for revenue and costing data (Elements 6.1, 6.2 and 6.3)

CONTENTS

PERFORMANCE CRITERIA

- Attribute overhead costs to production and service cost centres in accordance with agreed bases of allocation and apportionment (Element 6.2)
- Calculate overhead absorption rates in accordance with agreed bases of absorption (Element 6.2)
- Record and analyse information relating to overhead costs in accordance with the organisation's procedures (Element 6.2)

- Make adjustments for under and over recovered overhead costs in accordance with established procedures (Element 6.2)
- Review methods of allocation, apportionment and absorption at regular intervals in discussions with senior staff and ensure agreed changes to methods are implemented (Element 6.2)

1 Allocation and apportionment of overheads

1.1 Introduction

As with previous chapters, an understanding of overheads should be seen in the context of calculating a cost per unit for a product. For example:

	Cost / unit
	£
Direct labour cost	1.50
Direct material cost	3.20
Direct expenses	1.00
Prime cost	5.70
Production overheads	4.30
Total cost per unit	10.00

1.2 Marginal and absorption costing

In chapter 9 we shall study the difference between marginal and absorption costing. This distinction is based on the difference between fixed and variable costs that we studied earlier. In chapter 9 we shall see that if a business is using marginal costing fixed costs are excluded from the calculation of unit cost no matter whether they are production or non-production costs. If however a business is using absorption costing, the production fixed costs will be included in the cost of a unit.

In this chapter when we talk about absorbing costs into the cost of a unit, we are assuming that absorption costing is being used. This will all be clearer when we study chapter 9.

1.3 Direct expenses

The expenses that are identified as directly attributable to cost units are included in the prime cost of the cost units together with the direct materials costs and direct labour costs. These have already been dealt with in previous chapters.

1.4 Indirect costs or overheads

We have seen in earlier chapters of this text that there are three categories of indirect costs (making up total overheads):

- indirect materials
- indirect labour costs
- indirect expenses.

There are also two types of indirect costs or overheads:

- production overheads (included in cost per unit)
- non-production overheads (not included in cost per unit)

This inclusion of the indirect production costs, or overheads, in the total cost of the cost units is achieved by a process of allocation of overheads, apportionment of overheads and the absorption of overheads.

1.5 The process of allocation, apportionment and absorption

The purpose of allocation and apportionment is to attribute all production overhead costs to a production cost centre (remember we are not dealing with non- production overheads here). The purpose of absorption is to include the production overheads of a cost centre in the costs of the units produced by the cost centre.

Where a business has a mix of production and service cost centres, it may be necessary to allocate and apportion costs to both types of centre and then reapportion the service centres' costs to the production centres.

Overhead expenses incurred

Step 1: Overheads allocated or apportioned to cost centres using suitable bases

Cost centres

Step 2: Service centre costs reapportioned to production centres

Step 3: Overheads absorbed into units of production

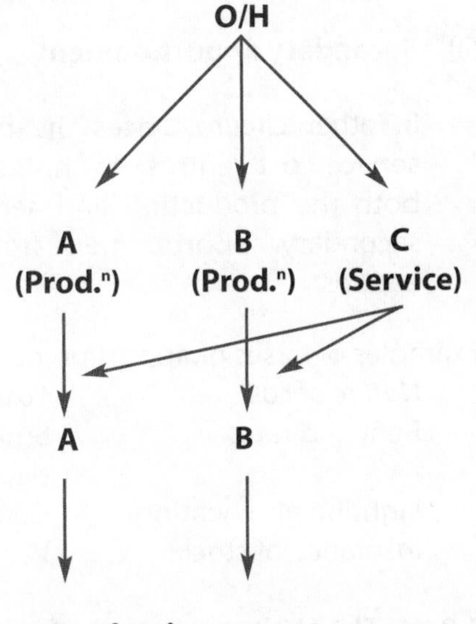

This process is detailed below.

1.6 Allocation of overhead costs

DEFINITION

Allocation attributes an entire cost to a single cost centre that has incurred that cost.

For example, if a cost centre rents its own premises then the whole rent cost of those premises is allocated to the cost centre.

Note that the cost centre may be either a production cost centre or a service cost centre.

Examples of costs that relate to one specific cost centre are given below:

Cost centre	*Allocated cost*
Canteen	Maintenance of kitchen equipment
	Chef's wages
Packing department	Depreciation of fork lift trucks

1.7 Cost apportionment

DEFINITION

Apportionment attributes a cost that is shared by two or more cost centres between those cost centres on a fair basis.

Thus if a business incurs a rent cost for premises shared by more than one cost centre, it will apportion that rent cost across the several centres.

(i) **Primary apportionment**

In some circumstances this may be done by apportioning all the indirect production costs to production centres.

(ii) **Secondary apportionment**

In other circumstances the business may have both production and service cost centres. In this case the primary apportionment will be to both the production and service cost centres. There will then be a secondary apportionment from the service centres to the production centres.

Examples of bases of apportioning overheads are as follows:

Nature of cost	*Possible bases of apportionment*
Rent and rates	Square footage occupied by various departments
Lighting and heating	Cubic capacity of locations or metered usage
Insurance of stocks	Value of stockholdings in various locations

1.8 The arbitrary nature of primary apportionment

With the exception of those costs that can be directly allocated to individual cost centres, the costs shown as attributable to a particular centre are **simply the result of using a particular basis to share out overall business costs.**

If different bases had been chosen, different figures would have resulted for each cost centre. Thus it is not appropriate to make generalised statements about the comparative levels of costs incurred by each department when the split has been done on an **essentially arbitrary basis.**

2 Primary apportionment

The following example and Activity 1 only use allocatioin and primary apportionment.

EXAMPLE

Example of cost allocation and apportionment

A Ltd has three departments: assembly, machining and administration. It incurs the following indirect costs in the year to December 20X4:

	£
Oil for machining department	2,000
Salary of assembly department supervisor	20,000
Insurance of machines in machining department	4,000
Rent of whole factory and offices	16,000
Administrative salaries	40,000
Canteen costs for whole factory and offices	15,000
	97,000

You are required to:

(a) Allocate the costs that can be allocated to the relevant department.

(b) Apportion the costs that cannot be allocated using the information below:

Department	Assembly	Machining	Administration
Area (sq ft)	3,000	3,000	2,000
No of employees	15	10	5

Solution

Overhead cost	Basis of allocation/ apportionment	Total £	Assembly £	Machining £	Administration £
Oil	Allocate	2,000		2,000	
Salary (supervisor)	Allocate	20,000	20,000		
Insurance	Allocate	4,000		4,000	
Rent	Floor area	16,000	6,000	6,000	4,000
Salaries (admin)	Allocate	40,000			40,000
Canteen	No of employees	15,000	7,500	5,000	2,500
		97,000	33,500	17,000	46,500

▷ ACTIVITY 1

This activity illustrates the apportionment of overheads using an overhead analysis sheet. Overhead costs are apportioned to service departments as well as production departments.

The activity stops at the point where general overheads have been apportioned to production departments and service departments. It does not show how service departments are apportioned to the production departments.

An organisation has two production departments, A and B, and two service departments, stores and the canteen.

The overhead costs for the organisation in total are as follows:

	£
Rent	32,000
Building maintenance costs	5,000
Machinery insurance	2,400
Machinery depreciation	11,000
Machinery running expenses	6,000
Power	7,000

There are also specific costs that have already been allocated to each cost centre as follows:

	£
Department A	5,000
Department B	4,000
Stores	1,000
Canteen	2,000

The following information about the various cost centres is also available:

	Total	Dept A	Dept B	Stores	Canteen
Floor space (sq ft)	30,000	15,000	8,000	5,000	2,000
Power usage	100%	45%	40%	5%	10%
Value of machinery (£000)	250	140	110	–	–
Machinery hours (000)	80	50	30		
Value of equipment (£000)	20	–	–	5	15
Number of employees	40	20	15	3	2
Value of stores requisitions (£000)	150	100	50	–	–

Task

Allocate and apportion the costs to the four departments.

Do not reapportion the service centre costs to the production departments.

[Answer on p. 112]

3 Secondary apportionment

3.1 Introduction

The next stage in the process is to allocate the service cost centre total costs to the production cost centres that make use of the service cost centre. This process is known as secondary apportionment.

The reason for doing this is that we want all the costs to be identified with a production cost centre so that we can then work out the cost of the units that the production cost centre produces.

3.2 Secondary apportionment with a single service centre

O EXAMPLE

A business has one service centre, the canteen, that serves two production centres. The overhead costs for a period have been allocated and apportioned between the three departments as given below.

	Production A	Production B	Canteen
Overhead	£10,000	£15,000	£12,000
Number of employees	100	200	

Reapportion the canteen's overheads to the production departments on the basis of the number of employees.

Solution

	Department A £	Department B £	Canteen £
Overhead	10,000	15,000	12,000
Number of employees 1:2	4,000	8,000	(12,000)
Total overhead for production department	14,000	23,000	

This method is known as direct apportionment and is appropriate either for one service cost centre or more provided that the service cost centres do not provide their service to other service cost centres.

▷ ACTIVITY 2

The cost of both the stores and the personnel departments of RFB plc have to be apportioned across the other cost centres. What bases would you recommend?

(a) Stores department
(b) Personnel department

[Answer on p. 113]

3.3 Secondary apportionment with two service centres

Problems may arise when there are two or more service centres with costs that have to be identified with production cost centres. (We shall only consider two service cost centres here.)

There are two situations

(a) The service centres only supply services to the production cost centres ie, they do not provide services to each other.
(b) The service centres provide services to the production cost centres and one of the service centres also provides services to the other service centre. (We do not consider the situation where the two service centres provide services to each other.)

3.4 Secondary apportionment with two service centres – direct method

This is used in situation (a) above ie, where the service centres do not supply services to each other.

You will typically be given the information about which centre provides services to whom as follows.

EXAMPLE

A business has two production centres, departments A and B, and two service centres, a canteen and a maintenance department. The proportion of the service departments services supplied to each department is as follows.

	Production A	Production B	Canteen	Maintenance
Usage of maintenance dept	40%	60%		
Usage of canteen	45%	55%		

This tells you that the maintenance department supplies 40% of its services to department A, 60% to department B and nothing to the canteen.

The canteen supplies 45% to department A, 55% to B and nothing to the maintenance department.

EXAMPLE

If we now add some numbers to the above percentage usage, the calculations will become clear.

The costs allocated and apportioned to the four departments are as follows before any of the service department costs have been apportioned to the production departments.

	£
Production A	50,000
Production B	60,000
Canteen	8,000
Maintenance	10,000

Apportion the service departments costs to the production departments.

Solution

	Dept A £	Dept B £	Canteen £	Maintenance £
	50,000	60,000	8,000	10,000
Secondary apportionment of maintenance	(40%) 4,000	(60%) 6,000		(10,000)
Secondary apportionment of canteen	(45%) 3,600	(55%) 4,400	(8,000)	

2.6 Secondary apportionment with two service centres – step down method

This is used in situation (b) above ie, where one of the service centres supplies services to the other.

EXAMPLE

We shall modify the above example so that the proportion of the service departments services supplied to each department is as follows

	Production A	Production B	Canteen	Maintenance
Usage of maintenance dept	40%	45%	15%	
Usage of canteen	45%	55%		

This tells you that the maintenance department supplies 40% of its services to department A, 45% to department B and 15% to the canteen.

The canteen supplies 45% to department A, 55% to B and nothing to the maintenance department.

Apportion the service departments costs to the production departments.

Solution

	Dept A £	Dept B £	Canteen £	Maintenance £
	50,000	60,000	8,000	10,000
Secondary apportionment of maintenance	(40%) 4,000	(45%) 4,500	(15%) 1,500	(10,000)
Secondary apportionment of canteen	(45%) 4,275	(55%) 5,225	(9,500)	

The method is as follows

Step 1 Identify the service department whose services are used by the other service department and apportion its costs to all the departments. In this case the maintenance department services the canteen so the maintenance costs are apportioned first.

Step 2 Now apportion the total costs of he canteen (ie its original costs (£8,000) plus its share of the maintenance costs (£1,500)) to the production departments.

This is referred to as the step down method.

EXAMPLE

Adam has a factory with two production departments, machining and painting, which are serviced by the maintenance and quality control departments. The maintenance department also spends some time in the quality control department.

Relevant information for a particular period is as follows:

	Machining	Painting	Maintenance	QC
Apportioned overheads (primary)	£20,000	£40,000	£10,000	£15,000
Usage of service departments Maintenance	30%	60%	–	10%
QC	50%	50%		

Show the secondary apportionment necessary using the step down method and the resulting total overheads to be attributed to each production department.

Solution

The service department costs should be charged out in the following order:

(1) Maintenance (since no charge is anticipated from other service cost centres and thus once this department's cost has been reapportioned, no further cost will be attributed to it from other centres).

(2) Quality control.

This leads to the following statement.

	Machining £	%	Painting £	%	Maintenance £	Quality control £	%
Apportioned overheads (primary)	20,000		40,000		10,000	15,000	
Secondary apportionment of maintenance	3,000	(30)	6,000	(60)	(10,000)	1,000	(10)
						16,000	
Secondary apportionment of quality control	8,000	(50)	8,000	(50)		(16,000)	
	31,000		54,000				

For this method you should always begin by apportioning the service cost centre which provides services to all centres, including the other service cost centre.

▷ ACTIVITY 3

A manufacturing business has two production departments and two service departments. The allocated overhead costs and apportioned general overhead costs for each department are as follows.

	£
Production department P1	140,000
Production department P2	200,000
Service department S1	90,000
Service department S2	120,000

Show how the overheads would be charged to each production department if it is assumed that the two service departments work as indicated in the table below.

	Apportionment ratio			
	Dept P1	Dept P2	Dept S1	Dept S2
Department S1	60%	40%	–	–
Department S2	25%	50%	25%	–

[Answer on p. 113]

3 Absorption of overheads

3.1 Introduction

Having collected all indirect costs in the production cost centres via overhead allocation and apportionment (primary and secondary), the total overhead of each production cost centre must be charged to the **output of the production cost centres.**

□ DEFINITION

Overhead absorption is the charging of a production cost centre's overhead costs to the cost units produced by the cost centre.

The **absorption rate** is normally calculated at the start of the period and is therefore **based on budgeted quantities** and on budgeted overheads. Various methods of absorption exist and the most suitable one should be chosen.

O EXAMPLE

Henry produces one product. Each unit of the product uses £20 worth of material and £10 of labour. Henry has two production centres, assembly and finishing. The following overheads are expected to be incurred:

Rent and rates	£12,000
Light and heat	£15,000

The assembly department occupies twice the floor area of the finishing department. Production is budgeted for 1,000 units.

Calculate the assembly overhead cost per unit, the finishing overhead cost per unit and hence the total cost per unit.

Solution

Step 1

Apportion the overheads to the cost centres, on the basis of size, therefore in the ratio of 2 to 1.

Overhead	Basis	Total	Assembly	Finishing
		£	£	£
Rent and rates	Area 2:1	12,000	8,000	4,000
Light and heat	Area 2:1	15,000	10,000	5,000
		27,000	18,000	9,000

Step 2

Calculate an overhead absorption rate per unit for each department.

Overhead per unit

Assembly

$$\frac{\text{Overhead}}{\text{Units produced}} = \frac{£18{,}000}{1{,}000} = £18 \text{ per unit}$$

Finishing

$$\frac{\text{Overhead}}{\text{Units produced}} = \frac{£9{,}000}{1{,}000} = £9 \text{ per unit}$$

Step 3

Total cost per unit:	£
Direct costs	
Materials	20
Labour	10
Overheads	
Assembly	18
Finishing	9
	57

The use of an absorption rate per unit is fine for one-product businesses/cost centres, but may be inappropriate for **multi-product businesses**.

O EXAMPLE

Sam produces pocket calculators and has one production department, having £15,000 overheads. Sam has planned production of 5,000 units.

$$\text{Overhead absorption rate per unit} = \frac{£15,000}{5,000} = £3/\text{unit}$$

Suppose Sam instead makes 3,000 pocket calculators and 2,000 complex computers. The complex computers take up twice as much time to produce as the calculators. The total overhead is the same as before. The overhead absorption rate per unit produced will be the same as before:

$$\text{Overhead absorption rate per unit} = \frac{£15,000}{3,000 + 2,000} = \frac{£15,000}{5,000} = £3/\text{unit}$$

Decide whether this is a reasonable basis to absorb overheads.

Solution

This is probably not a reasonable basis. The computer is likely to take longer to make and would involve the use of more of the indirect costs (e.g. supervisor's time). It is therefore necessary to choose an absorption basis that best reflects the demand of that product on the production department through which it passes.

3.2 Alternative absorption rate bases

Bases commonly used as an **alternative to the rate per unit**, when more than one product is involved, are as follows.

(a) rate per direct labour hour

(b) rate per machine hour.

Whichever method or combination of methods is used, the result will still only be an **approximate estimate** of what each product costs.

O EXAMPLE

Leo estimates that his total factory costs for the coming year will be as follows:

	£
Direct materials	40,000
Direct wages	60,000
Prime cost	100,000
Factory overhead	30,000
Total factory cost	130,000

The factory will produce 10,000 units of a variety of different products.

It is anticipated that during the year there will be 30,000 direct labour hours worked and 15,000 machine hours.

Compute the absorption rate per direct labour hour, per machine hour and per unit by which the factory overhead might be absorbed into the units produced.

Solution

(a) Direct labour hour rate $= \frac{£30,000}{30,000} = £1$ per direct labour hour

(b) Machine hour rate $= \frac{£30,000}{15,000} = £2$ per machine hour

(c) Rate per unit $= \frac{£30,000}{10,000} = £3$

▷ ACTIVITY 4

Bertram manufactures three products (A, B and C), the cost of each being:

	Product A	Product B	Product C
Direct materials	£14.40	£25.60	£36.00
Direct labour			
Machining @ £4.80 per hour	2 hours	1.5 hours	2 hours
Assembling @ £3.20 per hour	2 hours	2.5 hours	1 hour

Planned production is:

Product A	10,000 units
Product B	20,000 units
Product C	40,000 units

Production overheads for the forthcoming year are estimated at £120,000.

(a) Calculate the rate to be applied for absorbing the overheads into product costs using the direct labour hour rate.

(b) Calculate the production cost per unit of the three products.

[Answer on p. 113]

3.3 Choosing an absorption rate

The choice of which rate to be used depends largely on the nature of the operations concerned.

There is no correct method but in order to produce useful information it will always be preferable to choose an absorption rate which is in some way related to the costs being incurred.

Thus, for example, if the overhead consisted mainly of depreciation of machinery then it would be sensible to use the machine hour rate.

On the other hand, if the overhead consisted mainly of the salaries of supervisors who supervise the workforce then it would make sense to use the labour hour rate.

However, remember that at this stage of your studies you will only be using one absorption rate to cover the total of all the overheads. These overheads might comprise depreciation, supervisors' salaries, etc and there is therefore a fairly obvious dilemma as to which absorption rate to choose. If most of the overheads seem to relate to machinery costs or labour costs then choose the absorption rate accordingly. However, if you are in doubt, the most common rate to choose would be the labour hour rate.

A more modern approach is to use activity based costing (ABC). You do not need to know how this works but you could get a bonus mark if you mention it!

O EXAMPLE

A factory has two production departments, cutting and finishing. The budgeted overheads and production details are:

	Cutting	Finishing
Budgeted overhead	£100,000	£80,000
Budgeted direct labour hours	10,000	40,000
Budgeted machine hours	60,000	5,000

The cutting department is a machine intensive department whilst finishing is labour intensive.

The factory makes two products, the X and the Y. The production details for these are:

	X	Y
Direct labour hours		
Cutting	1	2
Finishing	4	6
Machine hours		
Cutting	8	6
Finishing	2	2

Calculate the overhead cost to be absorbed into each product using an appropriate absorption rate for each cost centre.

Solution

Step 1 Choose and calculate the absorption rates

It makes sense to use the machine hour rate for the machine intensive cutting department and the labour hour rate for the labour intensive finishing department.

Cutting – machine hour rate $= \frac{£100,000}{60,000}$

$=$ £1.67 per machine hour

Finishing – labour hour rate $= \frac{£80,000}{40,000}$

$=$ £2 per direct labour hour

Step 2 Absorption into unit costs

	£
Product X	
Cutting 8 hours x £1.67	13.36
Finishing 4 hours x £2	8.00
	21.36
Product Y	
Cutting 6 hours x £1.67	10.02
Finishing 6 hours x £2	12.00
	22.02

As the cutting cost centre is machine intensive then a machine hour absorption rate will best reflect how the overhead is incurred and, as the finishing cost centre is labour intensive, a direct labour hour rate is most appropriate in this cost centre.

Which rate should be used? Possibly both – **it depends upon the nature of the overheads.**

- If some overheads tended to be associated with labour time (heating costs, for example), then a direct labour hour rate could be used to absorb those.
- The machine hour rate could be used to absorb those costs associated with machine time (e.g. machine power costs).

▷ ACTIVITY 5

Pears plc manufactures children's clothing. The General Manager (GM) is concerned about how the costs of the various garments it produces are calculated. The material cost varies from one garment to another and the rates of pay in the various departments also vary to reflect the different skills offered. Both these prime costs are charged direct to individual garments so that any variation is taken into account.

	Overhead cost £000	Numbers employed	% of floor area	Material issued £000	Machine hours
Production departments					
Cutting	187	10	40	200	15,000
Sewing	232	15	30	250	25,000

Finishing	106	8	15	100
Service departments				
Stores	28	2	5	–
Maintenance	50	3	10	50

Using the overhead analysis sheet below, apportion:

(a) (i) stores department's costs to the production and maintenance departments

(ii) maintenance department's costs to the cutting and sewing departments only.

Select the most suitable basis for each apportionment and state the bases used on the overhead analysis sheet. (Calculations to the nearest £.)

Overhead analysis sheet **Date**

	TOTAL	PRODUCTION			SERVICE	
		Cutting	Sewing	Finishing	Stores	Maintenance
	£	£	£	£	£	£
Overheads	603,000	187,000	232,000	106,000	28,000	50,000
Apportion stores (Basis:)						
Apportion maintenance (Basis:)						
Total						

(b) Calculate overhead absorption rates for the three production departments using:

(i) machine hour rates for the cutting and sewing departments

(ii) labour hour rate for the finishing department given that 12,000 labour hours will be worked in the finishing department.

(Calculations to two decimal places of a £.)

(c) Explain briefly why it is appropriate to use machine hour rates in the cutting and sewing departments.

[Answer on p. 114]

4 Under/over absorption of overheads

4.1 Introduction

The overhead absorption rates that were calculated in the previous section are calculated at the start of the accounting period. Therefore they are based upon budgeted figures. This means that the calculation is based upon the budgeted overhead cost and the budgeted production details, be it units, labour hours, machine hours, etc.

The reason for this is that management will need to know the budgeted cost of each unit of production in order to be able to make decisions about the products and the sales and production. This requires not only budgeted figures for direct materials, direct labour and direct expenses, but also for overheads.

4.2 Absorption of overheads

During the accounting period the cost of each unit of production will include overheads based upon this budgeted overhead absorption rate.
But what happens if:

(a) the **actual production levels** are different from the budgeted levels and/or

(b) the actual overheads for the period are different from the budgeted overheads?

If either or both of these occur, the use of the predetermined absorption rate will result in an **over- or under-absorption of overheads**. (Sometimes referred to as over or under recovery of overheads.)

O EXAMPLE

A factory budgets to produce 10,000 units, its budgeted overhead is £30,000 and the budgeted direct labour hours are 4,000.

The factory actually produced only a total of 8,000 units in the coming year, due to a machine breakdown, in 3,200 labour hours. In addition, the cost of machine repairs resulted in actual factory overheads amounting to £34,000.

What is the under- or over-absorbed overhead?

Solution

The over-/under-absorbed overheads can be determined by the comparison of the actual total overhead cost with the overheads that will be absorbed at the budgeted overhead absorption rate.

$$\text{Budgeted overhead absorption rate (OAR)} = \frac{£30{,}000}{4{,}000}$$

= £7.50 per direct labour hour

	£
Actual overheads	34,000
Overheads absorbed: 3,200 hours x £7.50	24,000
Overheads under-absorbed	10,000

So the production costs in the profit and loss account for the year will only incorporate £24,000 of factory overheads, whereas in fact £34,000 was spent. If no adjustment is made, the profit figure will be £10,000 higher than it should be.

4.3 The adjustment for under-/over-absorption

The adjustment for this under- or over-absorbed overhead is made as a debit or credit to the costing profit and loss account.

	£
Sales	X
Cost of sales (using budgeted overhead absorption rates)	X
Gross profit	X
Less: Under-absorption of fixed overheads	(10,000)
Adjusted gross profit	X

The accounting entry for this adjustment would be as follows.

		£	£
Debit:	Profit and loss account	10,000	
Credit:	Production overheads		10,000

The double entry for this is covered in more detail in Chapter 10.

▷ ACTIVITY 6 

The actual overheads for a department were £6,500 last period and the actual output was 540 machine hours. The budgeted overheads were £5,995 and the budgeted output was 550 machine hours. Calculate the under- or over-absorbed overhead and state whether it would increase or reduce the profit for the period.

[Answer on p. 114]

5 Non-production overheads

5.1 Introduction

So far, only production overheads have been considered. There are other, non-production overheads which can be divided into the broad categories listed below, all of which can be absorbed into each cost unit using similar methods as described, if desired.

But remember, if the non-production overheads are absorbed into units, the cost per unit will not be the stock value per unit. The stock value per unit comprises only the production costs, direct and indirect.

5.2 Administrative overheads

Expenditure attributable to the general office, data processing, finance charges and audit fees.

5.3 Selling overheads

Expenditure attributable to the selling of the product, eg sales personnel, costs of advertising, cash discounts allowed, rent and rates of show rooms and sales offices.

5.4 Distribution overheads

Expenditure incurred in packing and delivery.

6 Test your knowledge

1. Define the term cost allocation.

2. Define the term cost apportionment.

3. List three items of overhead that might be apportioned to cost centres on the basis of area occupied.

4. Define the term overhead absorption.

5. Give three examples of commonly used bases for overhead absorption rates.

6. If overhead absorbed is greater than overhead incurred, the overhead is said to be?

[Answers on p. 115]

7 Summary

This chapter has considered how the overheads of a business are gathered together and traced through to the cost units to which they relate. Under the traditional cost accounting approach the budgeted overheads of the business are collected together in each of the cost centres, either by allocation, if the overhead relates to only one cost centre, or by apportionment on some fair basis if the overhead relates to a number of cost centres.

Once the overheads have been allocated and apportioned, the next stage is to reapportion any service cost centre overheads into the production cost centres. Care must be taken here where the service cost centres provide their service to other service cost centres. In these cases the step down method is required to reapportion the service cost centre overheads.

When all of the budgeted overheads are thus included in the production cost centres, an absorption rate must be chosen. In many cases this will be either on a direct labour hour basis or on a machine hour basis.

The overhead absorption rate is based upon the budgeted overheads and the budgeted production level. This rate is then used to include the overheads in the production throughout the accounting period. If the activity levels and/or the amount of the overhead is different to the budgeted figures, then the overhead will be either over- or under-absorbed. An adjustment is made for this when the costing profit and loss account is prepared.

Answers to chapter activities & 'test your knowledge' questions

ACTIVITY 1

OVERHEAD ANALYSIS SHEET PERIOD ENDING ....

	Total	Production		Service	
	£	Dept A £	Dept B £	Stores £	Canteen £
Overheads allocated directly to cost centres	12,000	5,000	4,000	1,000	2,000
Overheads to be apportioned					
Rent					
Basis: floor space					
15/30 x £32,000	32,000	16,000			
8/30 x £32,000			8,534		
5/30 x £32,000				5,333	
2/30 x £32,000					2,133
Building maintenance					
Basis: floor space	5,000				
15/30 x £5,000		2,500			
8/30 x £5,000			1,333		
5/30 x £5,000				834	
2/30 x £5,000					333
Machinery insurance	2,400				
Basis: machine value					
140/250 x £2,400		1,344			
110/250 x £2,400			1,056	–	–
Machinery depreciation	11,000				
Basis: machine value					
140/250 x £11,000		6,160			
110/250 x £11,000			4,840	–	–
Machinery running expenses	6,000				
Basis: machine hours					
50/80 x £6,000		3,750			
30/80 x £6,000			2,250	–	–
Power	7,000				
Basis: power usage percentages					
£7,000 x 45%		3,150			
£7,000 x 40%			2,800		
£7,000 x 5%				350	
£7,000 x 10%					700
Allocated and apportioned costs	75,400	37,904	24,813	7,517	5,166

ACTIVITY 2

(a) Stores – number of requisitions or value of issues per cost centre.

(b) Personnel – number of employees per cost centre.

ACTIVITY 3

Start by apportioning the costs of department S2.

	Total	Dept P1	Dept P2	Dept S1	Dept S2
	£	£	£	£	£
Allocated costs/ share of general costs	550,000	140,000	200,000	90,000	120,000
Apportion:					
S2 costs (25 : 50 : 25)		30,000	60,000	30,000	(120,000)
				120,000	
S1 costs (60 : 40)		72,000	48,000	(120,000)	
		242,000	308,000		

ACTIVITY 4

(a) Annual budget

	Product A	Product B	Product C	Total
Production (units)	10,000	20,000	40,000	70,000
Production hours				
Machining	20,000	30,000	80,000	130,000
Assembly	20,000	50,000	40,000	110,000
Total hours	40,000	80,000	120,000	240,000

Fixed overhead per direct labour hour: $\frac{£120,000}{240,000} = £0.50$

(b)

	Product A	Product B	Product C
	£	£	£
Direct materials	14.40	25.60	36.00
Direct labour			
Machining	9.60	7.20	9.60
Assembly	6.40	8.00	3.20
Overheads	(4 hr x £0.50) =	(4 hr x £0.50) =	(3 hr x £0.50) =
	2.00	2.00	1.50
	32.40	42.80	50.30

ACTIVITY 5

(a) Overhead analysis sheet Date: December 20X3

	Total	Production departments			Service departments	
		Cutting	Sewing	Finishing	Stores	Maintenance
	£	£	£	£	£	£
Overheads	603,000	187,000	232,000	106,000	28,000	50,000
Apportion stores (Basis: Material issues)		9,333	11,667	4,667	(28,000)	2,333
Apportion maintenance (Basis: Machine hours)		19,625	32,708	–	–	(52,333)
	603,000	215,958	276,375	110,667	–	–

(b)

	Cutting	Sewing	Finishing
Apportioned o/heads	£215,958	£276,375	£110,667
Machine hours	15,000	25,000	
Labour hours			12,000
Absorption rates	£14.40	£11.06	£9.22

(c) In the cutting and sewing departments, activity level and output can be best expressed by the machine hours worked. Therefore the absorption rates should be based on machine hours.

ACTIVITY 6

	£
Actual overhead	6,500
Absorbed 540 x $\frac{£5,995}{550}$	5,886
Under-absorbed overhead	614

It would reduce profits for the period.

Test your knowledge

1 The allotment of whole items of cost to a cost centre or cost unit.

2 The allotment of proportions of items of cost to cost centres or cost units.

3 Rent and rates, heat and light, and buildings insurance.

4 The charging of overhead to cost units.

5 Direct labour hour
Machine hour
Direct labour %

6 Over-absorbed (or over-recovered).

JOB AND BATCH COSTING SYSTEMS

INTRODUCTION

So far in this text we have looked at cost unit costing systems where all of the cost units are made in a manufacturing process and are all the same. We are now going to turn our attention to two other costing systems, those of job costing and batch costing. Job costing involves individual jobs with different materials and labour requirements (for example, car repairs). Batch costing, on the other hand, is suitable for businesses that produce batches of identical items (for example, bars of soap) though batch costs may vary from product to product.

KNOWLEDGE & UNDERSTANDING

- Calculation of product and service cost (Elements 6.1, 6.2 and 6.3)
- Costing systems appropriate to the organisation: job, batch, unit and process costing systems (Elements 6.1, 6.2 and 6.3)

CONTENTS

PERFORMANCE CRITERIA

- Identify direct costs in accordance with the organisation's costing procedures (Element 6.1)
- Record and analyse information relating to direct costs (Element 6.1)
- Calculate direct costs in accordance with the organisation's policies and procedures (Element 6.1)
- Record and analyse information relating to overhead costs in accordance with the organisation's procedures (Element 6.2)

1 Job costing

1.1 Introduction

So far in this text we have considered a unit costing system where direct costs are attributed to each cost unit and then overheads are included in the unit cost by absorption. This is the appropriate method of costing when production is made up of a number of identical individual cost units. However, there are other methods of costing which are appropriate for different manufacturing or service situations.

1.2 Job costing

Job costing is used in a business where the production is made up of individual large jobs, each of which is different and has different inputs of materials and labour. Each job is identified separately and the costs are identified for this specific job, coded to it and recorded as job costs. Effectively the job becomes the cost unit.

Typical examples of businesses that use job costing would be construction, aeroplane manufacture, printing and vehicle repairs.

1.3 Job card

Each job is given a separate identifying number and has its own job card. The job card is used to record all of the direct costs of the job and then eventually the overheads to be absorbed into the job.

A typical job card might look like this:

EXAMPLE

JOB NO 217

Materials requisitions	**Quantity**	**£**	**Total**
0254 G 3578	100 kg	4,200	
0261 K 3512	50 kg	3,150	
			7,350
Wages – employees	**Hours**	**£**	
13343	80	656	
15651	30	300	
12965	40	360	
	150		1,316
Overheads	**Hours**	**£**	
Absorption rate £12	150	1,800	1,800
Total cost			**10,466**

1.4 Materials requisitions

When materials are requisitioned then the requisition will be clearly coded to indicate the job to which it relates. The quantity and value of the material will then be recorded on the job card. This happens each time materials are requisitioned for this job.

1.5 Job analysis of gross pay

Where it is required to identify wages or salaries with particular jobs, then in addition to their attendance records the employees concerned will have to keep job time records, either a card or slip for each job on which they work or a daily or weekly timesheet listing the various jobs. Such records should be scrutinised and approved by a supervisor or other manager. When a bonus system is in operation, the record will also show the time allowed for each job.

The accounts department will reconcile the job time bookings for a period with the recorded attendance times, any discrepancy being investigated.

After reconciliation, the various job hours will be summarised and valued at gross pay rates.

1.6 Wages analysis sheet

A wages analysis sheet will be used to split the wages costs between each job. A typical wages analysis sheet is given below.

EXAMPLE

WAGES ANALYSIS SHEET

Department: Assembly
Average hourly rate: £5.25
Week ended: 17.5.XX

Employee	Productive work								Non-productive			Total hours
Clock No	Job No 10		Job No 15		Job No 17		Job No 21					
	Hrs	£	Hrs	£	Hrs	£	Hrs	£	Code	Hrs	£	
1214	12	63.00							107	4	21.00	40
1215			8	42.00	15	78.75	16	84.00				40
1216	30	157.50	15	78.75			10	52.50				40
1217	25	131.25	10	52.50	8	42.00			102	7	36.75	40
1218			12	63.00	20	105.00	4	21.00	107	4	21.00	40
Total hours	67		45		43		30			15		200
Total amount		351.75		236.25		225.75		157.50			78.75	1,050.00

The wages cost of each employee for each job is recorded on the job card.

1.7 Overhead costs

In just the same way as overheads are absorbed into cost units in a unit costing system, so the overheads must also be absorbed into each job in a job costing system. This absorption will be done according to the absorption basis that the business uses, probably either on a direct labour hour basis or a machine hour basis.

EXAMPLE

JOB NO 06255

Materials requisitions	**Quantity kg**	**£**	**Total**
5167 SHG 46	20	4,800	
0261 K 3512	30	5,400	
			10,200
Wages – employees	**Hours**	**£**	
895643	120	1,272	
095875	110	1,056	
325097	30	474	
	260		2,802
Overheads	**Hours**	**£**	
Total cost			

Show the total cost of the job.

Solution

JOB NO 06255

Materials requisitions	**Quantity kg**	**£**	**Total**
5167 SHG 46	20	4,800	
0261 K 3512	30	5,400	
			10,200
Wages – employees	**Hours**	**£**	
895643	120	1,272	
095875	110	1,056	
325097	30	474	
	260		2,802
Overheads	**Hours**	**£**	
Absorption @ £15.60 per hour	260		4,056
Total cost			**17,058**

The principles behind a job costing system are exactly the same as those in a unit costing system with the job being treated as the cost unit. What a job costing system does mean is that there must be tight control over the coding of all materials requisitions and hours worked to ensure that each job is charged with the correct direct costs and eventually overheads.

▷ ACTIVITY 1

Given below are the direct costs of job number 3362.

		£
Materials requisitions:		
15496		1,044
15510		938
15525		614
Wages analysis:		
Employee 13249	40 hours	320
Employee 12475	33 hours	231
Employee 26895	53 hours	312

Overheads are apportioned to jobs at the rate of £3.50 per direct labour hour.

What is the total cost of Job 3362?

[Answer on p. 124]

2 Batch costing

2.1 Introduction

A further costing system is that of batch costing. This is suitable for a business that produces batches of identical units, but each batch is for different units.

For example, a clothing manufacturer may have a production run for a batch of men's white shirts of collar size 16 inches. It may then have a production run for a batch of men's trousers with a waist size of 34 inches.

Each batch of production will have different costs but each unit within the batch should have the same cost. Therefore the total cost of the batch of production is calculated and divided by the number of units in that batch to find the cost per unit for that batch of production.

2.2 Costs included

As with any costing system the costs to be included in the batch cost are the direct costs of material, labour and any direct expenses plus the overheads that are to be absorbed into the batch.

Each batch of production is treated, for cost accounting purposes, as a cost unit.

EXAMPLE

A paint manufacturer is producing 1,000 litres of matt vinyl paint in 'sea blue'. The direct costs of the production run are:

	£
Materials	1,600
Labour 15 hours @ £10	150

Overheads are to be absorbed into the batch at a rate of £16 per direct labour hour.

What is the cost per litre of this batch of paint?

Solution

Batch cost		£
Materials		1,600
Labour		150
Overheads 15 hours @ £16		240
Total batch cost		1,990
Cost per litre	=	$\frac{£1,990}{1,000}$
	=	£1.99

ACTIVITY 2

A manufacturer of frozen meals produces a batch of 20,000 units of salmon tagliatelli. The direct costs of this batch are:

	£
Materials	15,000
Labour 1,000 hours	4,200

Overheads are to be absorbed at rate of £1.20 per direct labour hour.

What is the cost of each portion of salmon tagliatelli?

[Answer on p. 124]

3 Test your knowledge

1 Give three examples of businesses that would use job costing.

2 When material usage and cost is posted to a job card it is transferred from which stores document?

3 Give an example of a business that would use a system of batch costing.

4 A wages analysis sheet would classify labour cost as one of which two categories?

[Answers on p. 124]

4 Summary

In this short chapter we have considered different costing systems that are suitable for different types of organisation. A business that produces many identical products can cost those products on a cost per unit basis. A business that produces one-off products for customers, each of which is different, will use a job costing system. This treats each individual job as a cost unit and therefore attributes the direct costs to that job, as well as the overheads according to the organisation's overhead absorption basis.

In a business which produces a number of different products but produces them in batches of an identical unit then a batch costing system is appropriate. Here the costs of each batch of production are gathered together as though the batch was a cost unit and the actual cost per unit is calculated by dividing the batch cost by the number of units produced in that batch.

Answers to chapter activities & 'test your knowledge' questions

ACTIVITY 1

	£	£
Materials costs:	1,044	
	938	
	614	
		2,596
Labour costs:	320	
	231	
	312	
		863
Overhead costs:		
(40 + 33 + 53) hours x £3.50		441
Total cost		3,900

ACTIVITY 2

	£
Materials	15,000
Labour	4,200
Overheads 1,000 hours @ £1.2	1,200
Total cost	20,400
Cost per unit	20,400 / 20,000
	= £1.02

Test your knowledge

1 Motor vehicle repairs, jobbing builder and a printer.

2 Material requisition.

3 Shirt manufacturer.

4 Direct and indirect labour.

PROCESS COSTING

INTRODUCTION

In the last chapter we introduced you to two different types of costing system. In this chapter we are going to look at a very important costing system known as process costing. This type of costing is used when goods or services result from a sequence of continuous or repetitive operations or processes, for example in the manufacture of paint. We are going to look at how to calculate the cost of a unit of product (a tin of paint), what happens if some of the materials are 'lost' during the process and how to deal with work-in-progress. Most students find process costing to be a complex topic, but don't worry; with plenty of practice a sound technique can be developed that will help you to tackle questions on this topic.

KNOWLEDGE & UNDERSTANDING

- Calculation of product and service cost (Elements 6.1, 6.2 and 6.3)
- Costing systems appropriate to the organisation: job, batch, unit and process costing systems (Elements 6.1, 6.2 and 6.3)

CONTENTS

PERFORMANCE CRITERIA

- Identify direct costs in accordance with the organisation's costing procedures (Element 6.1)
- Record and analyse information relating to direct costs (Element 6.1)
- Calculate direct costs in accordance with the organisation's policies and procedures (Element 6.1)
- Record and analyse information relating to overhead costs in accordance with the organisation's procedures (Element 6.2)

1 Basics of process costing

1.1 When is it used?

Process costing is the costing method applicable where goods or services result from a sequence of continuous or repetitive operations or processes.

Process costing is sometimes referred to as continuous operation costing.

Examples include the chemical, cement, oil, paint and textile industries.

1.2 Illustration

Process costing is used when a company is mass producing the same item and the item goes through a number of different stages. Here is an example of a two-process manufacturing operation:

First stage	Input some material valued at £1 per kg Process (do some work to) the material (which costs money) Output the material now valued at £4 per kg
Second (final) stage	Input material from the first stage valued at £4 per kg Process the material again, increasing the cost Output the material now valued at £9 per kg. This now goes into finished goods ready to be sold. Cost of sales is £9 per kg

1.3 The basic process cost per unit

Process costing is very similar to batch costing, as we calculate the total costs for the process and divide by the number of units to get a cost per unit.

The main difference is that the process is ongoing so the costs and output for a particular time period are used.

We shall use a simple example to illustrate the basic approach.

A manufacturing operation involves two processes. The data for the first process during a particular period is as follows:

- At the beginning of the period, 2,500 kg materials are introduced to the process at a cost of £3,500.
- These materials are then worked upon, using £600 of labour and incurring/absorbing £450 of overheads.
- The resulting output is passed to the second process.

We need to ascertain the cost per kg of output that will be transferred to the second process:

Total process 1 costs	=	£3,500 + £600 + £450 = £4,550
Total output	=	2,500 kg

Thus, the output to process 2 would be costed at:

$$\frac{£4,550}{2,500 \text{ kg}} = £1.82 \text{ per kg output}$$

$$\text{So cost per unit of output} = \frac{\text{Total process costs}}{\text{Total output}}$$

1.4 Ledger accounts in process costing

To keep track of the costs we could prepare a process account for each process. This resembles a T account with extra columns. The reason for the extra columns is that we have to keep track of how many units we are working on as well as their value.

The usual costs appearing in such an account are those for materials, labour and overheads. (Labour and overheads are often combined under the heading 'conversion costs'.) In the case of materials we record both units and monetary amount; in the case of conversion costs we record the monetary amount only, because they do not add any units.

With process accounts the inputs into the process go into the left (debit) side of the account and output on the right (credit) side.

EXAMPLE

The process account for the above example might thus appear as follows.

Process 1 account

	Kg	£		Kg	£
Materials	2,500	3,500	Output materials to Process 2	2,500	4,550
Labour		600			
Overheads		450			
	2,500	4,550		2,500	4,550

1.5 Complications

There are two main complications to this procedure, which we shall now consider:

- What happens if some of the material to the process is lost?
- What happens if the process is not complete at the end of a period?

2 Normal and abnormal losses

2.1 Normal losses

In many industrial processes, some input is lost (through evaporation, wastage, etc) or damaged during the production process. The first thing we will look at in process costing is the concept of normal losses and abnormal losses or gains.

Normal loss represents items that you expect to lose during a process, and its cost is therefore treated as part of the cost of good production.

O EXAMPLE

At the start of a heating process 1,000kg of material costing £16 per kg is input. During the process, conversion costs of £2,000 are incurred. Normal loss (through evaporation) is expected to be 10% of input. During March 1,000kg were input and output was 900kg.

Compute the unit and total cost of output in March.

Solution

First we need to sort out the units. We can do this using the flow of units equation:

Input	=>	**Output**	+	**Loss**
1,000 kg	=>	900 kg	+	100 kg (to balance)

Thus the loss was as expected – 10% of input, i.e. it is all normal loss.

We now need to compute the cost per unit of good output.

Total input costs:		
Materials	£16 x 1,000 kg	£16,000
Conversion costs		£2,000
		£18,000

These costs will be spread over the good output units – thus the cost attributable to the normal loss units is absorbed into the good units.

Cost per unit of output:

$$= \frac{\text{Total process costs}}{\text{Input units – Normal loss units}}$$

$$= \frac{£18,000}{(1,000 - 100)}$$

$$= £20 \text{ per kg}$$

Total cost of output = 900 kg x £20 = £18,000.

This can be represented in a process account as follows.

Process account – March

	Kg	£		Kg	£
Input	1,000	16,000	Output	900	18,000
Conversion costs		2,000	Normal loss	100	–
	1,000	18,000		1,000	18,000

Notice that the units and the monetary amounts balance. Normal loss is valued at zero as its cost has been absorbed into that of good output.

2.2 Abnormal loss

Any actual loss in excess of the normal (expected) loss is known as abnormal loss. This is not treated as part of normal production cost and is separately identified and costed throughout the process. Its cost is then written off to profit and loss.

EXAMPLE

Abnormal loss – example

In April, 1,000 kg were input (at £16 per kg) to the same process as above and actual output was 800 kg. Conversion costs were £2,000 as before.

Required

Prepare the process account for the month of April.

Solution

Again look at the units only to start with.

Input	=>	**Output**	+	**Loss**
1,000 kg	=>	800 kg	+	200 kg (to balance)

The total loss is now 200 kg, when we only expected a (normal) loss of 100 kg.

The extra 100 kg is an abnormal loss. It represents items that we did not expect to lose. In this example it may have been that the temperature was set too high on the process, causing more of the input to evaporate.

To make the units balance we therefore need to include 100 units on the right of the process account to represent this abnormal loss:

Process account – April (units only)

	Kg	£		Kg	£
Input	1,000		Output	800	
Conversion costs	–		Normal loss	100	
			Abnormal loss	100	
	1,000			1,000	

Now we examine the costs.

Input, normal loss and output are valued at the same cost per kg as before. The value for abnormal loss is the same as that of output, i.e. £20 per kg.

Process account – April

	Kg	£		Kg	£
Input	1,000	16,000	Output	800	16,000
Conversion costs	–	2,000	Normal loss	100	–
			Abnormal loss	100	2,000
	1,000	18,000		1,000	18,000

The units and values are now balanced. The £2,000 value of the abnormal loss represents lost output. This output cannot be sold (it has evaporated) and therefore the profits of the company will be reduced. In the accounts, the value of abnormal loss is debited to the profit and loss account.

2.3 Abnormal gain

An abnormal gain occurs where losses are less than expected. Its treatment is the same as abnormal loss only the debits and credits are reversed.

O EXAMPLE

In May 2,000 kg at £16 per kg were input to the heating process and £4,000 conversion costs incurred. This month output was 1,950 kg.

Required

Prepare the process account for the month of May.

Solution

We begin by looking at the units flow.

Input	=>	Output	+	Loss
2,000 kg	=>	1,950 kg	+	50 kg (to balance)

The total loss is now only 50 kg, when we expected a (normal) loss of 2,000 x 10% = 200 kg. We have therefore made an abnormal gain of 150 kg.

To balance the units on the process account then, we need to put the normal loss (200 kg) on the right and the abnormal gain (150 kg) on the left.

The completed process account is shown below.

Process account – May

	Kg	£		Kg	£
Input	2,000	32,000	Output	1,950	39,000
Conversion costs	–	4,000	Normal loss	200	–
Abnormal gain	150	3,000			
	2,150	39,000		2,150	39,000

The abnormal gain has to go on the left to avoid having negative numbers in the T account.

Output and abnormal gain are both valued at £36,000/(2,000 – 200)kg = £20 per kg. Since we now have additional units to sell, the abnormal gain is **credited** to the profit and loss account. We have an additional 150 units to sell at £20 per unit.

▷ ACTIVITY 1

You are given the following information about the 'mashing' process of Mushypeas Ltd during June:

Ingredients input	1,600 kg @ £2.80 per kg
Labour	100 hours @ £6 per hour
Overheads	100 hours @ £2.50 per hour

Water loss from the process is expected to result in a 15% loss in input volume.

Calculate the cost per kg of output and show the mashing process account if actual output was:

(i) 1,360 kg

(ii) 1,250 kg

(iii) 1,540 kg.

[Answer on p. 142]

3 Scrap value of losses

3.1 Introduction

So far we have assumed that all losses are scrapped (i.e. they have nil value) but what happens if this is not the case?

EXAMPLE

Maine Ltd processes a liquid. When it is produced a residue forms on top of the liquid. This is skimmed off and sold off for 90p/litre. Normal waste is 10% of input. Costs for batch 975D were as follows.

	£
Materials (10,000 litres @ £2 per litre)	20,000
Labour	2,000
Overheads	500
Total	22,500
Actual output	8,500 litres

Required

Prepare the process account.

Solution

First, the units:

Input	=>	**Output**	+	**Loss**
10,000 litres	=>	8,500 litres	+	1,500 litres (to balance)

The total loss is 1,500 litres, when we only expected a (normal) loss of 10% x 10,000 = 1,000 litres. Thus, we have an abnormal loss of 500 litres.

The process account will include normal loss as before but this time it is **valued at its scrap value.** The sales value of the normal loss is then **subtracted** from the costs of the process before calculating value per unit.

In the example we would receive 1,000 litres @ £0.90 = £900 for selling the normal loss. This is entered in the process account. The same amount is then subtracted from the process costs, leading to the following valuation.

$$\text{Cost per unit} = \frac{\text{Total process costs} - \text{Normal loss proceeds}}{\text{Total input units} - \text{Normal loss units}}$$

$$\text{Cost per unit} = \frac{£22,500 - £900}{10,000 - 1,000} = £2.40 \text{ per litre}$$

Although we actually have 1,500 loss units to sell (1,000 litres of normal loss plus 500 units of abnormal loss), we only include the sales value of the **normal** loss in this calculation.

Process account

	Ltr	£		Ltr	£
Input	10,000	20,000	Output @ £2.40	8,500	20,400
Material Labour	–	2,000	Normal loss @ £0.90	1,000	900
Overheads		500	Abnormal loss @ £2.40	500	1,200
	10,000	22,500		10,000	22,500

3.2 Normal and abnormal loss accounts

We now require two additional T accounts to show the value of the normal and abnormal loss in this situation. These match the costs of the losses (from the process account) against the scrap proceeds. Here we show separate accounts for each type of loss, sometimes they will be combined into one 'process loss' account.

EXAMPLE

Show the normal and abnormal loss accounts for Maine Ltd.

Solution

Normal loss (scrap)

	Ltr	£		Ltr	£
Normal loss from process account	1,000	900	Cash proceeds (Debit bank)	1,500	1,350
Abnormal loss	500	450			
	1,500	1,350		1,500	1,350

Note: This account may also be called a 'scrap' account.

This T account takes the total sales of 1,500 units and cash proceeds received of £1,350 and divides it between the normal and abnormal loss units.

Abnormal loss

	Ltr	£		Ltr	£
Abnormal loss from process = full value of lost units @ £2.40	500	1,200	Cash received for abnormal loss @ £0.90	500	450
			P&L (balancing figure)		750
	500	1,200		500	1,200

If the scrap value of the losses was nil, then we would have written off £1,200 to the profit and loss account. However, in this case we were able to sell the abnormal loss for £0.90 per unit. Since we received £450 for selling the abnormal scrap, we are only £750 worse off than if we sold all the lost units at full value.

In effect we are worse off by (£2.40 – £0.90) = £1.50 per unit lost. Since the abnormal loss was 500 units then we are worse off by 500 x £1.50 = £750 which matches the P&L figure in the abnormal loss account.

In the above, the normal and abnormal loss accounts are being used purely to calculate the debit or credit to the profit and loss account.

Remember they are not needed if the losses have no scrap value since the value of abnormal loss may be debited straight to the profit and loss account.

Using a single losses account is simpler:

1. Complete the double entry for both normal and abnormal losses from the process account.
2. Put in the total cash proceeds.
3. The Balancing figure is the abnormal loss or gain.

Loss

	Ltr	£		Ltr	£
Normal loss from process account	1,000	900	Cash proceeds	1,500	1,350
Abnormal loss from process account	500	1,200	P&L (balancing figure)		750
	1,500	2,100		1,500	2,100

▷ ACTIVITIES 2, 3 & 4

2 X plc

X plc processes a chemical. Input to a batch was as follows.

	£
Materials (10,000 litres)	10,000
Labour and overheads	800
Total	10,800

Normal loss is 10% of input.

Actual output = 8,700 litres. The remaining liquid was skimmed off and sold for 36p per litre.

Required

Record this in a process account, a normal loss account and an abnormal loss account.

3 Y plc

Y plc runs a distillery making whisky. Input to a batch was as follows.

	£
Materials (1,000 litres)	5,000
Labour and overheads	427
Total	5,427

Normal loss is 10% of input as impurities are removed.

Actual output = 920 litres. The impurities separated off were sold for 27p per litre.

Required

Record this in a process account, a normal loss account and an abnormal loss account

4 Chemical compound

A chemical compound is made by raw material being processed through two processes. The output of Process A is passed to Process B where further material is added to the mix. The details of the process costs for the financial period number 10 were as shown below.

Process A	
Direct materials	2,000 kg @ £5 per kg
Direct labour	£7,200
Process plant time	140 hours @ £60 per hour

Process B	
Input from process A	?
Direct material	1,400 kg @ £12 per kg
Direct labour	£4,200
Process plant time	80 hours @ £72.50 per hour

The departmental overhead for period 10 was £6,840 and is absorbed into the costs of each process on direct labour costs in each process.

	Process A	Process B
Expected output	80% of input	90% of input
Actual output	1,400 kg	2,620 kg

Normal loss is contaminated material, which is sold as scrap for £0.50 per kg from Process A and £1.825 per kg from Process B.

Required

Prepare the following accounts:

(a) Process A
(b) Process B
(c) Normal loss (scrap)
(d) Abnormal loss/gain
(e) Finished goods (extract)
(f) Profit and loss (extract).

[Answers on p. 143]

4 Equivalent units and work-in-progress

4.1 Introduction

We begin with a word of warning. This next section on equivalent units is not easy to assimilate in one go: do not worry if you have to read it through a number of times.

Process costs are used for many products where the process may not be completed at the end of a period (e.g. manufacturing cars). Thus, some of the process costs are attributable to finished, complete units and some to incomplete, work-in-progress, units.

We need to decide how the costs should be split over these different categories of production. Note that you are only expected to deal with closing work-in-progress. Opening WIP is assumed to be nil.

To do this we use the concept of equivalent units.

Illustration

We have 1,000 units that are 50% complete at the end of a period. How many finished units is this equivalent to?

1,000 x 50% = 500 equivalent units (these are abbreviated to EUs).

In other words, we could have made 500 units and finished them instead of 1,000 half-finished units.

The calculation of equivalent units is quite straightforward.

Equivalent units = Number of physical units x percentage completion.

O EXAMPLE

DL Ltd is a manufacturer. In Period 1 the following production occurred.

Started and finished units	=	1,000
Closing work-in-progress (abbreviated as CWIP)	=	2,000 units each 25% complete

Required

How many finished units is this equivalent to?

Solution

		EUs
Started and finished	1,000 x 100%	1,000
Starting closing WIP	2,000 x 25%	500
Total		1,500

4.2 Valuing work-in-progress and finished goods

If we can calculate the cost of an equivalent unit we can calculate the cost of finished goods and closing WIP.

The cost per equivalent unit is simply calculated as total cost divided by the number of EUs produced. Assume that in DL above the costs in Period 1 were £6,000.

We calculated above that 1,500 EUs were produced in Period 1.

Thus, cost per EU = £6,000/1,500 = £4 per EU.

This can be used to calculate the value of the finished goods and closing WIP:

- Value of goods started and finished = 1,000 x £4 = £4,000.
  You can see that the value of finished goods is £4 per unit and the total value of finished goods is £4,000.
- Value of closing WIP = 500 x £4 = £2,000.
  This will go in the balance sheet for Period 1 (and will become the value of opening WIP for Period 2).

Note that closing WIP is valued using EUs and not physical units. Many students get this wrong in the exam.

Our process account for Period 1 would look as follows. (It is not usual to show units when WIP is involved as it can confuse.)

Process account – Period 1

	£		£
Costs	6,000	Finished goods	4,000
		Closing WIP c/f	2,000
	6,000		6,000

You can see that the method is quite straightforward:

- Calculate total equivalent units.
- Calculate total costs.
- Calculate cost per equivalent unit.
- Value finished goods and closing WIP as number of EUs x cost per EU.

▷ ACTIVITY 5

Process WIP

On 1 March 20X0 a process started work on 350 units and at the end of the month there were still 75 units in the process, each 60% complete.

The total cost of materials, labour, etc input during March was £3,696.

Required

Calculate the value of both finished goods and closing WIP.

[Answer on p. 146]

5 Treatment of materials and other costs

5.1 Different degrees of completion

So far we have talked about 'production costs' in general. In most questions, however, these will be split between various types of cost.

Assume that a process involves some direct materials and some direct labour and overheads.

Labour and overhead costs added together are often called conversion costs.

Usually, all the material is put in at the beginning of the process, whereas the conversion is 'added' as the product advances through the process. This means there may be a **different amount of equivalent units for conversion and materials.**

A good example is making a cake. All the materials (cake mix, fruit etc) are put in at the beginning, whereas cooking the cake advances through the process over time. So if the cake takes two hours to cook, after one hour the cake is 50% complete as regards the heating but is 100% complete with regard to materials.

Because of this, we have to keep track of the equivalent units for materials and for conversion separately.

For example, imagine we have a process in which all the materials are input at the beginning and that at the end of November there are 200 units 75% complete.

For conversion there are 200 x 75% = 150 EUs.

For materials all 200 units are complete (since all material went in at the beginning), i.e. 200 EUs.

EXAMPLE

Blue Ridge Ltd specialises in making disinfectants. Production requires several successive processes and the production details of the first process are as follows.

Units started in period	1,400 units
Closing work in process	400 units
Degree of completion:	
Materials	100%
Conversion	50%
Costs incurred in April:	
Materials	£81,060
Conversion	£71,940

Required

Calculate the value of closing work in process and completed units.

Solution

First start, as always, with a physical flow of units:

Units started	=	**Units completed**	+	**Closing WIP**
1,400	=	1,000	+	400

The 1,000 units completed is a balancing figure.

The effective units, costs and costs per unit are most clearly set out in a table as follows:

Input	Effective units			Costs	Costs per EU (£)
	Completed in period	c/f in CWIP	Total EU	Total costs (£)	
Materials	1,000	400 (100%)	1,400	81,060	57.90
Conversion	1,000	200 (50%)	1,200	71,940	59.95
				153,000	**117.85**

Work carefully through the table to ensure you are quite happy about where all the figures have come from.

Note that for the 'completed in period column' effective units = physical units, as they were wholly processed in this period. These units are then added to the effective units for the CWIP, to arrive at the total EU units processed in the period.

Total costs are then divided by the total EU to get a cost per EU for each type of input cost, and a total cost for each completed unit.

The costs may now be attributed to the categories of output as follows:

		£	£
Completed units:	1,000 x £117.85		117,850
Closing WIP:	Materials 400 x £57.90	23,160	
	Conversion200 x £59.95	11,990	
			35,150
			153,000

The process account would appear as follows. Note that if any units are entered in here, they would be physical units, not EU, as this would get too confusing!

Process account

	£		£
Materials	81,060	Completed goods	117,850
Conversion	71,940	Closing work-in-progress	35,150
	153,000		153,000

▷ ACTIVITY 6

NH Ltd

NH Ltd has two processes.

Material for 12,000 items was put into **process 1**. There were no opening stocks and no process losses. Other relevant information is:

Transfers to process 2	9,000 items
Direct material cost	£36,000
Direct labour cost	£32,000
Overheads	£8,530

The unfinished items were complete as to materials and 50% complete as to labour and overheads.

Information for process 2 is as follows:

Transfers from process 1	9,000 items (at a cost determined above)
Items completed	8,200 items
Labour cost	£34,596
Overheads	£15,300

There were no materials added in process 2 other than the units transferred from process 1. There were no process losses.

The unfinished items were deemed to be 25% complete in labour and overheads.

Required

Prepare process accounts for each process.

[Answer on p. 146]

6 Test your knowledge

1 For what type of manufacturing operation is process costing used?

2 What is the difference in treatment of costs attributable to normal and abnormal loss units?

3 Give the formula for computing cost per unit of output where there are losses that have a scrap value.

4 How are equivalent units calculated?

5 The value of output produced by Process A, and passed to Process B, is £3,400. Where will this figure appear in the process accounts?

[Answers on p. 148]

7 Summary

As you now know, process costing is used when a company is mass producing the same item and the item goes through a number of different stages. As the item goes through the different stages, losses may occur: normal losses, abnormal losses and abnormal gains. Losses may be scrapped or they may have a 'scrap value' which means that they can be sold (and that the revenue generated is used to reduce the costs of the process concerned).

Sometimes, at the end of an accounting period, a process may not be finished and there may be incomplete (work-in-progress) units. When this happens, it is necessary to use the concept of equivalent units to decide how the process costs should be split over work-in-progress and finished goods.

This chapter has shown you a whole new costing system that requires lots of question practice! In order to consolidate what has been covered in this chapter, make sure that you have a go at the key techniques questions in the workbook section of this book.

Answers to chapter activities & 'test your knowledge' questions

ACTIVITY 1

(i) **Actual output = 1,360 kg**

Flow of units:

Input	=>	**Output**	+	**Loss**
1,600 kg	=>	1,360 kg	+	240 kg (to balance)

Normal loss = 15% x 1,600 = 240 kg. We have no abnormal loss/gain.

Process costs = 1,600 x £2.80 + 100 x £6 + 100 x £2.50 = £5,330

$$\text{Cost per unit of output} = \frac{\text{Total process costs}}{\text{Input units} - \text{Normal loss units}} = \frac{£5,330}{(1,600 - 240)} = £3.92 \text{ per kg}$$

Mashing process – June

	kg	£		kg	£
Ingredients	1,600	4,480	Output	1,360	5,330
Labour		600	Normal loss	240	–
Overheads		250			
	1,600	5,330		1,600	5,330

Note that since the cost per unit is not exactly £3.92, the value of output has been rounded to balance the account.

(ii) **Actual output = 1,250 kg**

Flow of units:

Input	=>	**Output**	+	**Loss**
1,600 kg	=>	1,250 kg	+	350 kg (to balance)

Normal loss = 240 kg and we therefore have an abnormal loss of 110 kg.

Process costs = £5,330 as before.

$$\text{Cost per unit of output} = \frac{\text{Total process costs}}{\text{Input units} - \text{Normal loss units}} = \frac{£5,330}{(1,600 - 240)} = £3.92 \text{ per kg, as before}$$

The process account will now look like this:

Mashing process – June

	kg	£		kg	£
Ingredients	1,600	4,480	Output	1,250	4,900
Labour		600	Normal loss	240	–
Overheads		250	Abnormal	110	430
	1,600	5,330		1,600	5,330

(iii) **Actual output = 1,540 kg**

Flow of units:

Input	=>	**Output**	+	**Loss**
1,600 kg	=>	1,540 kg	+	60 kg (to balance)

Normal loss = 240 kg and we therefore have an abnormal gain of 180 kg.

Process costs = £5,330 as before.

Cost per unit of output = £3.92 per kg, as before.

The process account will now look like this:

Mashing process – June

	kg	£		kg	£
Ingredients	1,600	4,480	Output	1,540	6,036
Labour		600	Normal loss	240	–
Overheads		250			
Abnormal gain	180	706			
	1,780	6,036		1,780	6,036

△ ACTIVITY 2

X plc

Process account

	Ltrs	£		Ltrs	£
Input material	10,000	10,000	Output	8,700	10,092
Labour and overheads	–	800	Normal loss	1,000	360
			Abnormal loss	300	348
	10,000	10,800		10,000	10,800

Output valued at (£10,800 – £360)/9,000 = £1.16 per litre

Normal loss

	Ltrs	£		Ltrs	£
Process	1,000	360	Cash	1,300	468
Bal b/f to abnormal loss	300	108			
	1,300	468		1,300	468

Abnormal loss

	Ltrs	£		Ltrs	£
Process	300	348	Normal loss	300	108
			P&L		240
	300	348		300	348

ACTIVITY 3

Y plc

Process account

	Ltrs	£		Ltrs	£
Input material	1,000	5,000	Output	920	5,520
Labour and overheads	–	427	Normal loss	100	27
Abnormal gain	20	120			
	1,020	5,547		1,020	5,547

Output valued at (£5,427 – £27)/900 = £6.00 per litre

Normal loss

	Ltrs	£		Ltrs	£
Process	100	27	Cash	80	21.6
			Bal b/f to abnormal gain	20	5.4
	100	27		100	27

Abnormal loss

	Ltrs	£		Ltrs	£
Normal loss	20	5.4	Process	20	120
P&L		114.6			
	20	120		20	120

ACTIVITY 4

Chemical compound

(a)

Process A

	kg	£		kg	£ per kg	£
Direct material	2,000	10,000	Normal loss (W2)	400	0.500	200
Direct labour		7,200	To Process B (W3)	1,400	18.575	26,005
Process costs		8,400	Abnormal loss	200	18.575	3,715
Overhead (W1)		4,320				
	2,000	29,920		2,000		29,920

(W1) £6,840 x 7,200/(7,200 + 4,200) = £4,320

(W2) Normal loss = 20% of input = 2,000 x 20% = 400 kg

(W3) Value of output = £(29,920 – 200)/(2,000 – 400) = £18.575 per kg

(b)

Process B

	kg	£		kg	£ per kg	£
From Process A	1,400	26,005	Finished goods (W6)	2,620	21.7516	56,989
Direct material	1,400	16,800	Normal loss (W4)	280	1.825	511
Direct labour		4,200				
Overhead		2,520				
Process costs		5,800				
Total costs		55,325				
Abnormal gain (W5, W6)	100	2,175				
	2,900	57,500		2,900		57,500

(W4) Normal loss = 10% x (1,400 + 1,400) = 280

(W5) Expected output = 2,800 – 280 = 2,520 units; actual output 2,620; 100 units abnormal gain

(W6) Cost per unit = £(55,325 – 511) / (2,800 – 280) = £21.7516 (kept this accurate to avoid rounding errors)

(c)

Normal loss (scrap) account

	kg	£		kg	£
Process A	400	200	Cash – process A	600	300.00
Process B	280	511	Cash – process B	180	328.50
			Balance – transfer to abnormal loss	(100)	82.50
	680	711		680	711

(d)

Abnormal loss / gain account

	£		£
From normal loss a/c	82.50	Process B	2,175.00
Process A	3,715.00	P&L	1,622.50
	3,797.50		3,797.50

(e)

Finished goods

	kg	£		kg	£
Process B	2,620	56,989			

(f)

P & L

	£		£
Abnormal loss/gain	1,622.50		

△ ACTIVITY 5

Process WIP

Physical flow of units

Units started		Units completed		Closing WIP
350	=	275 (bal fig)	+	75

Equivalent units of production

Units started and finished	275
Closing WIP (75 x 60%)	45
	320

∴ Cost per equivalent unit = $\frac{£3,696}{320}$ = £11.55

Value of finished goods	=	275 x £11.55	=	£3,176.25
Value of closing WIP	=	45 x £11.55	=	£519.75
				£3,696

△ ACTIVITY 6

NH Ltd

Process 1

The physical flow of units:

Units started	=	Units completed	+	Closing WIP
12,000	=	9,000	+	3,000 (bal)

	Effective units			Costs	Costs per EU (£)
Input	Completed in period	CWIP	Total EU	Total costs (£)	
Materials	9,000	3,000 (100%)	12,000	36,000	3.00
Conversion	9,000	1,500 (50%)	10,500	40,530	3.86
				76,530	**6.86**

The costs may now be attributed to the categories of output as follows:

			£	£
Completed units	9,000 x £6.86			61,740
Closing WIP:	Materials	3,000 x £3	9,000	
	Conversion	1,500 x £3.86	5,790	
				14,790
				76,530

The process account will thus appear as follows:

Process 1 account

	Units	£		Units	£
Materials	12,000	36,000	Process 2	9,000	61,740
Labour		32,000	Work-in-progress	3,000	14,790
Overheads		8,530			
		76,530			76,530

Process 2

The physical flow of units:

Units started	=	Units completed	+	Closing WIP
9,000	=	8,200	+	800 (bal)

	Effective units			Costs	Costs per EU (£)
Input	Completed in period	CWIP	Total EU	Total costs (£)	
Process 1	8,200	800 (100%)	9,000	61,740	6.86
Conversion	8,200	200 (25%)	8,400	49,896	5.94
				111,636	**12.80**

The costs may now be attributed to the categories of output as follows:

			£	£
Completed units	8,200 x £12.80			104,960
Closing WIP:	Process 1	800 x £6.86	5,488	
	Conversion	200 x £5.94	1,188	
				6,676
				111,636

The process account will thus appear as follows:

Process 2 account

	No	£		No	£
Materials (process 1)	9,000	61,740	Finished goods	8,200	104,960
Labour		34,596	Work-in-process	800	6,676
Overheads		15,300			
	9,000	111,636		9,000	111,636

Test your knowledge

1. Process costing is used where goods are produced from a sequence of continuous or repetitive operations or processes.

2. The net costs attributable to normal loss units are absorbed into the cost of other units (good and abnormal loss). The costs attributable to abnormal loss units are accounted for separately and written off to profit and loss (net of any scrap proceeds).

3. Cost per unit of output =

$$\frac{\text{Total process costs} - \text{normal loss scrap proceeds}}{\text{Total input units} - \text{normal loss units}}$$

4. Equivalent units = physical units x % complete

5. It will appear as a credit (on the right) on the Process A account (output) and as a debit (left) on the Process B account (input).

COST BOOKKEEPING

INTRODUCTION

We are now going to turn our attention to the way in which we record transactions involving materials, labour and overheads in an integrated bookkeeping system. The concept of double entry should not be new to you as you will have studied it at Foundation Level. We will be looking at the basic accounting entries for costs and showing how they are transferred into the work-in-progress account and then into the finished goods account and then finally, into the costing profit and loss account.

KNOWLEDGE & UNDERSTANDING

- Recording of cost and revenue data in the accounting records (Elements 6.1 and 6.2)
- Relationship between the materials costing system and the stock control system (Element 6.1)
- Relationship between the labour costing system and the payroll accounting system (Element 6.2)
- Relationship between the accounting system and the expenses costing system (Elements 6.1 and 6.2)
- The sources of information for revenue and costing data (Elements 6.1, 6.2 and 6.3)

CONTENTS

PERFORMANCE CRITERIA

- Record and analyse information relating to direct costs (Element 6.1)
- Record and analyse information relating to overhead costs in accordance with the organisation's procedures (Element 6.2)

1 Integrated bookkeeping system

1.1 Introduction

The costs of a business have to be recorded in a bookkeeping system in just the same way as you have studied for financial accounting. Costs and expenses are debited to their relevant accounts and income is credited. A costing profit and loss account is then produced showing the income from sales less the costs of production and non-production expenses.

DEFINITION

An **integrated bookkeeping system** is one where the ledger accounts kept provide the necessary information for both costing and financial accounting.

In this chapter we only consider absorption costing. Marginal costing is not studied until the next chapter.

1.2 Ledger accounts

The main ledger accounts necessary to deal with the costs of production are as follows:

- **Materials cost account**
  The materials cost account is debited when materials are purchased.
  The account is credited when materials are taken out of stores and issued to production.
- **Labour cost account** – this is sometimes known as the wages control account.
  The total labour cost is recorded as a debit.
  The account is then credited with the different elements of this labour cost – production labour and non-production, or indirect, labour – effectively removing the costs from this account and transferring them into work-in-progress, overheads, etc.
- **Work-in-progress account** – this is where the cost of producing the cost units is recorded. On the debit side is recorded the cost of materials issued to production, the cost of direct labour and any production overheads.
  When the production is completed a credit entry is made transferring these costs to the finished goods account.
- **Finished goods account**
  This is debited with the transfer from the work-in-progress account for the production cost of the completed goods.
  The cost of goods actually sold during the period are then transferred to the costing profit and loss account by a credit entry to the finished goods account.
- **Production overhead control account**
  This is debited with the production overhead incurred and credited with the production overhead absorbed.
  The simple way to get the debits and credits the correct way round is to remember that with costs:
  - a debit entry puts costs into the account, and
  - a credit entry takes the costs out.

There are other ledger accounts that we will use but these are the main costing ledger accounts with which you must become familiar.

Cost bookkeeping

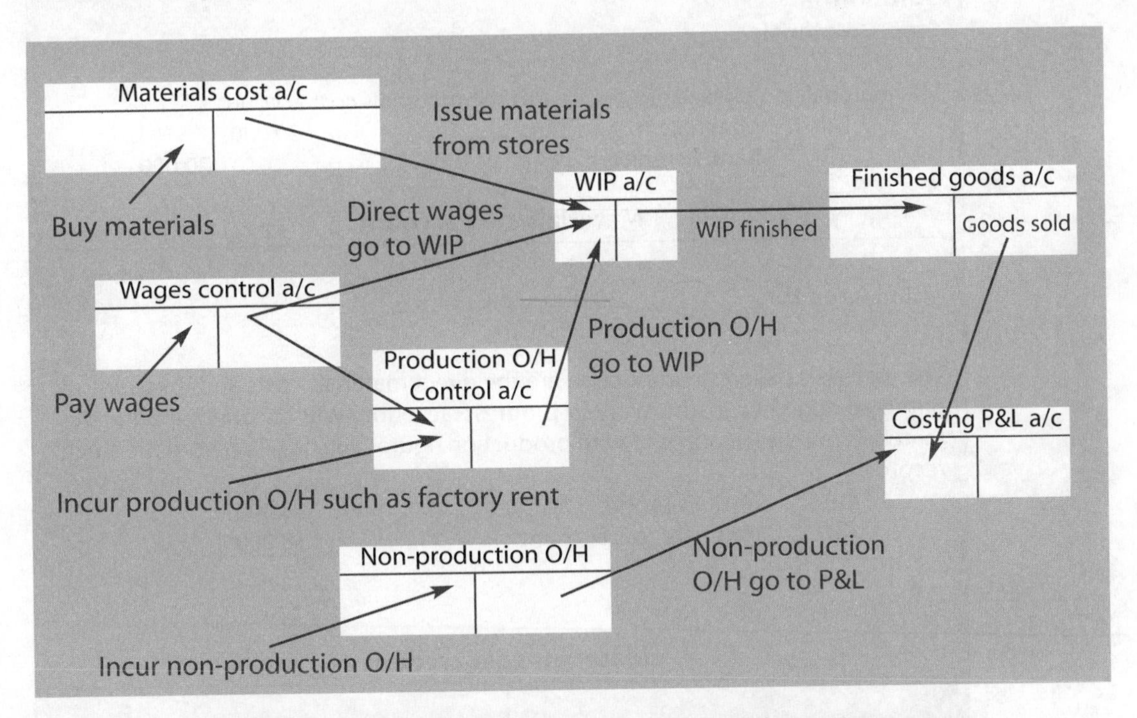

EXAMPLE

We will now work through a simple example to show how the cost bookkeeping works and how a costing profit and loss account is prepared. To keep it simple we have assumed that this is the first month of the business's transactions therefore there are no opening balances on any of the accounts.

A manufacturing business had the following transactions for its first month of production and trading:

	£
Materials purchased	20,000
Materials issued to production	18,000
Direct labour cost	15,000
Indirect production labour cost	3,000
Other production overheads incurred	6,000
Production overheads absorbed into production	8,000
Work-in-progress transferred to finished goods	35,000
Finished goods transferred to cost of sales	32,000
Sales	45,000
Non-production overheads incurred	2,000

We will now deal with the accounting entries for each of these transactions.

Note that when we make the initial entry for the above amounts into the ledger accounts, we enter the narrative 'bank/creditor' to indicate the other half of the double entry, e.g. for materials purchased £20,000, this means that we either paid cash of £20,000 or bought the goods on credit.

Solution

Step 1: Materials

The materials purchased are debited to the materials cost account:

DR	Materials cost account	20,000	
CR	Bank / creditors		20,000

Materials cost account

	£		£
Bank/creditors	20,000		

The materials issued to production are the direct materials costs and these are all gathered together in the work-in-progress account (WIP account) – both the materials purchased and issued to production figures will be taken from the stock records:

DR	Work-in-progress account	18,000
CR	Materials cost account	18,000

Materials cost account

	£		£
Bank/creditors	20,000	WIP account	18,000

Work-in-progress account

	£		£
Direct materials	18,000		

Step 2: Labour

The total labour cost is debited to the wages control account – this figure would be taken from the payroll system:

DR	Wages control account	18,000
CR	Bank	18,000

Wages control account

	£		£
Total wages cost (15,000 + 3,000)	18,000		

The direct labour cost is then transferred to the work-in-progress account and the indirect production labour cost is transferred to the production overhead control account:

DR	Work-in-progress account	15,000
CR	Wages control account	15,000
DR	Production overhead control account	3,000
CR	Wages control account	3,000

Wages control account

	£		£
Total wages cost (15,000 + 3,000)	18,000	WIP account	15,000
		Production overhead account	3,000

Work-in-progress account

	£		£
Direct materials	18,000		
Direct labour	15,000		

Production overhead control account

	£		£
Indirect labour	3,000		

Step 3: Production overhead

The other production overhead incurred is debited to the production overhead control account:

DR	Production overhead control account	6,000	
CR	Bank / creditors		6,000

Production overhead control account

	£		£
Indirect labour	3,000		
Bank/creditors	6,000		

The production overhead then has to be included in the cost of production, the work-in-progress account. As we have seen in earlier chapters, this is done by absorbing production overhead into production according to the predetermined absorption rate. This is done by making a transfer from the production overhead control account to the work-in-progress account. Notice that although £9,000 of production overhead has been incurred, only £8,000 is being absorbed into production – this will be dealt with later:

DR	Work-in-progress account	8,000	
CR	Production overhead control account		8,000

Production overhead control account

	£		£
Indirect labour	3,000	WIP account	8,000
Bank/creditors	6,000		

Work-in-progress account

	£		£
Direct materials	18,000		
Direct labour	15,000		
Production overhead	8,000		

Step 4: Work-in-progress transfer

Once the production is completed the production cost of the goods that are ready for sale is transferred out of the work-in-progress account and into the finished goods account.

DR	Finished goods account	35,000
CR	Work-in-progress account	35,000

Work-in-progress account

	£		£
Direct materials	18,000	Finished goods account	35,000
Direct labour	15,000		
Production overhead	8,000		

Finished goods account

	£		£
WIP account	35,000		

The finished goods account now holds the production cost of all of the goods completed in the month. However, only goods costing £32,000 were sold. When we prepare the costing profit and loss account, a transfer out of the finished goods account for £32,000 will be made, as we shall see later.

Step 5: Sales

The sales account is credited with the amount of sales for the period.

DR	Bank / debtors	45,000
CR	Sales account	45,000

Sales account

	£		£
		Bank/debtors	45,000

Step 6: Non-production overhead

Finally, the non-production overhead incurred is debited to the non-production overhead account:

DR	Non-production overheads account	2,000
CR	Bank/creditors account	2,000

Non-production overhead account

	£		£
Bank/creditors	2,000		

Step 7: Balancing the accounts

We are now in a position to balance each of the ledger accounts.

Materials cost account

	£		£
Bank/creditors	20,000	WIP account	18,000
		Balance c/d	2,000
	20,000		20,000
Balance b/d	2,000		

The balance on the materials cost account represents the raw materials unused and still in the stores department.

Wages control account

	£		£
Total wages cost (15,000 + 3,000)	18,000	WIP account	15,000
		Production overhead account	3,000
	18,000		18,000

There should never be a balance on the wages control account as the total cost of the labour is transferred either to the work-in-progress account or to overhead accounts.

Production overhead control account

	£		£
Indirect labour	3,000	WIP account	8,000
Bank/creditors	6,000	Balance c/d	1,000
	9,000		9,000
Balance b/d	1,000		

The balance b/d on the overhead account represents the under-absorbed overhead and we will deal with this later.

Work-in-progress account

	£		£
Direct materials	18,000	Finished goods account	35,000
Direct labour	15,000	Balance c/d	6,000
Production overhead	8,000		
	41,000		41,000
Balance b/d	6,000		

The balance on the work-in-progress account is the value of the production that is as yet incomplete and has not been transferred to the warehouse as finished goods.

The finished goods, sales and non-production overhead accounts are as they were before with no changes made to them as yet.

Finished goods account

	£		£
WIP account	35,000		

Sales account

	£		£
		Bank/debtors	45,000

Non-production overhead account

	£		£
Bank/creditors	2,000		

Step 8: We now complete the exercise by transferring the relevant amounts from the ledger accounts to the costing profit and loss account.

Finished goods account

	£		£
WIP account	35,000	Profit and loss account	32,000
		Balance c/d	3,000
	35,000		35,000
Balance b/d	3,000		

The production cost of the goods that have been sold, £32,000, is transferred to the profit and loss account as cost of sales. The remaining balance is the stock of finished goods still remaining in the warehouse.

The sales and the non-production overhead are transferred to the costing profit and loss account.

Sales account

	£		£
Profit and loss account	45,000	Bank/debtors	45,000

Non-production overhead account

	£		£
Bank/creditors	2,000	Profit and loss account	2,000

Production overhead control account

	£		£
Balance b/d	1,000	Profit and loss account	1,000

The balance b/d (the under-absorbed overhead) will be transferred to the costing profit and loss account as an additional expense for the period.

If the balance had been on the debit side of the account this would have been an over-absorbed overhead, which would be credited to the profit and loss account.

Costing profit and loss account

	£		£
Finished goods	32,000	Sales	45,000
Non-production overhead	2,000		
Production overhead (under absorbed)	**1,000**		
Profit	10,000		
	45,000		45,000

This can be presented in statement format as follows:

Costing profit and loss account

	£
Sales	45,000
Cost of sales	(32,000)
Gross profit	13,000
Non-production overhead	(2,000)
Under-absorbed overhead	(1,000)
Net profit	10,000

▷ ACTIVITY 1

Given below are the transactions of a manufacturing business for its first month of trading.

	£
Materials purchased	100,000
Materials issued to production	88,000
Direct labour cost	60,000
Indirect production labour cost	15,000
Other production overheads incurred	24,000
Production overheads absorbed into production	42,000
Work-in-progress transferred to finished goods	160,000
Finished goods transferred to cost of sales	140,000
Sales	200,000
Non-production overheads incurred	22,000

You are to record these transactions in the costing ledger accounts and to prepare a costing profit and loss account for the month.

[Answer on p. 161]

1.3 Alternative treatment of wages

There are several different ways that the double entry for costing purposes can be done. Wages in particular are subject to other methods and the examiner tested this in December 2004 with a short question as follows:

EXAMPLE

During November, gross direct labour costs of £33,000 were incurred as follows:

Net wages	20,500
Income tax deductions	7,400
Employee's national insurance contributions	2,100
Employer's national insurance contributions	3,000

The accounting codes used to record direct labour costs are as follows:

Code number	Description
1000	Work in progress
7000	Income tax payable
7001	National insurance contributions payable
9001	Net wages control account

Complete the table below to record the direct labour costs for November

Code	Dr £	Cr £
1000		
7000		
7001		
9001		

Solution

The solution is as follows

Code	Dr £	Cr £
1000	33,000	
7000		7,400
7001		5,100
9001		20,500

Method

You may be confused by some of the accounts the examiner refers to and may not have heard of one of them – the net wages control account.

The others however should be familiar to you:

Work in progress –
the account that collects the expenditure on products, which is debited to the work in progress account

Income tax payable and national insurance contributions payable –
the account that is the creditor for income tax and NI

Net wages control account –
This is effectively the creditor for net wages payable.

Even if you do not know the above, you can still work out the correct answer because the one thing you can be sure of is that the total cost of labour must end up as a debit in the WIP account. You will recognise that the tax and NI are credits in the income tax payable and national insurance contributions payable accounts, so it follows that the net wages must be credit in the net wages control account – otherwise the whole thing won't balance.

The examiner may occasionally ask this sort of question. The important thing is not to be confused by the names of the accounts. So long as you know the purpose of the double entry and know where the entries go in some of the accounts then you will be able to work out the rest.

2 Test your knowledge

1 Define the term integrated bookkeeping system.

2 List the main ledger accounts that comprise an integrated system to deal with costs of production.

3 What would be the double entry for transfer of goods to finished stock?

4 If the credit side of the production overhead control account is greater than the debit side then overhead is said to be?

5 A debit balance brought down on the work-in-progress account represents what?

[Answers on p. 162]

3 Summary

In this chapter we have looked at the bookkeeping entries for costs in an integrated bookkeeping system. The main ledger accounts used to record the costs of production are as follows.

- materials cost account
- labour cost account
- work-in-progress cost account
- finished goods account
- production overhead control account.

Questions on writing up the various accounts occur throughout the workbook in the materials, labour and overheads sections, so make sure that you practise your cost bookkeeping skills by having an attempt at these questions.

Answers to chapter activities & 'test your knowledge' questions

△ ACTIVITY 1

Materials cost account

	£		£
Bank/creditors	100,000	WIP account	88,000
		Balance c/d	12,000
	100,000		100,000

Wages control account

	£		£
Total labour cost		WIP account	60,000
(60,000 + 15,000)	75,000	Production overhead account	15,000
	75,000		75,000

Work-in-progress account

	£		£
Direct materials	88,000	Finished goods account	160,000
Direct labour	60,000	Balance c/d	30,000
Production overheads	42,000		
	190,000		190,000

Production overhead control account

	£		£
Indirect labour	15,000	WIP account	42,000
Bank/creditors	24,000		
Over-absorbed overhead (P&L)	3,000		
	42,000		42,000

Finished goods account

	£		£
WIP account	160,000	Profit and loss account	140,000
		Balance c/d	20,000
	160,000		160,000

Sales account

	£		£
Profit and loss account	200,000	Bank/debtors	200,000

Non-production overhead account

	£		£
Bank/creditors	22,000	Profit and loss account	22,000

Costing profit and loss account

	£
Sales	200,000
Less: cost of sales	(140,000)
Gross profit	60,000
Non-production overhead	(22,000)
Over-absorbed production overhead	3,000
Net profit	41,000

Test your knowledge

1 An integrated system is one where the ledger accounts maintained provide the necessary information for both costing and financial accounting.

2
- Materials control
- Labour control
- Production overhead control
- Work-in-progress control
- Finished goods control

3 DR Finished goods account
CR Work-in-progress

4 Over-recovered (or over-absorbed)

5 Stock of work-in-progress

ABSORPTION AND MARGINAL COSTING

INTRODUCTION

Absorption and marginal costing are two different ways of valuing the cost of goods sold and finished goods in stock. We looked at absorption costing when we studied Chapter 5: Accounting for Overheads, and we are now going to compare this method with that of marginal costing. With absorption costing, an element of fixed overhead is included in cost of sales and closing stock whereas, in marginal costing, fixed overheads are treated as period costs and are charged in full against the profit for the period. You need to understand the difference between the two methods and what the effect of stock valuation is on reported profits.

KNOWLEDGE & UNDERSTANDING

- Marginal costing (Elements 6.1 and 6.3)
- Absorption costing (Elements 6.2 and 6.3)
- Marginal versus absorption costing for costing and reporting purposes (Elements 6.1 and 6.2)
- Calculation of product and service cost (Elements 6.1, 6.2 and 6.3)

CONTENTS

1 Contribution and profit

1.1 Contribution

The concept of contribution is one of the most fundamental in cost accounting. Contribution measures the difference between the sales price of a unit and the variable costs of making and selling that unit.

Illustration

Sales price	£10	
Variable costs	(£6)	(materials, labour, variable overheads, etc)
Contribution	£4	

The concept of contribution is an extremely important one in cost and management accounting. It is important to remember that since contribution measures the difference between sales price and the variable cost of making a unit, if a product has a positive contribution it is worth making (since it will contribute some amount, however small, towards paying the fixed overheads; if enough units are made and sold such that total contribution exceeds fixed overheads then profit will start to be made).

1.2 Profit

Contribution does not include fixed overheads, so how do we account for them?

Assume that we sell 10,000 units of the above product, and that fixed overheads amount to £30,000.

Total contribution and profit is calculated as follows.

	£
Sales 10,000 x £10 =	100,000
Variable costs 10,000 x £6 =	60,000
Contribution	**40,000**
Fixed costs	30,000
Profit	**10,000**

1.3 Changes in activity level

It should be clear from the above that there is a direct link between the total contribution and the number of items sold. If sales doubled to 20,000 units the total contribution would also double to £80,000.

How does contribution and profit change if we double output and sales?

	10,000 units		20,000 units
	£		
Sales 10,000 x £10	100,000	20,000 x £10	200,000
Variable costs 10,000 x £6	60,000	20,000 x £6	120,000
Contribution	40,000		80,000
Fixed overheads	30,000		30,000
Profit	10,000		50,000
Contribution per unit	£4		£4
Profit per unit	£1		£2.50

What happens to profit if sales increase by one extra unit from 10,000 to 10,001? Does the profit go up by £1?

At first glance it looks obvious that the answer is yes, but remember that £3 of the revenue from each unit has been set aside to pay for fixed overheads. Once sales of 10,000 units have been achieved this is no longer needed, because the fixed overheads have been paid.

So what does happen if the company makes and sells an extra unit?

	£
Sales 10,001 x £10	100,010
Variable costs 10,001 x £6	60,006
Contribution	40,004
Fixed costs	30,000
Profit	10,004

Total contribution would go up by £4, but the total fixed overheads would not change. **Profit would therefore also go up by £4 (i.e. the same as contribution).**

There is therefore **no direct link between profit and output**. If output doubles, profits do not necessarily double.

2 Differences between absorption and marginal costing

2.1 Stock valuation

Absorption and marginal costing are two different ways of valuing cost of goods sold and finished goods in stock.

- Marginal costing values stock at the amount of variable costs required to produce each unit (the marginal cost). This means including direct materials, direct labour, direct expenses and any variable production overheads. No fixed overheads are absorbed into product costs; they are treated as a period cost and deducted lower down the profit and loss account.
  So, using the figures for the illustrative product above, under marginal costing each unit of stock would be valued at £6.
- Absorption costing adds an amount to the cost of each unit to represent the fixed production overheads incurred by that product. Remember that the amount added to each unit is based on estimates made at the start of the period. If these estimates are incorrect we may have under or over absorption (adjusted lower down).

Again, using the above illustrative product, if we planned to produce 10,000 units use of absorption costing would result in a unit stock valuation of £(6 + 3) = £9.

2.2 Layout of profit statements

The difference in treatment of fixed production overheads leads to a difference in the way profit statements under the two costing methods are presented.

2.3 Layout of profit statement – marginal costing

The proforma layout for calculating budgeted profit and loss under marginal costing is as follows (with illustrative figures).

		£	£
Sales (10,000 x £10)			100,000
Cost of sales (at marginal cost, £6)			60,000
Contribution			40,000
Less:	Fixed production costs	30,000	
	Fixed non-production costs (say)	2,000	
			(32,000)
Profit for the period			8,000

2.4 Layout of profit statement – absorption costing

Using absorption costing, the layout is somewhat different.

	£
Sales	100,000
Cost of sales (at absorption cost, £9)	(90,000)
Gross profit	10,000
Less: Fixed non-production costs	(2,000)
Profit for the period	8,000

Note in the above the different treatment of fixed production overheads. In the marginal costing statement these costs are not absorbed into cost of sales. Instead, they are deducted (in total) from the contribution. In the absorption costing statement, the fixed production overheads are absorbed into cost of sales. In both statements, the fixed non-production overheads are excluded from cost of sales.

▷ ACTIVITY 1

The following information has been provided.

	Cost per unit £
Direct material	8.50
Direct labour	27.20
Variable production overhead	11.30
Variable selling costs	2.20
Fixed production overhead	14.00
Fixed selling costs	4.95

Selling prices are set such that net contribution is 20% of revenue.

Note that the fixed costs per unit have been calculated by dividing the estimated fixed cost by the estimated output.

Required

Calculate each of the following in £/unit:

(a) prime cost
(b) full production cost
(c) full cost of making and selling
(d) marginal cost of making and selling
(e) absorption cost stock value
(f) selling price
(g) unit contribution.

[Answer on p. 172]

3 The effect of stock valuation on reported profit

3.1 Introduction

Another consequence of the difference in stock valuation between marginal and absorption costing is that reported profits will differ if there is closing stock. This is because:

- under **marginal costing** all the period's fixed production overheads are charged **in full** against that period's profit, whereas
- under **absorption costing** some of the period's fixed production overheads will be **carried forward** in the closing stock value and charged to the next period's profit and loss.

This is illustrated in the following example.

O EXAMPLE

Worked example of profit differences

	£ per unit
Sales price	£15
Materials	£4
Variable production costs	£2
Budgeted fixed production overheads	£40,000 per month
Budgeted production	10,000 units per month
Budgeted sales	8,000 units

No opening stock.

Required

(a) Compute the contribution per unit (on a marginal costing basis).

(b) Compute the profit per unit (on an absorption costing basis).

(c) Produce a budgeted marginal costing and an absorption costing profit and loss account for a month.

Solution

(a) **Marginal costing**

	£	£
Sales price		15
Materials	4	
Variable production costs	2	
Variable production cost of sales		(6)
Contribution per unit		9

(b) **Absorption costing**

	£	£
Sales price		15
Materials	4	
Variable production costs	2	
Fixed production overheads (W)	4	
Cost of sales		(10)
Profit per unit		5

Working

The fixed overhead absorbed by each unit is as follows.

$$\frac{\text{Budgeted fixed overheads}}{\text{Budgeted production}} = \frac{£40,000}{10,000} = £4 \text{ per unit}$$

(c) **Budgeted profit and loss accounts**

When calculating the profit we will need the number of units in closing stock. This is given by:
Opening stock + production – sales

This will be 0 + 10,000 – 8,000 = 2,000 units

If you are not given opening stock in a question assume it equals 0 units. You should also assume, unless told otherwise, that unit revenues and costs are as budgeted.

Marginal costing profit and loss account

	£	£
Sales (8,000x £15)		120,000
Opening stock	–	
Variable production costs (10,000 x £6)	60,000	
Closing stock (2,000 x £6)	(12,000)	
Variable cost of sales		(48,000)
Contribution		72,000
Fixed costs		(40,000)
Profit		32,000

Absorption costing profit and loss account

	£	£
Sales (8,000 x £15)		120,000
Opening stock	–	
Production costs (10,000 x £10)	100,000	
Closing stock (2,000 x £10)	(20,000)	
Cost of sales		(80,000)
Profit		40,000

Absorption costing reports an £8,000 higher profit than marginal costing.

Why?

- Under absorption costing the value of closing stock is £8,000 higher because we are carrying in closing stock 2,000 x £4 = £8,000 of fixed overheads.

▷ ACTIVITY 2

XYZ plc

XYZ plc manufactures toy horses and has produced a budget for the quarter ended 30 June 20X5 (Quarter 1) as follows.

Sales	190 units @ selling price of £12
Production	200 units
Variable production cost per unit	£8
Fixed production costs	£200

There was no opening stock.

Required

Draft the profit statement using:

(i) marginal, and

(ii) absorption costing principles.

[Answer on p. 173]

▷ ACTIVITY 3

McTack

McTack manufactures PCs and has produced a budget for the quarter ended 31 March 20X4 (Quarter 1) using absorption costing as follows.

	£	£
Sales (100 units @ £500 per unit)		50,000
Production cost of 120 units		
Materials	12,000	
Labour	24,000	
Variable overhead	6,000	
Fixed overhead	6,000	
	48,000	
Less:Closing stock (20 x £400)	(8,000)	
		(40,000)
		10,000

Required

Re-draft the profit statement using marginal costing principles.

[Answer on p. 174]

4 Advantages of absorption and marginal costing

4.1 Advantages of absorption costing

1 SSAP 9 requires its use for financial reporting.
2 The importance of fixed costs is revealed.
3 Where sales are seasonal and production steady the profit figure, being more consistent with production, will be more reasonable.

4.2 Advantages of marginal costing

1 Simplicity – avoiding apportionments and absorption problems.
2 Fixed costs logically relate to time and are so charged.
3 Profit figures more consistent with fluctuating sales.
4 Better for decision-making.

The choice between the two will depend on the requirements of and production/sales profile of the particular organisation.

5 Test your knowledge

1 Define the term marginal cost.

2 Define the term contribution.

3 When presenting a profit statement on absorption costing principles on what basis are stocks valued.

4 Under what method of presentation are fixed costs considered to be period costs?

[Answers on p. 174]

6 Summary

As you have learned in this chapter, the contribution concept is one of the most fundamental in cost accounting.

Contribution = Sales price – variable costs

Marginal costing calculates the contribution per unit of a product. In marginal costing stock units are valued at variable production cost and fixed overheads are accounted for as period costs. In absorption costing, stock units are valued at variable cost plus fixed production overheads absorbed using a pre-determined absorption rate. The differences in these methods give rise to different profit figures which are usually reconciled at the end of an accounting period.

Answers to chapter activities & 'test your knowledge' questions

ACTIVITY 1

Absorption costing

(a) **Prime cost per unit**

	£
Direct material	8.50
Direct labour	27.20
	35.70

(b) **Full production cost**

	£
Prime cost	35.70
Variable production overhead	11.30
Fixed production overhead	14.00
	61.00

(c) **Full cost of making and selling**

	£
Full production cost	61.00
Variable selling	2.20
Fixed selling cost	4.95
	68.15

(d) **Marginal cost of making and selling**

	£
Prime cost	35.70
Variable production overhead	11.30
Variable selling cost	2.20
	49.20

(e) **Absorption cost stock value**

	£
Prime cost	35.70
Variable production overhead	11.30
Fixed production overhead	14.00
	61.00

This is the same as (b).

(f) **Selling price**

NB: Net contribution =
Sales price less marginal cost of making and selling per unit
= Sales price – £49.20 (from (d)).

The cost structure is as follows:

Sales price	100%
Marginal cost	80%
Contribution	20%

Marginal cost = £49.20 = 80% of selling price.
Therefore selling price:

$$= \frac{£49.20}{80} \times 100$$

$$= £61.50$$

(g) **Unit contribution**

Selling price less marginal cost per unit

Selling price	61.50
Marginal cost per unit	49.20
	£12.30

ACTIVITY 2

There will be closing stock of 200 –190 = 10 units.

Under marginal costing, the closing stock will be valued at the variable production cost of £8 per unit.

With absorption costing the fixed production costs will also have to be included. The £200 fixed production costs will be absorbed into the 200 units of production, giving a fixed cost per unit of £1 and a total absorption cost of 8 + 1 = £9 per unit.

Marginal costing profit and loss account

	£	£
Sales (190 x £12)		2,280
Opening stock	–	
Variable production costs (200 x £8)	1,600	
Closing stock (10 x £8)	(80)	
Variable cost of sales		(1,520)
Contribution		760
Fixed costs		(200)
Profit		560

Absorption costing profit and loss account

	£	£
Sales (190 x £12)		2,280
Opening stock	–	
Production costs (200 x £9)	1,800	
Closing stock (10 x £9)	(90)	
Cost of sales		(1,710)
Profit		570

Absorption costing reports an £10 higher profit than marginal costing.

ACTIVITY 3

McTack – Budgeted profit statement quarter ended 31 March

Marginal costing format

		£	£
Sales (100 units @ £500/unit)			50,000
Production costs (120 units)			
Materials		12,000	
Labour		24,000	
Variable overhead		6,000	
		42,000	
Less:	Stocks (20 units x £350)	(7,000)	
			35,000
Contribution			15,000
Fixed overhead			6,000
Profit			£9,000

Reconciliation of profits

	£
Marginal costing	9,000
Add: Fixed overheads in closing stock (20 x £50)	1,000
Absorption costing profit	10,000

Test your knowledge

1 Marginal cost is defined as total variable costs.

2 Contribution is sales revenue less total variable costs.

3 Stocks would be valued at full cost of production (including an element of fixed production cost).

4 Marginal costing.

CVP ANALYSIS AND LIMITING FACTORS

INTRODUCTION

CVP (cost-volume-profit) analysis is based on cost behaviour and marginal costing principles and is a key decision-making tool. CVP analysis analyses the effect that different levels of activity have on contribution and profit. The breakeven point is an important calculation in CVP analysis as it represents the level of activity at which there is no profit and no loss. Other key calculations include the margin of safety and the P/V ratio. We shall also be looking at a topic known as key factor analysis which is the technique of allocating resources which are in short supply between products according to the amount of contribution that they earn.

KNOWLEDGE & UNDERSTANDING

- Analysis of the effect of changing activity levels on unit costs (Elements 6.1, 6.2 and 6.3)
- The identification of fixed, variable and semi-variable costs and their use in cost recording, cost reporting and cost analysis (Elements 6.1, 6.2 and 6.3)
- Cost-volume-profit analysis (Element 6.3)
- The identification of limiting factors (Element 6.3)

CONTENTS

PERFORMANCE CRITERIA

- Identify information relevant to estimating current and future revenues and costs (Element 6.3)
- Prepare estimates of future income and costs (Element 6.3)
- Calculate the effects of variations in capacity on product costs (Element 6.3)

- Analyse critical factors affecting costs and revenues using appropriate accounting techniques and draw clear conclusions from the analysis (Element 6.3)
- State any assumptions used when evaluating future costs and revenues (Element 6.3)
- Identify and evaluate options and solutions for their contribution to organisational goals (Element 6.3)
- Present recommendations to appropriate people in a clear and concise way and supported by a clear rationale (Element 6.3)

1 Contribution

DEFINITION

Remember, contribution is defined as the **difference between selling price and the variable cost of producing and selling that item**. This is in contrast to profit per unit, which is the difference between selling price and the total absorption cost of producing and selling that item, which includes an element of fixed cost.

We need to decide between courses of action and **which course of action will be most beneficial**, looking at the revenues and costs under each alternative.

Fixed costs, by definition, are unavoidable and do not change with the level of production. Therefore, in any decision which is connected with varying the level of production, **fixed costs are not a relevant cost** as they do not change regardless of which course of action is taken.

EXAMPLE

Katie Limited is currently producing decorated mirrors. Each mirror sells at £10 each and has a variable cost of production of £8 per unit. Current production is 900 units per period. Fixed costs are expected to be £900 for the coming period, and therefore are charged at £1 per unit to production.

Katie has been approached to supply a new customer with 100 mirrors but at a discounted price of £8.25 per mirror.

Should she accept the order?

Solution

If we look at profit per unit, then the decision would be to reject the order, as we would not sell for £8.25 per unit something which has cost us (£8 + £1) = £9 to produce.

However, if we look at total profits generated by the business before and after the acceptance of project, we find the following.

		Reject	Accept
		£	£
Revenue	(900 @ £10)	9,000	9,000
	(100 @ £8.25)		825
			9,825
Variable costs	(900/1,000 @ £8)	(7,200)	(8,000)
Fixed costs		(900)	(900)
Profit		900	925

Therefore we can see that profits are improved by accepting the contract. Whilst revenue is increasing by £825, costs only increase by £800 as **fixed costs do not change.**

We could have derived the same answer by looking at contribution generated by the contract.

Remember contribution is calculated as selling price – variable cost. On a per unit basis for the contract, this is £8.25 – £8 = £0.25 contribution on each extra unit sold. As we sell 100 units more, this generates a total increase in contribution, and thus profit, of £25 (100 x £0.25).

We should accept the project; the use of **contribution analysis** enables us to determine this quickly.

▷ ACTIVITY 1

Roger Morton

Roger makes a single product, the Morton. During 20X9 he plans to make and sell 10,000 Mortons and accordingly has estimated the cost of each to be £50 (see below). Each Morton sells for £75.

	Cost of a Morton
	£
Material	12
Labour	24
Variable overhead	10
Fixed overhead	4
	50

Required

(a) Calculate Roger's total fixed overhead.

(b) Calculate the contribution per unit earned by each Morton.

(c) What is the total profit earned if Roger sells 2,000 Mortons?

[Answer on p. 192]

2 Cost-volume-profit (CVP) analysis

2.1 Introduction

How many units do we need to sell to make a profit? By how much will profit fall if price is lowered by £1? What will happen to our profits if we rent an extra factory but find that we can operate at only half capacity?

All of the above are **realistic business questions**. One solution would be to set up a model of the business on a PC and feed in the various pieces of information. Packages such as Lotus 1-2-3 and Microsoft Excel mean that this is an easy option.

But we have to appreciate that the PC is simply performing **cost-volume-profit (CVP) analysis** by another route. We can do this without a PC.

2.2 Approach to CVP

- Costs are assumed to be either **fixed** or **variable**, or at least **separable into these elements**.
- Economies or diseconomies of scale are ignored; this ensures that **the variable cost per unit is constant.**
- We look at the effect a change in volume has on **contribution** (not profit).
- Contribution per unit = selling price per unit – total variable cost per unit.

3 Breakeven analysis

DEFINITION

Breakeven point

The **breakeven point** is the volume of sales at which neither a profit nor a loss is made.

Calculations are made easier, however, if we think in terms of contribution rather than profit. Breakeven is then the volume of sales at which total contribution (contribution per unit multiplied by number of units sold) is equal to fixed costs.

Note that fixed costs here are total fixed costs, i.e. fixed production and fixed selling costs.

The breakeven point can then be found using the following formula.

$$\text{Breakeven point} = \frac{\text{Fixed cost}}{\text{Contribution/unit}}$$

EXAMPLE

Breakeven point

Rachel's product, the 'Steadyarm', sells for £50. It has a variable cost of £30 per unit. Rachel's total fixed costs are £40,000 per annum.

What is her breakeven point?

Solution

To break even we want just enough contribution to cover the total fixed costs of £40,000.

We therefore want total contribution of £40,000.

Each unit of sales gives contribution of 50 – 30 = £20.

Therefore the breakeven point in units

$$= \frac{\text{Total fixed costs}}{\text{Contribution per unit}} = \frac{£40,000}{£20} = 2,000 \text{ units}$$

We can show that this calculation is correct as below.

	£
Total contribution (2,000 units x £20)	40,000
Total fixed costs	(40,000)
Profit/loss	0

3.1 Margin of safety

The margin of safety is the amount by which the anticipated (budgeted) sales can fall before the business makes a loss. It can be expressed in absolute units or relative percentage terms.

In units: Margin of safety = Budgeted sales units – Breakeven sales units

In %: Margin of safety =

$$\frac{\text{Budgeted sales units – Breakeven sales units}}{\text{Budgeted sales unit}} \times 100\%$$

For the 'Steadyarm' product above, if Rachel is expecting to achieve sales of 3,600 units:

Margin of safety (units) = 3,600 – 2,000 = 1,600 units

As a %: $\frac{1,600}{3,600} \times 100 = 44.4\%$

Actual sales can fall by 44.4% of budgeted level before the Steadyarm will start to make a loss.

Margin of safety can also be expressed in sales revenue terms.

▷ ACTIVITY 2

Camilla Ng

Camilla makes a single product, the Wocket. During 20X5 she plans to make and sell 3,000 Wockets and has estimated the following:

	Cost per unit
	£
Material	3
Labour	5
Variable overhead	2
Total variable cost per unit	10

Total fixed costs are budgeted to be £12,000

Estimated selling price £15

Required

(a) Calculate the contribution per unit earned by each Wocket.

(b) Calculate Camilla's budgeted profit.

(c) Calculate Camila's breakeven point and margin of safety.

[Answer on p. 192]

3.2 Achieving a target profit

A similar approach can be used to find the sales volume at which a particular profit is made.

Sales volume to achieve a particular profit

$$= \frac{\text{Total fixed costs + required profit}}{\text{Contribution/unit}}$$

O EXAMPLE

Achieving a target profit

Information as with Rachel above but we now want to know how many units must be sold to make a profit of £100,000.

To achieve a profit of £100,000, we require sufficient contribution firstly to cover the fixed costs (£40,000) and secondly, having covered fixed costs, we require sufficient contribution to give a profit of £100,000. Therefore our required contribution is £140,000.

Sales volume to achieve a profit of £100,000

$$= \frac{\text{Total fixed costs + required profit}}{\text{Contribution/unit}}$$

$$= \frac{£40,000 + £100,000}{£20}$$

= 7,000 units

We can show that this is the case with a summarised profit and loss account.

	£
Sales (7,000 x £50)	350,000
Variable cost (7,000 x £30)	(210,000)
Total fixed costs	(40,000)
Profit	100,000

4 CVP charts

4.1 Breakeven charts

We can show our analysis diagrammatically in a breakeven chart.

Breakeven chart showing fixed and variable cost lines

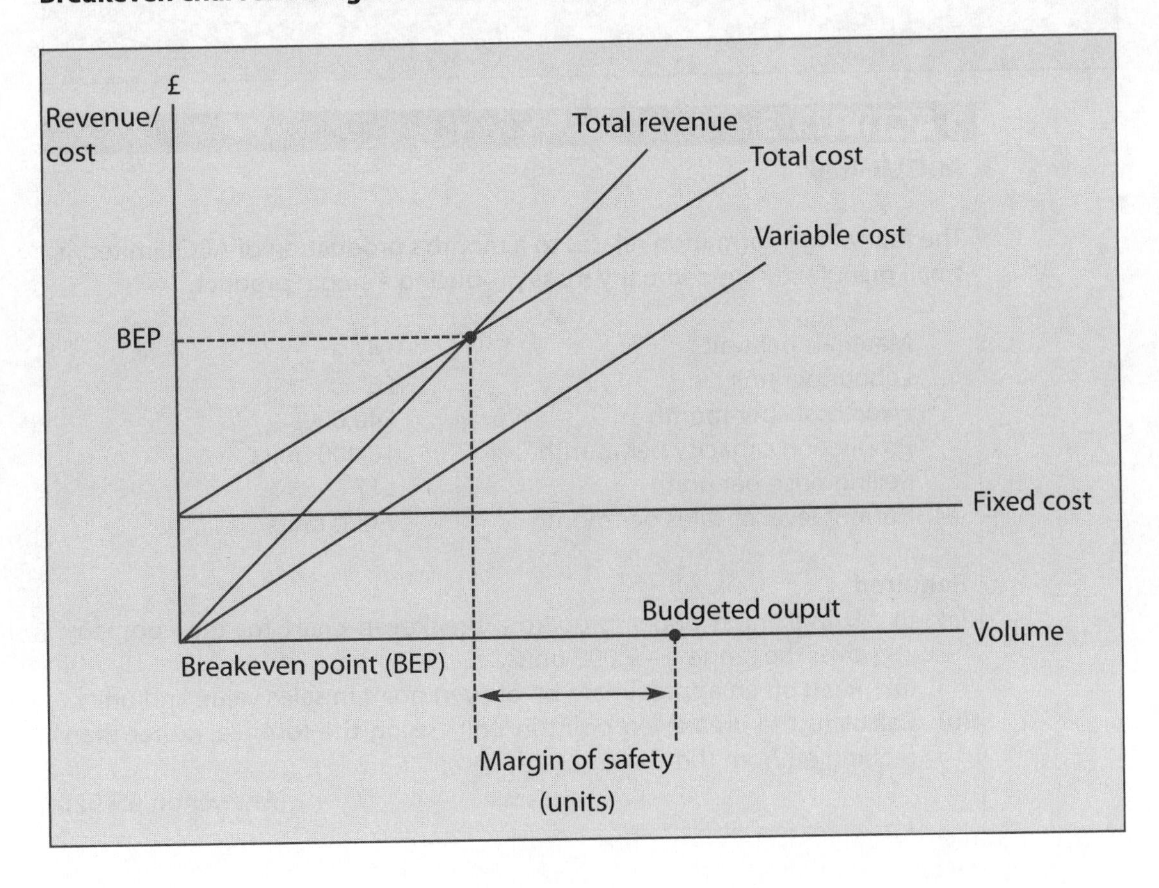

The variable cost and fixed cost line add little to the diagram, so we normally show it as below.

Breakeven chart showing total cost line

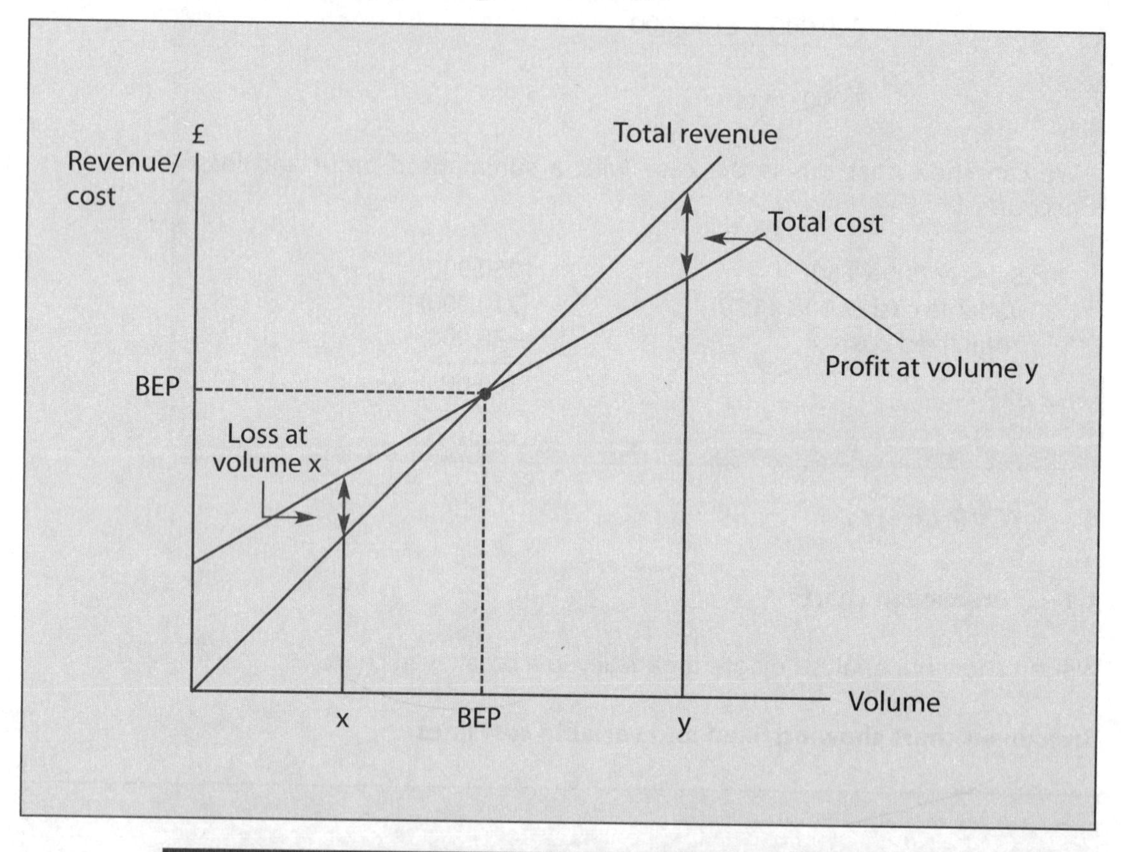

▷ ACTIVITY 3

ABC Limited

The following information relates to a month's production of ABC Limited, a small manufacturing company mass producing a single product.

Materials per unit	£4
Labour per unit	£6
Fixed costs per month	£40,000
Production capacity per month	10,000 units
Selling price per unit	£17
Current level of sales per month	7,000 units

Required

(a) (i) Using graph paper, prepare a breakeven chart for the company over the range 0 – 7,000 units.

(ii) Read off an approximate breakeven point in sales value and units.

(b) Calculate the breakeven point in units using the formula, rather than reading off from the chart.

[Answer on p. 192]

4.2 Profit-volume (P/V) chart

A P/V chart is another way of presenting the information.

P/V chart

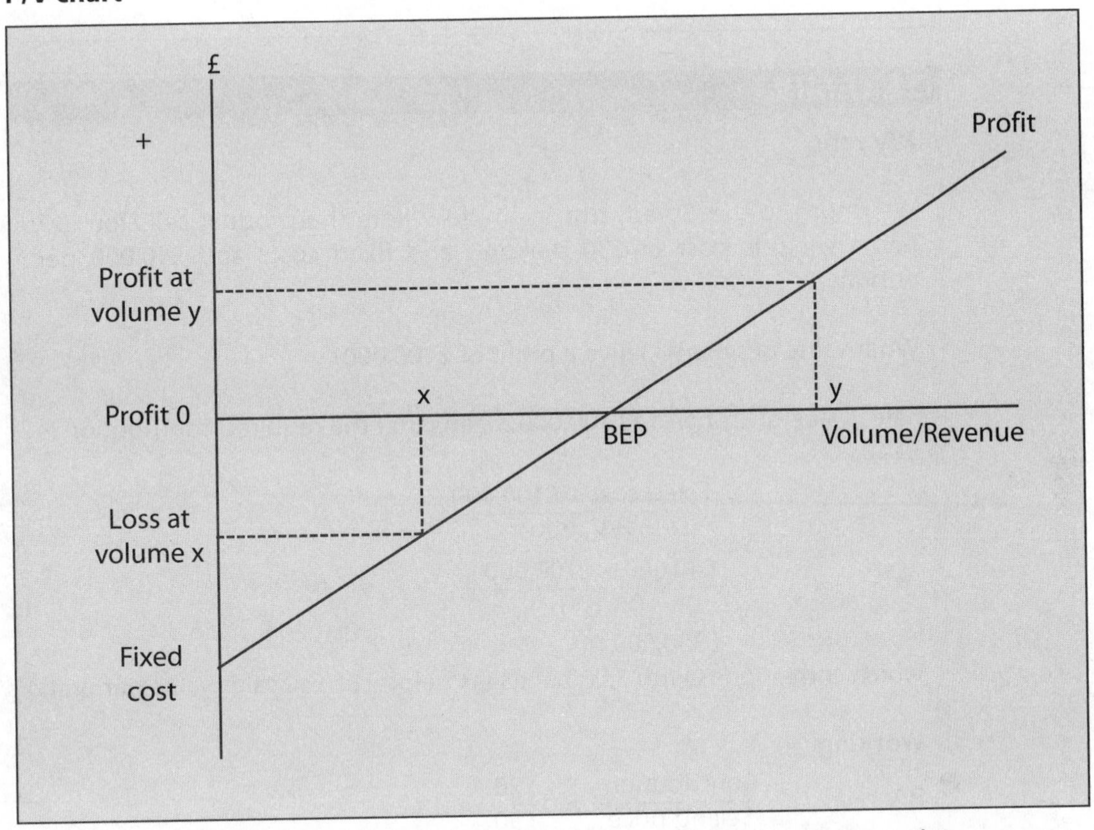

Note that at a **sales volume of nil**, the **total loss** will be the same as the business's **fixed costs**.

5 Profit volume ratio (P/V ratio)

DEFINITION

P/V ratio

The P/V ratio is a measure of the rate at which profit (or, strictly, contribution) is generated with sales volume, as measured by revenue. An alternative name which provides a more accurate description is the contribution/sales (C/S) ratio.

$$\text{P/V ratio} = \frac{\text{Contribution per unit}}{\text{Selling price}}$$

It tells us what proportion of the selling price is contributing to our fixed overhead and profits. It is comparable to the contribution margin.

If, for example, the P/V ratio was 40% this would mean that 40% of the selling price was contribution which means therefore that the remaining 60% is variable cost.

It can be used to find the breakeven point or the point at which profit is £x in terms of sales value (rather than volume).

$$\text{Sales value giving a profit £X} = \frac{\text{Fixed cost + profit}}{\text{P/V ratio}}$$

EXAMPLE

P/V ratio

We return to the 'Steadyarm' example, where the product sells for £50, has a variable cost of £30 per unit and fixed costs and £40,000 per annum.

What value of sales will give a profit of £100,000?

Sales value giving profit £100,000 means that the required contribution is £140,000

$$= \frac{\text{Fixed cost + £100,000}}{\text{P/V ratio}}$$

$$= \frac{\text{£40,000 + £100,000}}{\text{0.4 (W)}}$$

$$= \text{£350,000}$$

which corresponds with 7,000 units (as before) at £50 sales value per unit.

Working

$$\text{P/V ratio} = \frac{\text{Contribution}}{\text{Selling price}} = \frac{\text{£20}}{\text{£50}} = 0.4$$

ACTIVITY 4

Security services

The company for which you work provides security services for corporate clients. It currently charges £30 per hour for the service and the cost structure of the service is as follows:

Variable cost per hour	£22
Fixed cost for one month	£18,000

The marketing director has suggested that the company should provide extra benefits to its services. Research conducted amongst current customers suggests that they would be prepared to pay £33 per hour for the improved service. The cost structure would be altered as follows:

Revised variable cost per hour	£20
Revised fixed cost for one month	£39,000

It is not expected that sales levels would alter from the current level of 5,200 hours per month.

Required

(a) Calculate the breakeven point in hours per month both in the present situation and with the changes proposed by the marketing director.

(b) Calculate the monthly profit both in the present situation and with the changes proposed by the marketing director.

(c) Comment briefly on the way in which the revised cost and selling price structure will affect future profit changes if sales increase or decrease from their current level.

[Answer on p.193]

6 Assumptions of CVP analysis

CVP analysis makes a number of assumptions as follows.

- Fixed costs remain fixed throughout the range charted.
- Variable costs change in direct proportion to volume.
- Selling prices do not change with volume.
- Efficiency and productivity do not change with volume.
- It is applied to a single product or static mix of products.
- Volume is the only factor affecting cost.
- Linearity is appropriate.

While some of the assumptions may seem unrealistic, over the limited range of activity usually considered, they are often a **reasonable approximation** to the true position.

7 Limiting factors

DEFINITION

Key factor analysis

Key factor analysis is a technique that we can use when we have one resource (such as materials, labour or machine time) that is in scarce supply and we can make more than one type of product using that resource. Naturally, we wish to use that resource in the most efficient manner to maximise profits. Key factor analysis will identify that manner.

(If there are two or more resources in restricted supply, we would use the technique of linear programming, which is not in this syllabus.)

7.1 Approach to key factor analysis

- Determine the **resource** that is in scarce supply (the limiting factor or key factor).
- Calculate the contribution per unit generated by each type of product we want to make.
- For each product **divide its contribution per unit by the number of units of scarce resource needed** to make one unit of that product.
- Pick the product with the **highest contribution per unit of scarce resource**.

EXAMPLE

Key factor analysis 1

Helen makes two products as set out below:

	H	L
	£	£
Selling price	100	30
Material @ £10 per kg	(50)	(10)
Contribution	50	20

Helen can sell all the goods she can make.

Next year she will be able to purchase only 1,000 kg of material.

Find Helen's optimal production plan for next year.

Approach

First note that looking at contribution per unit is not sufficient here – whilst H has the highest unit contribution, it also uses the most amount of the scarce resource, material, per unit. Thus, making H may not maximise the contribution earned from the material available.

One approach would be trial and error – compute the total contribution earned from making all H, all L or some combination.

Solution

However, we will adopt the much more efficient key factor approach, ie identifying the product with the greatest contribution per unit of scarce resource. The scarce resource, which in this case is material, becomes the key factor.

Calculate the contribution per unit of scarce resource as this measures how efficiently the scarce resource is used.

H: $\dfrac{\text{Contribution/unit}}{\text{kg material used}}$

$= \dfrac{£50}{5\text{ kg (W)}} = £10/\text{kg}$

Working

Kg used: £50 ÷ £10/kg = 5 kg per unit

L: $\dfrac{£20}{1\text{ kg}} = £20/\text{kg}$

As L has the higher contribution per unit of scarce resource, Helen should make L. Calculate the total contribution from making either L or H and compare the two to assure yourself this is the case.

In principle, this is all there is to key factor analysis. In examinations the question is often embellished in a similar manner to the following example. Try this example before looking at the solution.

EXAMPLE

Key factor analysis 2

Helen's sister Louise is subject to the same restriction of 1,000 kg of material next year.

She makes two products:

	L	U
	£	£
Selling price	30	70
Material @ £10 per kg	(10)	(20)
	20	50

Louise can sell as much of either product as she can make; however she has signed a contract with William guaranteeing to supply him with 200 L each year.

What is Louise's optimal production plan for next year?

Solution

Again we must calculate contribution per unit of scarce resource.

L: $\frac{£20}{1} = £20$

U: $\frac{£50}{2} = £25$

This time we do not apply this knowledge immediately. Here Louise is compelled to produce at least 200 L whether it has the highest contribution per scarce resource or not.

After she has produced 200 L she will have 800 kg of material left.

We can determine the use of this 800 kg by key factor analysis. It should be used on U, which has the higher contribution per unit of scarce resource.

Production plan 200 L
400 U (800 kg/2 kg)

EXAMPLE

Key factor analysis 3

Louise's husband John is subject to a restriction of £3,200 worth of labour hours in one month. He makes three products.

	A	B	C
	£	£	£
Selling price	10	15	20
Labour cost	(3)	(5)	(6)
Other variable costs	(4)	(4)	(5)
Contribution	3	6	9

Maximum demand levels in any one month are expected to be 400 units for products A and C and 200 units for B.

What is John's optimal production plan for the next month?

Solution

Here we have the commonly occurring 'maximum demand' additional constraints. The approach is basically as before, ranking each option according to contribution per unit of scarce resource (labour hours). We allocate labour hours to the highest ranking product up to its maximum demand; then move onto the next best and so on until all labour hours are used.

Note that the labour constraint is actually expressed in monetary terms. We could convert this to hours and calculate each product's usage in hours, but a quicker way is to rank the products in terms of **contribution per £ labour**.

	A	B	C
Contribution per unit	£3	£6	£9
Labour £ per unit	£3	£5	£6
Contribution per £ of labour	£1	£1.20	£1.50
Rank	3	2	1

The optimum allocation will thus be as follows:

	Units	£ labour	Contribution
			£
Product C (up to maximum 400)	400	2,400	3,600
Product B (W)	160	800 (balance)	960
Product A	–	–	–
		£3,200	£4,560

Working

	£
Total labour cost available	3,200
Used by production of C	2,400
Balance	800

Units of B produced by £800 of labour = $\frac{£800}{5}$ = 160 units.

▷ ACTIVITY 5

ABC

ABC makes three products with the following estimated costs and revenues.

	A	B	C
Selling price (£)	20	25	30
Variable cost per unit (£)	10	11	14
Fixed cost per unit (£)	3	5	6
Profit per unit (£)	7	9	10
Amount of material X used per unit (kg)	2	2	4
Maximum demand (units)	250	100	200

Due to a shortage in the market, only 800 kg are available.

Required

Determine the production schedule that will optimise profit, bearing in mind the limiting factor; also assuming that the actual sales per product will not exceed the forecast figures quoted.

[Answer on p. 194]

▷ ACTIVITY 6

Dunnsports

Dunnsports make a variety of sports goods. One of its product groups is cricket boots and they make a range of five styles. You are given the following data for the forthcoming quarter.

	'Gower'	'Boycott'	'Willis'	'Taylor'	'Miller'
Selling price	£27.50	£30.00	£28.50	£29.00	£25.00
Variable costs per unit:					
Direct material	£8.00	£8.50	£8.25	£8.50	£7.75
Direct labour					
– hours	1.2	1.3	1.1	1.25	1.0
– at £7.50 per hour	£9.00	£9.75	£8.25	£9.38	£7.50
Budget/forecast sales and production per month quarter	500 pairs	510 pairs	520 pairs	500 pairs	510 pairs
Forecast labour hours for period	2,970				

Shortly after the budgeted output was agreed a machine breakdown occurred and, as parts are not available immediately, labour hours will be limited to 2,675.

Required

Determine the production schedule that will optimise profit, bearing in mind the limiting factor; also assuming that the actual sales per product will not exceed the forecast figures quoted.

[Answer on p. 195]

8 Test your knowledge

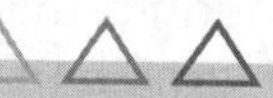

1 Define the term contribution.

2 What is the formula for calculating the breakeven point in units of output?

3 What is the formula for calculating the breakeven point in sales value?

4 Define the term margin of safety.

5 Define the term limiting or key factor.

6 What is the formula for determining sales volume in units when a target profit is set?

[Answers on p. 196]

9 Summary

In this chapter we have considered the approaches required to make short-term decisions about operating levels. CVP analysis recognises that changes in profit arise from changes in contribution which, in turn, is directly related to activity levels. Thus, we can use contribution per unit to compute the required activity level to achieve a particular profit level, including zero (breakeven point).

$$\text{Breakeven point in units} = \frac{\text{Fixed cost}}{\text{Contribution /unit}}$$

$$\text{Sales volume to achieve a particular profit} = \frac{\text{Total fixed costs + required profit}}{\text{Contribution/unit}}$$

If we know the beakeven point, then we can also calculate the margin of safety

Margin of safety (units) = Budgeted sales units – Breakeven sales units

$$\text{Margin of safety (\%)} = \frac{\text{Budgeted sales units – breakeven sales units}}{\text{Budgeted sales units}} \times 100\%$$

The contribution/sales (C/S) ratio, or P/V ratio is given by

$$\text{P/V ratio} = \frac{\text{Contribution per unit}}{\text{Selling price}}$$

Replacing the contribution per unit with the C/S ratio in the above formulae gives

$$\text{Breakeven point in sales revenue terms (£)} = \frac{\text{Fixed cost}}{\text{C/S ratio}}$$

$$\text{Sales revenue (£) to achieve a particular profit} = \frac{\text{Total fixed costs + required profit}}{\text{C/S ratio}}$$

Key factor analysis is a technique that we can use when we have a resource (materials, labour or machine time, for example) that is in short supply. Scarce resources should be allocated between products on the basis of the contribution that they earn per unit of scarce resource. It is common for examination tasks to ask you to allocate scarce resources between different products, so make sure that you get lots of question practice on this topic.

Answers to chapter activities & 'test your knowledge' questions

△ ACTIVITY 1

Roger Morton

(a) **Total fixed overhead**
Fixed overhead per unit based on planned output.
£4 per unit x 10,000 = £40,000

(b) **Contribution per unit**
Selling price per unit – Variable cost per unit
£75 – £46 = £29

(c) **Profit**
Contribution – Fixed costs
£29 x 2,000 – £40,000 = £18,000

△ ACTIVITY 2

(a) **Contribution per unit**
= Selling price per unit – Variable cost per unit
= £15 – £10 = £5

(b) **Budgeted Profit**
= Total contribution – Fixed costs
= £5 x 3,000 – £12,000 = £3,000

(c) **Breakeven point**
= Total fixed costs / Contribution per unit
= £12,000/£5 = 2,400 units

Margin of safety
= (budgeted sales – breakeven point)/budgeted sales x 100%
= (3,000 – 2,400)/3,000 x 100% = 20%

△ ACTIVITY 3

ABC Limited

(a) (i) **Figures for breakeven chart**

Sales 7,000 @ £17	£119,000	
Variable cost per unit	£10 per unit	
at 7,000 units		£
Variable cost	7,000 x £10 =	70,000
Fixed cost		40,000
Total cost		110,000

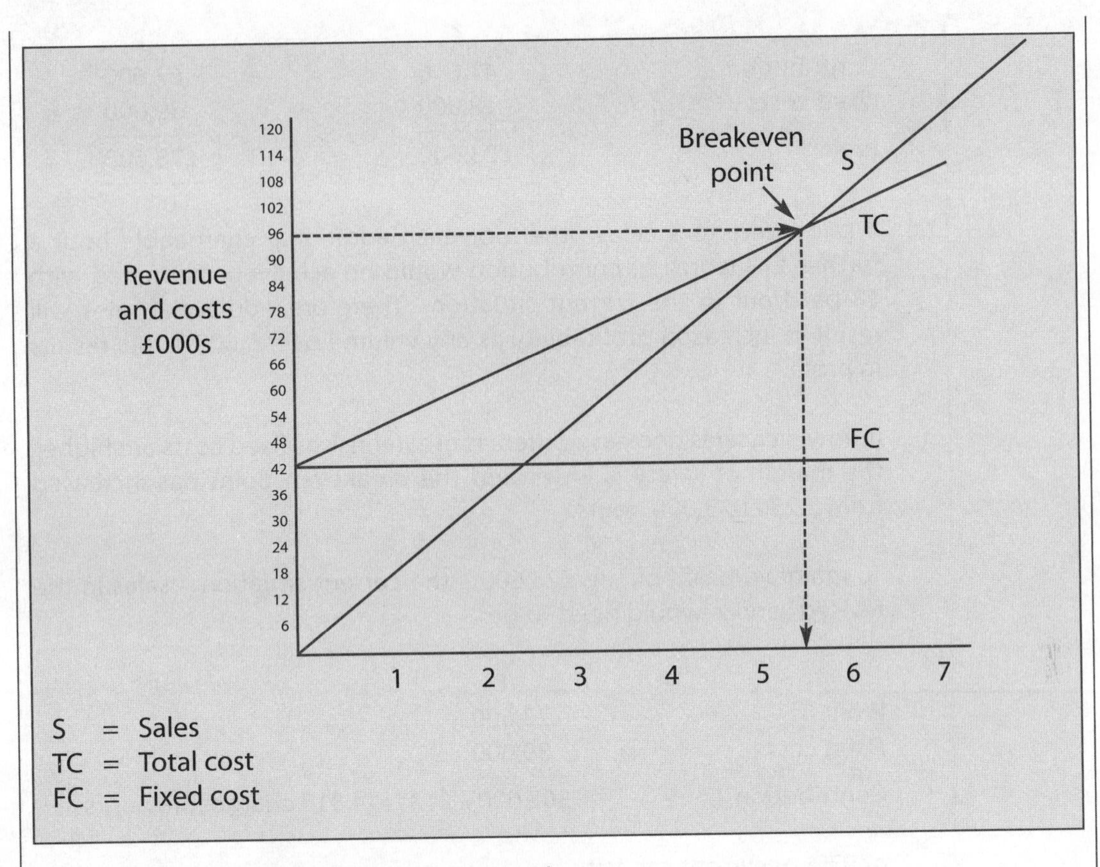

(ii) Breakeven point from graph
Approx £97,000 sales, 5,600 units.

(b) Breakeven point in units

$$\frac{\text{Fixed costs}}{\text{Contribution per unit}}$$

$$= \frac{£40,000}{£7}$$

= 5,715 units (rounding up)

ACTIVITY 4

Security services

(a) **Breakeven point in hours per month**

$$= \frac{\text{Fixed costs}}{\text{Contribution per hour}}$$

	Present position	Revised position
	$\frac{£18,000}{£30 - £22}$	$\frac{£39,000}{£33 - £20}$
=	2,250 hours	3,000 hours

(b) **Profits**

Present position	*Revised position*
5,200 chargeable hours	5,200 chargeable hours
x £8 contribution per hour	x £13 contribution per hour

	£	£
Contribution	41,600	67,600
Fixed costs	18,000	39,000
Profit	£23,600	£28,600

(c) If sales were to increase then for each additional chargeable hour a further £13 worth of contribution would be achieved, compared with £8 per hour in the current situation. Therefore, additional sales will result in increased profitability as any volume over 3,000 hours results in profit.

If, however, sales decreased there is greater risk as fixed costs are higher, the margin of safety is lower and the breakeven point has increased from 2,250 to 3,000 hours.

To maintain profit of, say, £23,600 – the current situation – sales in the revised service would need to be:

	£
Profit	23,600
Fixed cost	39,000
Contribution	£62,600 / £13 = 4,815 chargeable hours

or 93% of current capacity

ACTIVITY 5

ABC

	A	B	C
Selling price (£)	20	25	30
Variable cost per unit (£)	10	11	14
Contribution per unit	10	14	16
Amount of material X used per unit (Kg)	2	2	4
Contribution per kg of material X	5	7	4
Ranking	2	1	3

ABC should first make 100 B using up 200 kg of material X. This leaves 600 kg.

They should next make 250 A using up another 500 kg. This leaves 100 kg.

Finally, the 100 kg of material X left should be used to make 25 units of C.

ACTIVITY 6

Dunnsports

Contribution per limiting factor, ie the labour hour

Products	'G'	'B'	'W'	'T'	'M'
£	£	£	£	£	
Selling price	27.50	30.00	28.50	29.00	25.00
Less variable costs	17.00	18.25	16.50	17.88	15.25
Contribution per unit	10.50	11.75	12.00	11.12	9.75
Labour hours per unit	1.2	1.3	1.1	1.25	1.0
Contribution per direct labour hour	£8.75	£9.04	£10.91	£8.90	£9.75
Ranking	(5)	(3)	(1)	(4)	(2)

Revised production schedule

Revised direct labour hours	2,675
Produce 520 pairs 'Willis' x 1.1 hours/unit	572
Available	2,103
Produce 510 pairs 'Miller' x 1.0 hour/unit	510
Available	1,593
Produce 510 pairs 'Boycott' x 1.3 hours/unit	663
Available	930
Produce 500 pairs 'Taylor' x 1.25 hours/unit	625
Available	305

305 remaining hours/1.2 hours unit = 254 pairs 'Gower'

The revised optimum production plan is thus to produce the originally budgeted quantities for the Boycott (510), Willis (520), Taylor (500) and Miller (510) and a reduced quantity of Gower (254).

Test your knowledge

1 Contribution = sales revenue less total variable costs.

2 $$\frac{\text{Total fixed costs}}{\text{Contribution per unit of output}}$$

3 $$\frac{\text{Total fixed costs}}{\text{Contribution/sales}} \text{ or } \frac{\text{Total fixed costs}}{\text{PV ratio}}$$

4 The margin of safety is the difference between the breakeven point in sales revenue or units of output and the budgeted level in terms of sales revenue or output.

This difference can be expressed in absolute or relative terms.

5 The limiting factor is a resource that is in short supply and is termed a scarce resource.

6 $$\text{Sales volume} = \frac{\text{Total fixed costs + target profit}}{\text{Contribution per unit}}$$

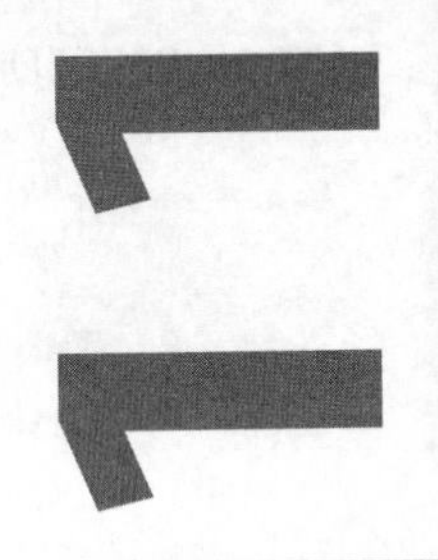

INVESTMENT APPRAISAL

INTRODUCTION

In the previous chapter we looked at how contribution can be used to make short-term decisions, such as which products to make when we have a shortage of resources (e.g. materials, labour).

In this chapter the focus is on long-term investment decisions – usually lasting more than one year.This could vary from the decision to build a new factory to whether or not to discontinue a product range.

There are many different investment appraisal techniques that could be used but the ones relevant to Unit 6 focus on predicting and evaluating future cash flows. The payback period, net present value method and the internal rate of return method are presented here.

KNOWLEDGE & UNDERSTANDING

- Methods of project appraisal: payback and discounted cash flow methods (NPV and IRR) (Element 6.3)
- The principles of discounted cash flow (Element 6.3)

CONTENTS

PERFORMANCE CRITERIA

- Prepare estimates of future income and costs (Element 6.3)
- State any assumptions used when evaluating future costs and revenues (Element 6.3)
- Identify and evaluate options and solutions for their contribution to organisational goals (Element 6.3)

1 Predicting future cash flows

The first stage in evaluating a proposed investment is to estimate the future cash flow implications. This will involve estimating future sales, costs, capital expenditure, disposal proceeds and so on.

As well as knowing what the future cash flows will be, we also need to know when they will occur. To simplify matters, we start the clock (time t = 0) when the initial investment happens.

To simplify things further, subsequent future cash flows are assumed to happen at year-ends, e.g. all of the sales and costs for the first year are assumed to be paid at the end of the first year – call this t = 1.

If we do this for all the future cash flows of the project, then we will typically end up with a table like the following:

	t = 0 £000	Year 1 (t = 1) £000	Year 2 (t = 2) £000	Year 3 (t = 3) £000	Year 4 (t = 4) £000	Year 5 (t = 5) £000
Invest	(100)					
Sales		40	50	60	50	40
Variable costs		(10)	(12)	(15)	(13)	(11)
Net cash flow	(100)	30	38	45	37	29

Note that when estimating future cash flows we want to identify what difference the project will make – only future incremental cash flows are relevant, e.g. the factory rent may be unaffected by the proposed project and would not be included when assessing the investment.

2 Payback period

2.1 Calculation

One way of assessing the predicted cash flows is to calculate a payback period. This simply asks how long it will take before the initial investment is recovered.

If the annual cash flows are constant, then the calculation is very straightforward e.g. if I invest £100,000 and get cash back of £20,000 each year, then it will take 100/20 = 5 years to recover my investment.

However, if the annual cash flows vary, then we need to calculate the cumulative net position at the end of each year.

Using the example above:

Time	Cash flow £000	Cumulative position £000	Working
t = 0	(100)	(100)	
t = 1	30	(70)	(100) + 30
t = 2	38	(32)	(70) + 38
t = 3	45	13	(32) + 45
t = 4	37	50	13 + 37
t = 5	29	79	50 + 29

From this table we can see that we would recover the initial investment sometime in the third year.

To be more precise we need to examine the cash flows in the third year in more detail. Here they relate to sales and variable costs, so are likely to occur throughout the year, rather than all being paid at the year-end. This means that we will break even part way through the third year, rather than waiting until the year-end.

Here we can see that we need a further £32,000 coming into the third year and that the total receipt in the year is £45,000. The payback period is therefore

$= 2\ ^{32}/_{45}$ or 2.71 years.

This can then be compared with the target payback that has been set. e.g. this company may have decided only to accept projects with paybacks lower than four years, in which case this project is acceptable.

2.2 Merits and demerits of payback period

Merits

(a) It is **easy to calculate**.

(b) It is **easy to understand**.

(c) It is **less affected by uncertainty**.
One limitation of any measure is that we are making a decision with estimates of revenue into the future. These estimates might be wrong but one would expect to be more confident of the accuracy of the earlier forecasts than the more distant forecasts, and payback period is dependent only on the earlier forecasts.

(d) It can obviously be very useful in specific circumstances such as when the company has **liquidity problems**.

Demerits

(a) **Flows outside the payback period are ignored**. If, for the same example as before, the receipt in the fifth year had been £20,000 instead of £2,000, the payback period would be unaltered at 2.5 years.

(b) **The timing of flows within the payback period is ignored**. If, again for

the same example, the first two years' receipts had been:
1st year £44,000
2nd year £1,000
then again the payback period would be unaltered at 2.5 years.

(c) It **ignores the time value of money** i.e. the interest that capital can earn. We shall see the relevance of this in the next sections on discounted cash flow.

▷ ACTIVITY 1 

A machine costs £100,000 now. We expect cash receipts of £30,000 in one year's time, £40,000 in two years' time, £60,000 in three years' time and £10,000 in four years' time.

Calculate the payback period for the investment.

[Answer on p. 207]

3 The time value of money and discounting

3.1 The time value of money

A key concept in long-term decision-making is that of money having a time value.

Suppose you were offered £100 now or £100 in one year's time. Even though the sums are the same, most people would prefer the money now. The £100 in the future is effectively worth less to us than £100 now – the timing of the cash makes a difference.

The main reasons for this are as follows:

- *Investment opportunities:* the £100 received now could be deposited into a bank account and earn interest. It would therefore grow to become more than £100 in one year.
- *Inflation:* the £100 now will buy more goods than £100 in one year due to inflation.
- *Cost of capital:* the £100 received now could be used to reduce a loan or overdraft and save interest.
- *Risk:* the £100 now is more certain than the offer of money in the future.

What if the offer were changed to £100 now or £105 in one year? Many would still prefer the £100 now, even though it is the smaller amount!

To do calculations using the time value of money it needs to be expressed as an interest rate (often known as a cost of capital, a required return or a discount rate)

Suppose we felt that £100 now was worth the same to us as £110 offered in one year's time. We could say that our time value of money was estimated at 10% per annum.

While this would incorporate all four of the factors mentioned above (investment opportunities, inflation, costs of capital and risk), it is easiest to imagine that we have a bank account paying 10% interest per annum.

The £100 now could be invested for a year and would grow to £110.

Therefore £100 now is worth the same as £110 offered in one year. Alternatively we say that the £110 in one year has a present value of £100 now. This process of taking future cash flows and converting them into their equivalent present value now is called discounting.

To calculate the present value of any future cash flow we multiply the cash flow by a suitable discount factor (or present value factor):

Present value = future cash flow x discount factor

Discount factors are provided in assessments and simulations – you do not need to be able to calculate them.

For example, with a 10% discount rate, the discount factor for a cash flow at t=1 is 0.909. Thus the offer of receiving £100 in one year's time is worth in today's terms

Present value = 100 x 0.909 = £90.90

3.2 Net Present Value (NPV)

The main implication of the time value of money is that we cannot simply add up and net off cash flows at different times – they are not comparable.

To get round this we do the following:

Step 1 Identify future incremental cash flows.

Step 2 Discount the cash flows so they are in today's terms (present values).

Step 3 Now the present values can be added up and netted off to give a net present value or NPV.

Step 4 If the NPV is positive, then it means that the cash inflows are worth more than the outflows and the project should be accepted.

Using the previous example with a discount rate of 10%, this could be set out as follows:

	t = 0 £000	Year 1 (t = 1) £000	Year 2 (t = 2) £000	Year 3 (t = 3) £000	Year 4 (t = 4) £000	Year 5 (t = 5) £000
Net cash flow	(100)	30	38	45	37	29
Discount factor	1	0.909	0.826	0.751	0.683	0.621
Present value	(100)	27.3	31.4	33.8	25.3	18.0

Net Present Value = (100) + 27.3 + 31.4 + 33.8 +25.3 + 18.0 = 35.8

This is positive, so the project should be undertaken.

An alternative layout could be as follows:

Time	Cash flow £000	Discount factor @ 10%	Present Value £000
t = 0	(100)	1	(100)
t = 1	30	0.909	27.3
t = 2	38	0.826	31.4
t = 3	45	0.751	33.8
t = 4	37	0.638	25.3
t = 5	29	0.621	18.0
	Net Present Value		35.8

▷ ACTIVITY 2

A machine costs £80,000 now. We expect cash receipts of £20,000 in one year's time, £50,000 in two years' time, £40,000 in three years' time and £10,000 in four years' time. The rate of interest applicable is 15%. Should we accept or reject the machine?

The relevant present value factors are:

	Year 1	Year 2	Year 3	Year 4
15%	0.870	0.756	0.658	0.572

[Answer on p. 207]

▷ ACTIVITY 3

Machine A costs £100,000, payable immediately. Machine B costs £120,000, half payable immediately and half payable in one year's time.
The cash receipts expected are as follows.

	A £	B £
at the end of 1 year	20,000	–
at the end of 2 years	60,000	60,000
at the end of 3 years	40,000	60,000
at the end of 4 years	30,000	80,000
at the end of 5 years	20,000	–

With interest at 5%, which machine should be selected?

The relevant present value factors are:

	Year 1	Year 2	Year 3	Year 4	Year 5
5%	0.952	0.907	0.864	0.823	0.784

[Answer on p. 208]

3.3 The internal rate of return (IRR)

For most projects, a graph of NPV against discount rate looks like the following:

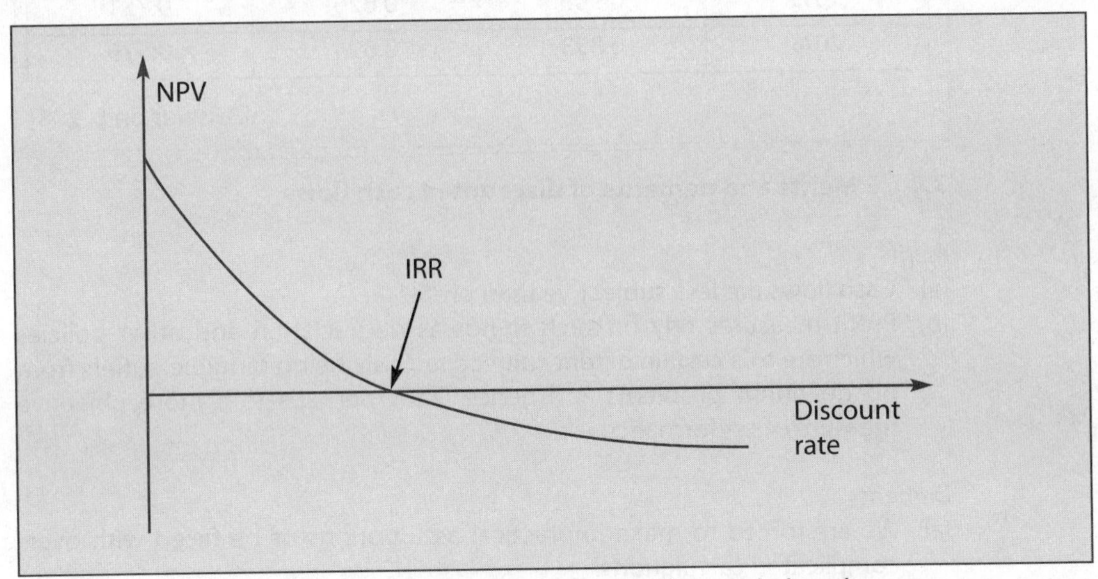

As the discount rate gets larger, the NPV gets smaller and then becomes negative:

The internal rate of return (IRR) is the discount rate that will cause the cash flow of a project to have a net present value equal to zero.

From the graph, for discount rates less than the IRR, the NPV is positive and the project acceptable.

If we are not sure which discount rate to use, then knowledge of the IRR still allows us to make an investment decision. If our estimated discount rate were somewhere between 10% and 15%, and the IRR of a project was 22% then we can still accept the project as our rate is less than the IRR, giving a positive NPV.

You will not have to calculate IRRs.

▷ ACTIVITY 4

Suppose a machine will cost £80,000 immediately, and will generate cash inflows of:

Time	£
Year 1	40,000
Year 2	50,000
Year 3	10,000

(a) Calculate the Net Present Value when the interest rate is 10% and 20%.
(b) Draw a graph of NPV against the rate of interest based upon this data.
(c) From your graph, read off the approximate IRR.

The relevant present value factors are:

	Year 1	Year 2	Year 3
10%	0.909	0.826	0.751
20%	0.833	0.694	0.579

[Answer on p. 208]

3.4 Merits and demerits of discounted cash flows

Merits

(a) Cash flows are less subjective than profits.

(b) Profit measures rely on such things as depreciation and other policies which are to a certain extent subjective. Cash, being tangible, suffers from no 'definition' problems and hence leads perhaps to a more objective measure of performance.

Demerits

(a) We are forced to make impractical assumptions or be faced with over-complicated calculations.
In the examples given so far we have assumed flows at yearly intervals, ignored taxation, ignored inflation – to mention just three simplifying assumptions.

(b) Discounted cash flow as a concept is more difficult for a layman to grasp. It would clearly be beneficial for the person on whose behalf we are performing the calculation to have a grasp of the basic concept underlying the technique.

4 Long-term investments in more detail

DEFINITION

Capital investment project

The key characteristic of a capital investment project is the tying up of capital for a number of years, in order to earn profits or returns over the period. Pulling out of the project earlier than originally intended will normally cause the return on investment to be considerably lowered and may even cause a loss.

This differentiates this type of investment from the type more commonly undertaken by **individuals**, such as the purchasing of shares or depositing money at a building society, where the capital can often be recovered with a reasonable return at any time.

4.1 What will the capital be invested in?

The most common investment you will encounter will be in **tangible fixed assets**, such as a new machine, factory or premises from which to operate a new service business.

Other less tangible forms of investment include **research and development, patent rights or goodwill** obtained on the purchase of an existing business.

4.2 What form will the returns take?

The purchase of a new fixed asset will often be with the intention of starting a new line of business – say the manufacturing of a new product, or the provision of a new or extended service. The returns will be the **net income** generated by the new business.

Alternatively, the investment may be to benefit the existing operations, such that **sales are increased** (where existing products/services are improved technologically or in quality) or **costs are reduced** (where production processes are updated or personnel reorganised). The returns will be measured as the **increase in net income or net reduction in costs** resulting from the investment.

4.3 Authorisation for a capital project

For projects involving a significant amount of capital investment, **authorisation** for its go-ahead will usually be given by the main board, or a sub-committee formed from the board for this purpose. Smaller projects (such as the replacement of an existing machine) may be within the authorisation limits of the manager of the area of business involved.

The decision will be based upon a **project proposal** using methods such as payback or discounted cash flow.

4.4 Importance of non-financial factors

Although these appraisal methods will usually give a basis for a **recommendation as to whether or not the project should be accepted**, they will only be able to take account of monetary costs and benefits. **Qualitative factors** will also need to be considered when reaching a final decision – such as possible effects on staff morale (for example, if the project involves increased automation or considerable overtime), the environment, customer satisfaction and the business's status/reputation.

5 Test your knowledge

1 What does the payback period measure?

2 What is meant by money having a time value?

3 What are the four reasons why money has a time value?

4 What is the main purpose of calculating the internal rate of return?

[Answers on p. 209]

6 Summary

In this chapter we have considered the mechanics, the advantages and the disadvantages of various investment appraisal techniques. In the context of an examination, you must be able to calculate the payback period and the Net Present Value of a project.

The payback period calculates how long it will take to recover the initial investment in a project. The Net Present Value, on the other hand, is an appraisal technique that takes the time value of money into account. As a general rule, if a project has a positive NPV, then it should be accepted, whereas a project with a negative NPV should be rejected.

You do not need to be able to calculate the IRR of a project, but you do need to use it to make investment decisions. Since the IRR is the discount rate at which a project has a NPV equal to zero, a cost of capital (or discount rate) which is less than the IRR will give rise to a positive NPV (and is therefore considered to be an 'acceptable investment').

The investment appraisal techniques that we have covered here are commonly tested in the Unit 6 examination.

Answers to chapter activities & 'test your knowledge' questions

ACTIVITY 1

Time	Cash flow £000	Cumulative position £000	Working £000
t = 0	(100)	(100)	
t = 1	30	(70)	(100) + 30
t = 2	40	(30)	(70) + 40
t = 3	60	30	(30) + 60
t = 4	10	40	30 + 10

From this table we can see that we would recover the initial investment sometime in the third year.

To be more precise we need to examine the cash flows in the third year in more detail. Here they probably relate to sales and variable costs, so are likely to occur throughout the year, rather than all being paid at the year-end. This means that we will break even part way through the third year, rather than waiting until the year-end.

Here we can see that we need a further £30,000 coming into the third year and that the total receipt in the year is £60,000. The payback period is therefore:

$= 2\ ^{30}/_{60}$ or 2.5 years.

ACTIVITY 2

Year		Cash flows	DF @ 15%	Present value
		£		£
0	Cost	(80,000)	1	(80,000)
1	Inflows	20,000	0.870	17,400
2		50,000	0.756	37,800
3		40,000	0.658	26,320
4		10,000	0.572	5,720
				NPV = 7,240

Since the net present value is positive (i.e. a cash surplus) we should accept the machine.

ACTIVITY 3

Machine A

Year	Cash flows	DF @ 5%	Present value
	£		£
0	(100,000)	1	(100,000)
1	20,000	0.952	19,040
2	60,000	0.907	54,420
3	40,000	0.864	34,560
4	30,000	0.823	24,690
5	20,000	0.784	15,680
			NPV = 48,390

Machine B

Year	Cash flows	DF @ 5%	Present value
	£		£
0	(60,000)	1	(60,000)
1	(60,000)	0.952	(57,120)
2	60,000	0.907	54,420
3	60,000	0.864	51,840
4	80,000	0.823	65,840
			NPV = 54,980

Since machine B has the higher NPV, our decision should be to select machine B.

ACTIVITY 4

(a) **Interest rate 10%**

Year		DF @ 10%	P/V
	£		£
0	(80,000)	1	(80,000)
1	40,000	0.909	36,360
2	50,000	0.826	41,300
3	10,000	0.751	7,510
			NPV = 5,170

(b) **Interest rate 20%**

Year		DF @ 20%	P/V
	£		£
0	(80,000)	1	(80,000)
1	40,000	0.833	33,320
2	50,000	0.694	34,700
3	10,000	0.579	5,790
			NPV = (6,190)

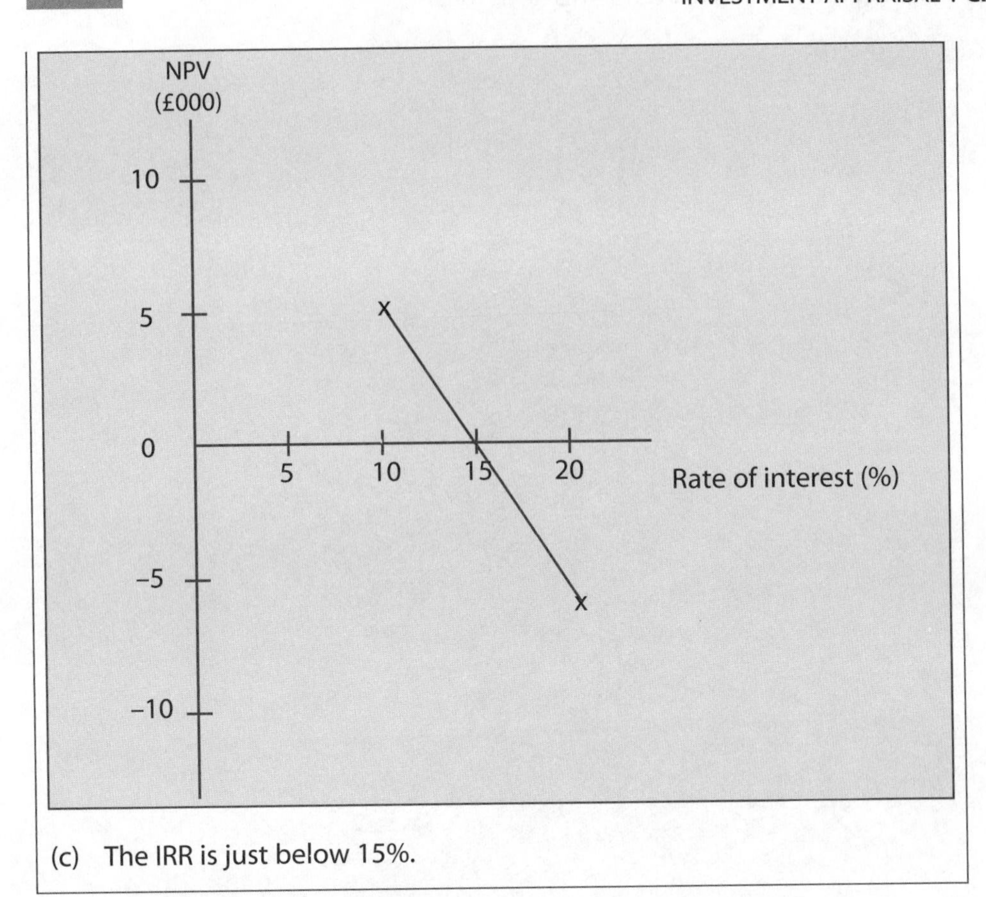

(c) The IRR is just below 15%.

Test your knowledge

1 The payback period measures the amount of time it takes to recover the cash outlay of the original investment.

2 The concept of the time value of money is that cash flows are worth more to us the sooner they are likely to occur. For example, £100 now is worth more to us than £100 expected to be received in , say, a year's time.

3 The main reasons for money having a time value are as follows:
- *Investment opportunities:* £100 received now could be deposited into a bank account and earn interest. It would therefore grow to become more than £100 in one year.
- *Inflation:* £100 now will buy more goods than £100 in one year due to inflation.
- *Cost of capital:* £100 received now could be used to reduce a loan or overdraft and save interest.
- *Risk:* £100 now is more certain than the offer of money in the future.

4 The main purpose of calculating the internal rate of return is to get an indication of the ranges of interest rates at which a project will be profitable or loss making. It is a sort of benchmark interest rate.

KEY TECHNIQUES QUESTIONS

Chapter 1
Principles of cost accounting

▷ ACTIVITY 1

Define the term cost accounting and list the possible benefits that accrue from a cost accounting system.

▷ ACTIVITY 2

Define the term management accounting and list the functions it fulfils to assist management to run a successful business.

▷ ACTIVITY 3

For cost and management accounting information to be used effectively it must possess a number of attributes.

List at least four such attributes and give examples from an information system with which you are familiar.

▷ ACTIVITY 4

Define the term cost unit and list cost units relevant to the following business activities:

- Accountancy practice.
- Brewery.
- Steel works.
- Cereal farmer.
- University.
- Railway company.
- Airline company.
- Restaurant.
- Motor manufacturer.
- Hospital.

▷ ACTIVITY 5

A cost centre is a production or service location, function, activity or item of equipment for which costs are accumulated.

Give six examples of cost centres you are likely to find in an hotel.

▷ ACTIVITY 6

Crescent Feeds Ltd have produced the following set of cost and management accounting figures for its current accounting period.

	£	
Production and sales tonnage	–	2,500 tonnes
Direct labour	102,000	
Admin overheads	16,500	

Direct materials	210,000
Direct expenses	5,250
Production overheads	40,400
Selling and distribution costs	52,300
Financial overhead	2,100

Calculate for the period:

- Prime cost
- Cost of production
- Cost of admin, sales and distribution and financial overhead
- Total cost
- Prime cost per tonne of product
- Production cost per tonne of product
- Total cost per tonne of product

▷ ACTIVITY 7

Kiveton Cleaning Services provide contract cleaning to schools, hotels, hospitals and offices.

They have three operational sites which are responsibility centres:

- Kiveton
- Whitby
- Birmingham

The company analyses its sales income by responsibility area and category of business by codes.

Coding structure:

Responsibility area (first three numbers of code):

- Kiveton 100
- Whitby 110
- Birmingham 120

Category of business (last three numbers of code):

- Schools 200
- Hotels 210
- Hospitals 220
- Offices 230

Code the following sales invoices:

- Whitwell High School (Kiveton area)
- White Swan Hotel (Kiveton area)
- Worcester Royal Hospital (Birmingham area)
- Dudley Council Offices (Birmingham area)
- Brown's Hotel, Malvern (Birmingham area)
- Eskdale School (Whitby area)
- Royal Victoria Hotel (Whitby area)
- Dunn and Musgrove, offices (Whitby area)
- Rother Valley Hospital (Kiveton area)

▷ ACTIVITY 8

Define the terms fixed cost and variable cost.

Identify the fixed and variable costs, in the following list of costs, incurred by a cricket bat manufacturer.

- Direct materials
- Direct labour (paid on piecework)
- Heat and light (workshop)
- Power (used in production machinery)
- Consumable materials used in production
- Accounts department salaries
- Insurance of sales cars
- Depreciation of workshop building
- Insurance of machinery
- Training costs for new production employees
- Stores department salary
- Agents sales commission
- Audit fees
- Petrol for managing directors' vehicle
- Advertising

▷ ACTIVITY 9

Refer to the above list and classify the expenditure to the following headings.

- Direct costs
- Production overhead
- Administration overhead
- Sales and distribution overhead

Chapter 2
Material costs

▷ ACTIVITY 10

When reviewing the balance of stock on a stock record card, at what level would a purchase requisition be raised?

▷ ACTIVITY 11

What is the purpose of a purchase requisition and who should sign and authorise its completion?

▷ ACTIVITY 12

What is the purpose of a goods received note?

How many copies of a GRN should be generated and to which departments should they be distributed?

▷ ACTIVITY 13

Kiveton Cleaning Services supplies its employees with protective clothing. One such item is protective gloves.

Records from the stores department for January showed:

1 Jan	Opening stock 150 pairs @ £2 each
7 Jan	Purchases 40 pairs @ £1.90
15 Jan	Issues 30 pairs
29 Jan	Issues 35 pairs

Calculate the value of the issues and the closing stock if the FIFO method is used to price the usage.

▷ ACTIVITY 14

Cavernelli runs a pizza house.

The stock and usage of pizza bases for December was:

		Units	Value £
Opening stock	1 Dec	200	180
Purchases	3 Dec	800	800
Purchases	20 Dec	1,200	1,140
Usage	w/e 7 Dec	400	
	w/e 14 Dec	350	
	w/e 21 Dec	410	
	w/e 28 Dec	475	

Calculate the value of issues and the closing stock using both the FIFO and LIFO methods of pricing usage (show figures to the nearest £).

The issues are priced at the end of each week.

▷ ACTIVITY 15

Define the following terms:

- Maximum stock level
- Minimum stock level
- Re-order level
- Re-order quantity or economic order quantity

▷ ACTIVITY 16

List six factors which need to be taken into account when setting stock levels.

▷ ACTIVITY 17

Crescent Engineering use a standard component AB3 and the stock, receipts and issues for the month of September were:

Opening stock 75 units @ £40 = £3,000.

Date	Receipts (units)	Unit cost £	Issues to production (units)
1 Sept	100	40	
10 Sept	75	42	
15 Sept			60
20 Sept			55
23 Sept	45	42	
30 Sept			50

The company uses the weighted average cost method for pricing issues and valuing stock.

Calculate the value of the usage for the month and the value of closing stock (figures to the nearest £1).

▷ ACTIVITY 18

Ravenscar Engineering use a standard component XZ7.

It estimates the following information regarding this unit:

Maximum weekly usage		600 units
Minimum weekly usage		400 units
Delivery period	max	6 weeks
	min	4 weeks
Re-order quantity		2,500 units

Calculate:

- Re-order level
- Maximum stock level
- Minimum stock level
- Average stock level

▷ ACTIVITY 19

Biscuit Making Company

The administration department is responsible for the purchase of sugar that is used in the production of biscuits. The price of sugar is volatile and company policy is to issue it from the stores department to the mixing department on a First-In-First-Out (FIFO) basis.

Task 19.1

Complete the stores ledger card using the First-In-First-Out basis to cost issues and value stocks of sugar for the month of November 20X8.

Note: Entries in the cost columns should be to three decimal places. Workings for the value column should be shown.

Stores Record Card

Material: Month:

Date	Receipts			Issues			Balance		
	Quantity (kilos) 000s	Cost (per kilo) £	Value £	Quantity (kilos) 000s	Cost (per kilo) £	Value £	Quantity (kilos) 000s	Cost (per kilo) £	Value £
Balance b/f November 1							50	0.175	8,750
November 4	34	0.180	6,120						
November 10				46					
November 15	29	0.200	5,800						
November 19	16	0.240	3,840						
November 22				52					
November 26	32	0.220	7,040						
November 28				39					

Task 19.2

Data on file shows that the maximum the factory uses is 35,000 kilos of sugar per week. There is a lead-time of one week and the company policy is to hold a buffer stock of one week's maximum usage.

Complete the following table

	Quantity (kilos)
Buffer stock	
Re-order level	

Task 19.3

(a) In Task 19.1 you costed issues of sugar to the mixing department on a First-In-First-Out (FIFO) basis. The general manager wants a costing method for issues that charges the mixing department with the most recent prices. Does FIFO meet this objective? Give a reason for your answer.

(b) In Task 19.2 you calculated the reorder level and buffer stock. Explain the difference between these two terms.

▷ ACTIVITY 20

Retail Store Company

Task 20.1

Issues are costed from the warehouse and transport department using the weighted average method.

Complete the stores ledger card below for an item of stock in the clothing department for the month of May 20X8 using the weighted average method for costing issues and valuing stock.

Note: Figures in the total columns should be shown to the nearest £.
The company's policy is to round prices per unit to three decimal places.

Stores Record Card

Department: Month:

Date	Receipts			Issues			Balance		
	Quantity	Price £	Total £	Quantity	Price £	Total £	Quantity	Price £	Total £
1/5 Balance							2,420	5.200	12,584
7/5	2,950	5.500	16,226						
11/5	3,200	5.700	18,239						
14/5				4,105					
21/5	1,535	5.400	8,289						
27/5				1,800					
30/5				2,600					

Task 20.2

Write a memo to the warehouse and transport manager which:

- explains the weighted average method and states its strengths
- comments upon the suitability of the method given the changes in receipt prices for May 20X8 in the stores ledger card.

Task 20.3

(a) In Task 20.1 you used the weighted average method for costing issues and valuing stock in the clothing department.
Explain why a costing method had to be used to cost issues and value stock in preference to identifying the cost of each unit of stock separately.

(b) Identify two other methods for costing issues and valuing stock.

ACTIVITY 21

The production cost centres in Curtains Ltd are cutting, finishing and packing; these are supported by three non-producing cost centres: stores, maintenance and canteen.

The operations in the cutting section are machine intensive. The machines are operated by a number of direct employees. The activity in both finishing and packing is labour intensive.

The company use the FIFO method for valuing stores issues to production and for valuing stock.

Task 21.1

Refer to the sales invoices (representing purchases for Curtains Ltd) and material requisitions below. Using the information you are required to complete the stores ledger accounts below for the month of March 20X1. The company uses the FIFO method for stores issues and stock valuation. You may assume that suppliers raise invoices on the same day as goods are delivered.

STORES LEDGER ACCOUNT

Material description:
Cotton lining material
50 metre rolls

Code: C310

Control levels:

Maximum	200
Minimum	60
Reorder level	90
Reorder quantity	100

	Receipts			Issues			Balance		
Date	Quantity	Unit price	Total	Quantity	Unit price	Total	Quantity	Unit price	Total
1 Mar							80	87.00	6,960.00

STORES LEDGER ACCOUNT

Material description:
Cotton red
50 metre rolls

Code: C322

Control levels:

Maximum	150
Minimum	45
Reorder level	80
Reorder quantity	50

	Receipts			Issues			Balance		
Date	Quantity	Unit price	Total	Quantity	Unit price	Total	Quantity	Unit price	Total
1 Mar							75	100.00	7,500.00

SALES INVOICE

DUNN & MUSGRAVE LTD
CRESCENT GARDENS
WHITBY
YO21 3EJ

VAT Reg: 292 8751 40
Date/Tax Point: 2 March 20X1

Invoice No: 2172
Your Order No: 3100

To:
Curtains Ltd
The High Street
Whitby

Item Description	Quantity	Unit price £	Total £
Cotton lining material 50 metre rolls	100	87.00	8,700.00
		VAT 17.5%	1,522.50
			£10,222.50

Net 30 days

SALES INVOICE

Heyes & Thistle Ltd
Bay Road Industrial Estate
Scarborough
N Yorks YO29 4EF

VAT Reg: 393 7142 51
Date/Tax Point: 9 March 20X1

Invoice No: 9213
Your Order No: 3105

To:
Curtains Ltd
2 The High Street
Whitby, North Yorkshire

Item Description	Quantity	Unit price £	Total £
Cotton material red, code 322 50 metre rolls	50	102.00	5,100.00
		VAT 17.5%	892.50
			£5,992.50

Net 30 days

SALES INVOICE

DUNN & MUSGRAVE LTD
CRESCENT GARDENS
WHITBY
YO21 3EJ

VAT Reg: 292 8751 40
Date/Tax Point: 9 March 20X1

Invoice No: 2274
Your Order No: 3110

To:
Curtains Ltd
The High Street
Whitby

Item Description	Quantity	Unit price £	Total £
Cotton lining material 50 metre rolls	75	90.00	6,750.00
		VAT 17.5%	1,181.25
			£7,931.25

Net 30 days

SALES INVOICE

Heyes & Thistle Ltd
Bay Road Industrial Estate
Scarborough
N Yorks YO29 4EF

VAT Reg: 393 7142 51
Date/Tax Point: 16 March 20X1

Invoice No: 9347
Your Order No: 3210

To:
Curtains Ltd
2 The High Street
Whitby, North Yorkshire

Item Description	Quantity	Unit price £	Total £
Cotton material red, code 322 50 metre rolls	50	102.00	5,100.00
		VAT 17.5%	892.50
			£5,992.50

Net 30 days

SALES INVOICE

DUNN & MUSGRAVE LTD
CRESCENT GARDENS
WHITBY
YO21 3EJ

VAT Reg: 292 8751 40
Date/Tax Point: 16 March 20X1

Invoice No: 2320
Your Order No: 3305

To:
Curtains Ltd
The High Street
Whitby

Item Description	Quantity	Unit price £	Total £
Cotton lining material 50 metre rolls	80	90.00	7,200.00
		VAT 17.5%	1,260.00
			£8,460.00

Net 30 days

SALES INVOICE

DUNN & MUSGRAVE LTD
CRESCENT GARDENS
WHITBY
YO21 3EJ

VAT Reg: 292 8751 40
Date/Tax Point: 23 March 20X1

Invoice No: 2375
Your Order No: 3317

To:
Curtains Ltd
The High Street
Whitby

Item Description	Quantity	Unit price £	Total £
Cotton lining material 50 metre rolls	100	87.00	8,700.00
		VAT 17.5%	1,522.50
			£10,222.50

Net 30 days

MATERIAL REQUISITION

Date: 5 March 20X1
Cost Centre: Cutting
Number: 950

Quantity	Code	Description
100	C310	Cotton lining material 50 metre rolls

Signature: R Keynes

MATERIAL REQUISITION

Date: 10 March 20X1 Number: 981
Cost Centre: Cutting

Quantity	Code	Description
60	C322	Cotton red 50 metre rolls

Signature: R Keynes

MATERIAL REQUISITION

Date: 12 March 20X1 Number: 996
Cost Centre: Cutting

Quantity	Code	Description
100	C310	Cotton lining material 50 metre rolls

Signature: R Keynes

MATERIAL REQUISITION

Date: 19 March 20X1 Number: 1020
Cost Centre: Cutting

Quantity	Code	Description
80	C310	Cotton lining material 50 metre rolls

Signature: R Keynes

MATERIAL REQUISITION

Date: 20 March 20X1 Number: 1031

Cost Centre: Cutting

Quantity	Code	Description
60	C322	Cotton red 50 metre rolls

Signature: R Keynes

MATERIAL REQUISITION

Date: 27 March 20X1 Number: 1052

Cost Centre: Cutting

Quantity	Code	Description
10	C322	Cotton red 50 metre rolls

Signature: R Keynes

Task 21.2

Refer to the stores ledger accounts in Task 21.1 above for materials codes C310 and C322 and prepare a memo for the general manager, Neil Barker, highlighting any unusual matters relating to the stock levels, issues and receipts during the month.

▷ ACTIVITY 22

The situation

Your name is Paul Goodenough and you are employed as an accounting technician by Esk Valley School. The school is a private establishment and caters for 500 pupils between the ages of 11 and 18; half of whom are boarders.

The academic department includes the following cost centres: maths and science, business studies, humanities, art and design, and sports. These are supported by administration, estates and catering. The centres are coded 200, 210, 220, 230, 240, 250, 260 and 270 respectively.

The school employs a team of full-time teachers but also has a number who work part-time. You are responsible for the entire accounting function at the school and have developed management accounting systems based on costing principles.

The situation is based on the first quarter's accounting period ended 31 March 20X1.

Task 22.1

Refer to the material requisitions below and complete the stores ledger account which follows. The school's policy is to charge out supplies to departments based on the FIFO method of stores valuation.

STORES REQUISITION

Cost Centre: Maths and Science 200.100 — No: 721 — Date: 15 January

Quantity	Detail	Code
200	A4 100 page notebooks	4.100

Signature: J Brown — Authorised: Susan Woodhouse

STORES REQUISITION

Cost Centre: Humanities 220.100 — No: 750 — Date: 2 February

Quantity	Detail	Code
500	A4 100 page notebooks	4.100

Signature: M Atkins — Authorised: Susan Woodhouse

STORES REQUISITION

Cost Centre: Business Studies 210.100
No: 761
Date: 15 January

Quantity	Detail	Code
400	A4 100 page notebooks	4.100

Signature: F Edgar Authorised: Susan Woodhouse

STORES REQUISITION

Cost Centre: Sports 240.100
No: 772
Date: 4 March

Quantity	Detail	Code
350	A4 100 page notebooks	4.100

Signature: M Kent Authorised: Susan Woodhouse

STORES REQUISITION

Cost Centre: Art and Design 230.100
No: 781
Date: 21 March

Quantity	Detail	Code
500	A4 100 page notebooks	4.100

Signature: S Husband Authorised: Susan Woodhouse

STORES LEDGER ACCOUNT

Material 100 page A4 notebooks

Code 4.100

Stock levels

Maximum	1,200
Minimum	50
Re-order level	300
Re-order quantity	1,000

	Receipts			Issues			Balance		
Date	Quantity	Unit price	Total	Quantity	Unit price	Total	Quantity	Unit price	Total
1 Jan							250	0.80	200.00
30 Jan	1,000	0.82	820.00						
28 Feb	1,000	0.80	800.00						
31 Mar	1,000	0.81	810.00						

Task 22.2

Refer to the cost schedule provided below and complete this summary for the period. Supplies are coded 100.

COST SCHEDULE

Issues of A4 notebooks for the quarter ended 31 March 20X1

Cost Centre and expense code	*Cost of issues*
	£
200.100	
210.100	
220.100	
230.100	
240.100	
250.100	
£	

Chapter 3
Labour costs

▷ ACTIVITY 23

(a) What is the purpose of a timesheet in labour costing?

(b) Why would an organisation wish to record its hourly paid employees' hours of work?

▷ ACTIVITY 24

Dunn and Musgrove is a firm of Licensed Accounting Technicians. In addition to the two partners there are three employees; two of whom work on clients' accounts, the other is on reception.

The two employees working on clients' accounts fill out timesheets to record their time; the partners keep separate diaries of time worked.

Each client is given a job number. The accounting assistants are Louise Astbury and Simon White. Their charge out rates are £8.00 and £12.00 per hour.

The partners' charge out rates are £25.00 per hour.

For the week ended 8 January 20X1 the individual timesheets together with notes from partners' diaries showed:

TIMESHEET

Name: L Astbury **Date:** w/e 8 Jan

Client job no	M	T	W	Th	Fr	Sat	Total hours
701	3.50	4.00		2.50	3.00		13.00
704	2.50			4.00			6.50
706		2.00		0.50			2.50
707	2.00	2.00			2.00		6.00
708			3.00		3.00		6.00
709			5.00	1.00			6.00
	8.00	8.00	8.00	8.00	8.00		40.00

Notes from partners' diaries (relevant to the jobs listed)

Pauline Dunn	Job 701	3 hours
	Job 709	4 hours

TIMESHEET

Name: Simon White **Date:** w/e 8 Jan

Client job no	M	T	W	Th	Fr	Sat	Total hours
701			4.00				4.00
704		4.50					4.50
710				4.50	3.50		8.00
711	8.00		4.00		2.00		14.00
712		3.50		3.50	2.50		9.50
	8.00	8.00	8.00	8.00	8.00		40.00

Notes from partners' diaries (relevant to the jobs listed)

James Musgrove	Job 712	4 hours
	Job 711	5 hours

Using the timesheets given and the charge out rates, determine the charge to the jobs shown.

▷ ACTIVITY 25

Shorts Ltd produce various garments. One of its products is 'boxer shorts'. The normal working week is 37½ hours and an individual productivity bonus of £4 is paid per batch of 15 shorts produced (bonus is only paid on complete batches).

There are two employees engaged on this product line.

During the week ending 14 August 20X1 the details on this activity were:

Employee	Carter	Noble
Basic hourly rate	£4	£4
Total hours worked	40½ hrs	41 hrs
Overtime hours paid @ time and a half	3 hrs	3½ hrs
Total output (shorts)	164	180
Reject rate (% of total)	3%	2½%

Calculate the gross wage for each employee for the week ending 14 August.

▷ ACTIVITY 26

List possible advantages of paying employees by output achieved.

▷ ACTIVITY 27

The Victoria Hotel is divided into a number of cost centres which are coded as follows:

Reception	100
Bar	110
Restaurant	120
Hairdressing salon	130
Swimming pool/gym	140
Housekeeping (inc bedrooms)	150
Exterior building fabric	160
Car park	170
External grounds	180

The hotel employs one person, Jan Fenster, who is solely responsible for the maintenance duties at the hotel. Jan fills in a weekly timesheet, so that accurate maintenance costs can be recorded.

Jan Fenster is paid £8.50 per hour for all hours worked.

The timesheet for the week ended 18 August 20X1 showed the following:

TIMESHEET

Name: Jan Fenster **Date:** w/e 18 August

Cost centre	Activity	Hours	M	T	W	Th	Fr	Sat	Total
140	Swimming pool cleaning and maintenance		8.00	0.50	0.50	0.50	0.50		10.00
130	Repair to hairdryer			2.50					2.50
150	Plumbing Bedroom 9			5.00					5.00
160	Window cleaning				4.00	4.00			8.00
170	Car park fence repair						3.00		3.00
180	External ground maintenance				3.50	3.50	4.50		11.50
			8.00	8.00	8.00	8.00	8.00	–	40.00

Calculate and list the maintenance labour cost for each cost centre for the week ending 18 August.

▷ ACTIVITY 28

Brown and Jones are a firm of joiners.

They have a workshop and employ six craftsmen. One of the employees is engaged on the production of standard doors for a local firm of builders.

This employee is paid a bonus based on time saved. The time saved is paid at a rate of 50% of the basic hourly rate.

In addition to the bonus, hours worked over the basic 40 per week are paid at time and a half.

In the week ended 13 February 20X1 the following details were available.

Basic hourly rate	£6.00
Time allowed per standard door	2 hours
Doors produced	25
Time worked	45 hours

Calculate the employee's gross pay for the week ended 13 February 20X1.

ACTIVITY 29

Cost centres

The production cost centres in Curtains Ltd are cutting, finishing and packing; these are supported by three non-producing cost centres: stores, maintenance and canteen.

The operations in the cutting section are machine intensive. The machines are operated by a number of direct employees.

The activity in both finishing and packing is labour intensive.

Cost accounting records and policies

The company use the FIFO method for valuing stores issues to production and for valuing stock.

The management accounting coding system includes the following:

Cost centre codes		*Expenditure codes*	
100	Cutting	200	Direct materials
110	Finishing	210	Indirect materials
120	Packing	220	Direct labour
130	Stores	230	Indirect labour
140	Maintenance	240	Production overhead
150	Canteen		

Task 29.1

The timesheets for two employees are shown below. These employees work on the production of a run of product C3220 108" drop, red curtains. Using the information contained in the internal policy document reproduced in the data below, you are required to analyse their wages for the week ended 23 March 20X1 as follows:

- Complete the total columns on the timesheets.
- Check for discrepancies and highlight these as a note on the face of the timesheet.
- Calculate the piecework earnings, training, sick or holiday pay; and applying where necessary the guaranteed fallback daily earnings determine the gross pay per employee.
- Complete the analysis of wages for the week.
- Calculate the direct labour cost per unit of output.
- Enter this analysis on the cost ledger data entry sheet below.

TIMESHEET

Week ending: 23 March 20X1

Employee name: John Collinson   Employee No: 157

Cost centre: Cutting

Activity	*Monday output*	*Tuesday output*	*Wednesday output*	*Thursday output*	*Friday output*	*Total output*
Cutting am	–	–	12	10	10	
Cutting pm	–	–	12	12	10	
Total output	–	–	24	22	20	
Hours on production	-	-	8	8	8	
Training	–	–	–	–	–	
Sick pay	–	–	–	–	–	
Holiday	8	8	–	–	–	
Total hours						
Reject units			2	1	1	
Gross pay:						
Piecework earnings						
Training						
Sick pay						
Holiday						

Guaranteed pay: £

Gross pay: £

TIMESHEET

Week ending 23 March 20X1

Employee name: June Mullhen   Employee No: 158

Cost centre: Cutting

Activity	*Monday output*	*Tuesday output*	*Wednesday output*	*Thursday output*	*Friday output*	*Total output*
Cutting am	13	12	–	12	10	
Cutting pm	14	13	–	12	10	
Total output	28	25		24	20	
Hours on production	8	8	–	8	6	
Training	–	–	–	–	2	
Sick pay	–	–	8	–	–	
Holiday	–	–	–	–	–	
Total hours						
Reject units	–	2		1	1	
Gross pay:						
Piecework earnings						
Training						
Sick pay						
Holiday						

Guaranteed pay: £

Gross pay: £

Internal policy document

Document No: **Curtains 150**

Subject: **Remuneration of Labour**

Date: **June 20X0**

Extract from product listing:
Piecework rates per unit of output:
Product C3220 108" drop red curtains.
Cutting process.
£1.20 per pair of good production.
Guaranteed minimum wage per day £25.00.
Employees work an eight-hour day, no overtime is worked.
Rate per hour for training, sick pay and holiday pay is £4.75 per hour. The hours paid on training are paid in addition to piecework earnings.

Analysis of wages:
Direct labour – piecework earnings on production or guaranteed minimum.
Indirect labour – training, sick pay and holiday pay.

Discrepancies on time sheets
Curtains Ltd wish to facilitate the prompt payment of wages and early reporting of labour costs.
Employees are paid from details on their timesheets. Any discrepancies are temporarily adjusted within direct labour pending the outcome of the review and enquiries.

Wages analysis week ending 23 March 20X1

	Employee 157 £	*Employee 158* £	*Total* £
Direct labour			
Indirect labour:			
Training			
Holiday			
Sick pay			

Direct labour cost per unit of output:

$$\frac{\text{Total direct labour}}{\text{Total good production}} = \underline{\hspace{4cm}} = £$$

COST LEDGER DATA ENTRY SHEET

Week ending:

Debit accounts:

Cost Centre Codes	*Expenditure Code*	£
100	220	
	230	
110	220	
	230	
120	220	
	230	
130	220	
	230	
140	220	
	230	
		£

Task 29.2

Prepare a memo to the production manager, Karl Meyer, highlighting any discrepancies on the two timesheets and requesting assistance in resolving the query.

Task 29.3

At a recent management meeting it was suggested that the system of piecework in the cutting cost centre may be replaced by a single rate per hour worked on production.

Currently holiday pay, sick pay and training is paid at £4.75 per hour.

It has been suggested that a consolidated rate of £5 per hour will be paid for all activities.

Using the proforma provided below, compare the production cost per good unit of output for the week ended 23 March with that if hours spent on production had been paid at the suggested consolidated rate.

Direct labour cost per unit of output for the week ended 23 March 20X1

$\frac{\text{Total direct labour}}{\text{Total good production}}$ = ______________________ = £

Alternative – consolidated rate per hour

	Employee 157	Employee 158	Total (hours)
Direct labour hours			
Total hours x Rate per hour =	x		= £

Direct labour cost per unit of output based on alternative

$\frac{\text{Direct labour cost}}{\text{Total good units}}$ = ______________________ = £

▷ ACTIVITY 30

The situation

Your name is Paul Goodenough and you are employed as an accounting technician by Esk Valley School. The school is a private establishment and caters for 500 pupils between the ages of 11 and 18; half of whom are boarders.

The academic department includes the following cost centres: maths and science, business studies, humanities, art and design, and sports. These are supported by administration, estates and catering. The centres are coded 200, 210, 220, 230, 240, 250, 260 and 270 respectively.

The school employs a team of full-time teachers but also has a number who work part-time. You are responsible for the entire accounting function at the school and have developed management accounting systems based on costing principles.

The situation is based on the first quarter's accounting period ended 31 March 20X1.

Task

Refer to the policy document concerning part-time wages and salaries below, and the timesheets for part-time staff provided below. Complete the timesheets and calculate the gross pay for each member of staff for the week ending 28 March 20X1.

No: 21 W&S

POLICY DOCUMENT

Prepared by: Susan Woodhouse, Bursar
Date: 7 December 20X0
Subject: Part time wages and salaries (including casual staff)

Cost centre	Cost centre code	Expenditure	Expense code
Teaching units:			
Maths and Science	200	Wages and salaries (Teaching)	110
Business Studies	210		
Humanities	220		
Art and Design	230	Wages and Salaries (Catering)	120
Sports	240		
Administration	250	Wages and Salaries (Estates)	130
Estates	260		
Catering	270	Wages and Salaries (Admin)	140

The following daily rates for part-time staff have been fixed for 20X1.

Teaching unit	Daily rate (£)
Maths and Science	135
Business Studies	135
Humanities	125
Art and Design	120
Sports	125

Estates	Rate per hour
Gardening staff	£5.25
Catering	
Canteen staff	£5.00

For both gardening and canteen staff any time over seven hours per day is paid as overtime at time and a half.

PART TIME STAFF
TIMESHEET – TEACHING

Cost Centre: Sports
Cost Centre Code:
Expense Code:
Date: Week ended 28 March 20X1
Name: Raymond Staniland

Please ✓ each completed am/pm session

	am	pm
Monday	✓	✓
Tuesday	–	–
Wednesday	✓	–
Thursday	✓	✓
Friday	–	–

Gross pay: days x £ per day
= £
Authorised by: S Woodhouse

PART TIME STAFF
TIMESHEET – TEACHING

Cost Centre: Art and Design
Cost Centre Code:
Expense Code:
Date: Week ended 28 March 20X1
Name: James Parker

Please ✓ each completed am/pm session

	am	pm
Monday	✓	✓
Tuesday	–	–
Wednesday	–	–
Thursday	–	–
Friday	✓	✓

Gross pay: days x £ per day
= £
Authorised by: S Woodhouse

PART TIME STAFF
TIMESHEET – TEACHING

Cost Centre: Business Studies
Cost Centre Code:
Expense Code:
Date: Week ended 28 March 20X1
Name: Elizabeth Jones

Please ✓ each completed am/pm session

	am	pm
Monday	✓	–
Tuesday	✓	✓
Wednesday	✓	–
Thursday	–	–
Friday	✓	✓

Gross pay: days x £ per day
= £
Authorised by: S Woodhouse

PART TIME STAFF
TIMESHEET – TEACHING

Cost Centre: Maths and Science
Cost Centre Code:
Expense Code:
Date: Week ended 28 March 20X1
Name: John Brewster

Please ✓ each completed am/pm session

	am	pm
Monday	✓	–
Tuesday	✓	–
Wednesday	✓	–
Thursday	✓	–
Friday	✓	–

Gross pay: days x £ per day
= £
Authorised by: S Woodhouse

PART TIME STAFF
TIMESHEET – ESTATES AND CATERING

Cost Centre: Catering
Cost Centre Code:
Expense Code:
Date: Week ended 28 March 20X1
Name: Carol Heyes

	am	pm	Total hours
Sunday	4	5	
Monday	4	3	
Tuesday	4	3	
Wednesday	4	6	
Thursday	4	6	
Friday	4	3	
Saturday	4	4	
	___	___	___

Basic time hours x £ = £

Overtime hours x £ = £ ______

Gross pay £ ______

Authorised by: *S Woodhouse*

PART TIME STAFF
TIMESHEET – ESTATES AND CATERING

Cost Centre: Estates
Cost Centre Code:
Expense Code:
Date: Week ended 28 March 20X1
Name: Simon Jones

	am	pm	Total hours
Sunday	–	–	
Monday	4	3	
Tuesday	–	–	
Wednesday	4	4	
Thursday	–	–	
Friday	4	5	
Saturday	–	–	
	___	___	___

Basic time hours x £ = £

Overtime hours x £ = £ ______

Gross pay £ ______

Authorised by: *S Woodhouse*

Chapters 4 and 5
Expenses and Accounting for overheads

▷ ACTIVITY 31

Define the terms:

- capital expenditure
- revenue expenditure.

▷ ACTIVITY 32

The following is a list of expenditure incurred by a firm of agricultural engineers.

Which of these items would be classed as capital expenditure?

- Repairs to machinery.
- Purchase of new delivery vehicle.
- Depreciation of delivery vehicle.
- Painting and sign-writing of new vehicle in firm's livery and colours.
- Firm's cost of own labour in building extension to workshop.
- Installation of air conditioning unit in new workshop extension.
- Redecoration of office.
- Installation and setting up of new machinery in workshop (own labour).

▷ ACTIVITY 33

Define the terms:

- overhead allocation
- overhead apportionment
- overhead absorption.

▷ ACTIVITY 34

What bases of apportionment or reapportionment would you normally use for the following items of overhead?

- Depreciation of plant.
- Power.
- Heat and light.
- Rent and rates.
- Insurance of plant.
- Insurance of buildings.
- Canteen costs (total cost).
- Stores department costs (total cost).
- Shop floor administration.
- Consumable tools.
- Consumable materials (oils, greases, cleaning materials).
- Minor maintenance.

▷ ACTIVITY 35

R Noble and Sons are a firm of agricultural engineers based in North Yorkshire.

They have a large workshop from which they operate, but also visit customers to maintain equipment.

The business is divided into cost centres which include:

- Machining.
- Fabrication.
- Fitting shop.
- Outside client work.
- Canteen.
- Stores.
- Maintenance.

A summary of their budgeted overhead for the three months ended 31 March 20X1 showed:

		£
	Depreciation of machinery	5,000
	Insurance of machinery	2,100
	Insurance of buildings	1,500
	Heat and light	800
	Power	1,750
	Rent and rates	2,250
(m/c, fab, and fitting only)	Shop floor admin	500
(m/c, fab,fit and outwork only)	Consumable tools	900
(m/c, fab, fit and outwork only)	Consumable materials	410
(all cost centres except canteen)	Supervisory salaries	4,000
		19,210

Other relevant costs and data for the period showed:

	Machining	Fabrication	Fitting	Outside work	Canteen	Stores	Main-tenance
Value of buildings	£30,000	£35,000	£25,000	–	£7,500	£10,000	£12,500
No of employees	3	2	1	2	1	1	1
Value of plant	£40,000	£19,000	£10,000	£20,000	£1,000	£2,500	£7,500
Indirect labour	–	–	–	–	£1,375	£2,750	£3,125
Indirect materials	£1,625	£1,125	£275	£150	£188	£287	£1,375
Vehicle insurance				£475			
Vehicle tax				£75			
Vehicle running cost				£1,400			
Floor area (sq m)	300	350	250	–	75	100	125
Kilowatt hours (power used) ratio	40	30	16	–	2	2	10
Direct labour hours	1,600	1,067	540	1,100	260	520	520
Material requisitions	195	150	120	200	–	–	100

Task 35.1

Prepare an overhead analysis sheet for the quarter using the proforma below based on the budget.

Task 35.2

Determine overhead recovery rates for each of the four directly operational cost centres per direct labour hour, namely:

- machining
- fabrication
- fitting
- outside contracts.

OVERHEAD ANALYSIS SHEET (TASK 35.1)

R Noble Agricultural Engineers Budget Period End 31 March 20X1

Overhead Item	Total	Basis	Machining	Fabrication	Fitting	Outside work	Canteen	Stores	Maintenance
	£		£	£	£	£	£	£	£
Indirect labour									
Indirect materials									
Vehicle costs									
Depreciation m/c									
Insurance m/c									
Insurance buildings									
Heat and light									
Power									
Rent and rates									
Shop floor admin									
Consumable tools									
Consumable mats									
Supervision sals									
Reapportionment:									
Canteen		Number of employees							
Stores		No of material req							
Maintenance		DL hours							

▷ ACTIVITY 36

R Noble and Sons, agricultural engineers have four directly operational cost centres:

- machining
- fabrication
- fitting shop
- outside contract work.

The predetermined overhad recovery rates per direct labour hour were: £7.77, £7.99, £8.47 and £7.18 respectively.

For budget period 4, the month of April 20X1, the direct labour hours worked were:

· machining	500 hours
· fabrication	350 hours
· fitting shop	180 hours
· outside contract work	400 hours

The actual overhead for the period was:
machining £4,150, fabrication £2,600, fitting shop £1,450 and outside contract work £2,950.

Calculate the overhead recovered in each cost centre for period 4 showing any under- or over- recovery of overhead per cost centre and in total.

▷ ACTIVITY 37

During period 6, the month of June 20X1, R Noble and Sons receive an order to produce a replacement set of doors for a grain drier unit. They estimate the job as follows:

Direct materials	£3,500
Direct labour	
machining	15 hrs
fabrication	8 hrs
fitting shop	5 hrs

The predetermined overhead recovery rates per direct labour hour were: £7.77, £7.99 and £8.47 respectively.

All skilled craftsmen are paid £7.50 per hour.

Using the information above determine the production cost of the doors, showing clearly the direct material, direct labour and overhead recovered.

▷ ACTIVITY 38

During period 5, the month of May 20X1, R Noble and Sons under- and over-recovery of overhead per cost centre was:

Cost centre	*Overhead recovered*	*Actual overhead*	*(under)/over-recovered*
	£	£	£
Machining	3,950	4,250	(300)
Fabrication	2,950	3,150	(200)
Fitting shop	1,640	1,600	40
Outside work	2,750	2,600	150
	£11,290	£11,600	(310)

Post these total figures to the overhead account, showing the transfer of the under-recovery to the costing profit and loss account.

▷ ACTIVITY 39

Biscuit Making Company

The general manager has given you the task of supplying cost data for the manufacture of a specific brand of chocolate biscuit for 20X9 on the basis of projected costs. A cost clerk has given you data on variable and fixed costs, which is relevant over the range of production.

(a) Complete the budgeted cost schedule for the different levels of production.

BUDGETED COST SCHEDULE		**YEAR 20X9**		
		ACTIVITY (Packets)		
		175,000	**200,000**	**225,000**
Description	**Cost**	**£**	**£**	**£**
Direct material	8p per packet			
Direct labour	6p per packet			
Packing costs	1p per packet			
Depreciation costs	£12,000			
Rent and rates	£26,000			
Supervisory costs	£12,000			
Administration costs	£8,000			

(b) Using your data from part (a) complete the table below for costs at the three levels of production.
Costs per packet should be rounded to three decimal places.

	ACTIVITY (Packets)		
	175,000	200,000	225,000
COST	£	£	£
Total variable cost			
Total fixed cost			
Total cost			
Cost per packet			

▷ ACTIVITY 40

Using your results from Activity 39:

(a) Identify the trend in cost per packet of biscuits for production between 175,000 and 225,000 packets.

(b) Give reasons for this trend.

▷ ACTIVITY 41

(a) In addition to fixed and variable costs, two other classifications of cost behaviour are semi-variable costs and stepped fixed costs.

Sketch graphs below and give an example of each.

Semi-variable **Stepped fixed**

Cost £ | Activity

Cost £ | Activity

(b) Justify/explain your choice of examples in part (a).

▷ ACTIVITY 42

Biscuit Making Company

The general manager has asked you to monitor the absorption of overheads for the production departments for November 20X8.

Company policy is to absorb overheads on the following basis.

Department	**Basis**
Mixing	Per £ of labour cost
Baking	Machine hours
Packing	Labour hours

Budgeted and actual data for November 20X8 is:

	Mixing	**Baking**	**Packing**
Budgeted overheads	£164,000	£228,900	£215,000
Actual labour hours worked			16,000
Budgeted labour hours			17,200
Actual machine hours		16,100	
Budgeted machine hours		16,350	
Actual labour costs	£63,700		
Budgeted labour costs	£65,600		

Task 42.1

Calculate the budgeted overhead absorption rate for each department.

	Mixing £	**Baking £**	**Packing £**
Budgeted overhead Absorption rate			

Task 42.2

Complete the production overhead schedule below.

Note: Overheads should be absorbed on the basis of actual performance.

PRODUCTION OVERHEAD SCHEDULE			
Month:			
	Mixing £	**Baking £**	**Packing £**
Budgeted overheads			
Actual overheads	171,500	224,000	229,000
Overhead absorbed			

Task 42.3

Complete the table below.

	Mixing £	Baking £	Packing £
Over-absorbed overheads			
Under-absorbed overheads			

Task 42.4

You were given the budgeted production overheads for the mixing, baking and packing departments to arrive at overhead absorption rates for each department.

(a) Explain why you do not have to calculate a budgeted overhead absorption rate for the stores department.

(b) Explain what will have happened to the budgeted overheads for the stores department.

Task 42.5

The budgeted overhead absorption rates for the baking and packing departments were based upon time, whilst the rate for the mixing department was based upon value.

State which approach to overhead absorption is more appropriate, giving a reason for your answer.

▷ ACTIVITY 43

You have been looking at the following budgeted overhead data relating to the individual departments of a store for the year ended 31 May 20X9. You have determined that some overheads will be attributable solely to a particular department and these overheads are listed below:

Department	Overhead £
Electrical	224,600
Household	213,200
Clothing	203,000
Food	194,600
Buying	42,200
Admin	102,300
Warehouse and transport	51,300

You have also ascertained that the following overheads will be incurred for all departments and not one department in particular:

	£
Rent and rates	380,400
Canteen Services	94,800

You have gathered the following information concerning the departments:

Department	Floor area (sq metres)	Number of employees
Electrical	2,844	51
Household	2,952	52
Clothing	3,900	54
Food	1,920	41
Buying	180	6
Admin	300	21
Warehouse and transport	3,120	12
Total	15,216	237

Task 43.1

Complete the budgeted department overhead schedule by:

- allocating the attributable overheads above to each department
- apportioning rent and rates and canteen services across all the departments.

BUDGETED DEPARTMENT OVERHEAD SCHEDULE
YEAR ENDED 31 MAY 20X9

	Electrical £	Household £	Clothing £	Food £	Buying £	Admin £	Warehouse and trans £	Total £
Allocated overhead								1,031,200
Rent and rates								380,400
Canteen services								94,800
Total								1,506,400

Task 43.2

Write notes to the chief accountant that:

- identify the departments that will need to have their overheads reapportioned
- identify the departments that will need to have overheads reapportioned to them
- explain the reasons for the reapportionment of overheads.

Task 43.3

(a) The store uses a system of coding each cost. Identify two reasons why a coding system is used in practice.

(b) A machine was bought in the warehouse and transport department for £20,000 on 1 June 20X6. Depreciation is provided for at the rate of 20% using the reducing balance method. Calculate the depreciation charge for the year ended 31 May 20X8.

(c) Show the double entry that will appear in the cost accounts for the depreciation charge you calculated in part (b) for the year ended 31 May 20X8.

▷ ACTIVITY 44

Cost centres

The production cost centres in Curtains Ltd are cutting, finishing and packing; these are supported by three non-producing cost centres: stores, maintenance and canteen.

The operations in the cutting section are machine intensive. The machines are operated by a number of direct employees.

The activity in both finishing and packing is labour intensive.

Cost accounting records and policies

The company use the FIFO method for valuing stores issues to production and for valuing stock.

The management accounting coding system includes the following:

Cost centre codes		*Expenditure codes*	
100	Cutting	200	Direct materials
110	Finishing	210	Indirect materials
120	Packing	220	Direct labour
130	Stores	230	Indirect labour
140	Maintenance	240	Production overhead
150	Canteen		

Task 44.1

Refer to the internal policy document on overhead recovery rates for 20X1 shown in the data below, which has details of the budgeted hours for each cost centre for the quarter ended 31 March 20X1.

Using the proforma provided below which gives details of actual activity and costs for the quarter:

- calculate the overhead recovered per cost centre and in total for the period (to the nearest £)

- calculate the under or over recovery for each cost centre and in total and tabulate your results.

Internal policy document

Subject: **Production Overhead**

Date: **December 20X0**

Cost centre	*Cutting*	*Finishing*	*Packing*
Overhead recovery rate	£9.50 per machine hour	£8.50 per direct labour hour	£7.25 per direct labour hour

The cutting department is machine intensive, whereas the finishing and packing activity is more labour intensive.

Budgeted data for the quarter ended 31 March 20X1:

Cost centre	*Cutting*	*Finishing*	*Packing*
Machine hours	5,200	–	–
Direct labour hours	–	4,200	3,700

Proforma for Task 44.1

The actual level of activity for the quarter ended 31 March 20X1 was:

Cost centre	Cutting	Finishing	Packing
Machine hours	5,450		
Direct labour hours		4,390	3,870
Actual cost (overheads)	£52,000	£36,500	£27,750

Overhead recovered

Cost centre:

Cutting Actual machine hours x Overhead recovery rate

x = £

Finishing Actual direct labour hours x Overhead recovery rate

x = £

Packing Actual direct labour hours x Overhead recovery rate

x = £

Under or over recovery of overhead for the quarter ended 31 March 20X1

Cost centre	Overhead recovered £	Actual cost £	(Under)/ over-recovered £
Cutting			
Finishing			
Packing			

Task 44.2

The company uses an integrated accounting system and maintains a production overhead account.

Using the proforma provided below, complete the production overhead control account for the period, showing the transfer of the under or over recovery to the costing profit and loss account.

Production overhead control account

31 Mar	£	31 Mar	£
Creditors and wages control (i.e. overheads)			
Cutting		Cutting	
Finishing		Finishing	
Packing		Packing (overhead recovered)	
	£		£

▷ ACTIVITY 45

The situation

Your name is Adele Clarking and you work as an accounting technician for Ravenscar Motors, a company which has three main activities: motor repairs, car valeting service and tow bar fitting for cars and commercial vehicles. The budgeted turnover for the year is £800,000.

The business is divided into three profit centres: motor repairs, car valeting and tow bars which are supported by a cost centre, stores. In addition to this there is also the administration unit which deals with accounting, purchasing, personnel and administration.

Task 45.1

Refer to the first memo from Richard Fielder reproduced below, and prepare the overhead analysis sheet for the budget period.

Then calculate the overhead recovery rate for each of the profit centres: motor repairs, car valeting and tow bar fitting. Use the proforma provided below (showing your workings to four decimal places when calculating the recovery rates).

MEMORANDUM

To: Adele Clarking
From: Richard Fielder
Date: 30 December 20X0
Subject: Overhead absorption rates

I list below a summary of the overheads for the budget period for the quarter to 31 March 20X1, together with other data.

Can you please complete the overhead analysis sheet and determine the overhead for the three profit centres after reapportioning the stores cost centre.

Then calculate overhead recovery rates for each based on direct labour hours.

Overheads	Budget for quarter to 31 March 20X1
	£
Depreciation	18,000
Rent and rates	30,000
Heat and light	2,100
Power	3,100
Workshop managers salary	21,000
Stores salary	12,500
Consumables	1,850
Insurance plant	2,500
Insurance buildings	4,100

Statistics and other data

Profit and cost centres	Motor repairs	Valeting	Tow bars	Stores
Area occupied (sq metres)	300	100	75	25
Power consumption ratio	0.4	0.2	0.3	0.1
Plant value	£100,000	£35,000	£43,000	£2,000
Direct labour hours (standard)	8,000	4,000	2,000	–
No of employees	4	2	1	1
Material requisitions	1,000	500	300	

OVERHEAD ANALYSIS SHEET

Overhead	Total	Basis	Motor Repairs	Valeting	Tow Bars	Stores
	£		£	£	£	£
Depreciation	18,000	Plant value				
Rent and rates	30,000	Area				
Heat and light	2,100	Area				
Power	3,100	Consumption ratio				
Workshop manager's salary	21,000	No of employees				
Stores salary	12,500	Allocated				
Consumables	1,850	Dir lab hours				
Insurance plant	2,500	Plant value				
Insurance buildings	4,100	Area				
Reapportionment of stores		Material requisitions				( )
			£	£	£	
Direct labour hours						
Recovery rate per DL hour						

Task 45.2

Refer to the second memo from Richard Fielder reproduced below and complete the overhead schedule provided below.

MEMORANDUM

To: Adele Clarking
From: Richard Fielder
Date: 31 March 20X1
Subject: Overhead recovery for the quarter ended 31 March 20X1

The following summary shows the details relevant to overhead cost for the current period.

	Motor repairs	Valeting	Tow bars
Standard hours produced	8,200	4,050	2,025
Actual direct labour hours	8,150	3,950	2,100
Actual overhead cost	£57,100	£23,400	£17,750

Could you please complete the overhead schedule showing for each centre: the overhead recovered, the actual overhead and the (under)/over recovery of overhead for the period.

Many thanks.
Richard

OVERHEAD SCHEDULE FOR QUARTER ENDED 31 MARCH 20X1

Profit centre	Overhead recovered £	Actual overhead £	(Under)/Over-recovered £
Motor repairs			
Valeting			
Tow bars			
	£	£	£

Working

Overhead recovered		£
Motor repairs	Standard hours x Hourly rate	
Valeting	Standard hours x Hourly rate	
Tow bars	Standard hours x Hourly rate	

▷ ACTIVITY 46

The situation

Your name is Paul Goodenough and you are employed as an accounting technician by Esk Valley School. The school is a private establishment and caters for 500 pupils between the ages of 11 and 18; half of whom are boarders.

The academic department includes the following cost centres: maths and science, business studies, humanities, art and design, and sports. These are supported by administration, estates and catering. The academic centres are coded 200, 210, 220, 230, 240 respectively. The administration is coded 250.

The school employs a team of full-time teachers but also has a number who work part-time. You are responsible for the entire accounting function at the school and have developed management accounting systems based on costing principles.

The situation is based on the first quarter's accounting period ended 31 March 20X1.

Task 46.1

Refer to the policy document concerning overheads below and the overhead schedule provided below.

Complete the overhead schedule and calculate the overhead recovery rates for each of the teaching units.

No: 25 overhead

POLICY DOCUMENT

Prepared by: S Woodhouse
Date: 8 December 20X0
Subject: Teaching unit overheads
Period: January –December 20X1

Teaching unit salaries and salary related costs are fixed and are recovered along with other overheads.

Allocated costs	200	210	220	230	240	Total
	Cost centres					
	£	£	£	£	£	£
Wages and salaries	155,000	130,000	141,000	125,000	140,000	691,000
Pension – employer's contribution 6% of salaries						
Employer's NI contribution 8% of salaries						
Consumables	15,000	12,000	14,500	11,900	18,000	71,400
Central services costs						
Estate costs – general	131,500					
buildings insurance	12,500					
heat and light	23,500					
equipment insurance	4,750					
Catering	85,000					
Administration (inc Head's office)	72,400					

Estimated student hours 600,000

Split of estimated hours by cost centre:

200	210	220	230	240	Total
105,000	115,000	125,000	121,000	134,000	600,000

Reapportion central services costs in the following order – catering, estates, admin.

Catering costs – reapportion on basis of student hours.
Estate costs – reapportion on basis of area occupied.
Admin costs – reapportion on basis of student hours.
Ratio of area occupied:

Cost centre	200	210	220	230	240	250
	15%	12%	10%	10%	39%	14%

ESK VALLEY SCHOOL – OVERHEAD SCHEDULE

Overhead	Total £	Basis £	Maths and Science £	Business Studies £	Human -ities £	Art and Design £	Sports £	Admin £	Estates £	Catering £
Wages and salaries	691,000	Allocated								
Pension costs	41,460	% of salaries								
Employer's NI	55,280	% of salaries								
Consumables	71,400	Allocated								
Buildings insurance	12,500	Estates							12,500	
Heat and light	23,500	Estates							23,500	
Equipment insurance	4,750	Estates							4,750	
Estate costs	131,500	Allocated							131,500	
Catering	85,000	Allocated								85,000
Admin-istration	72,400	Allocated						72,400		
	1,188,790									
Reappor-tionment:										
Catering		Student hours								(85,000)
										–
Estates		Area							( )	
									–	
Admin-istration		Student hours						( )		
								–		
	1,188,790									

OVERHEAD RECOVERY RATES

Teaching Cost Centres	Maths and Science £	Business Studies £	Humanities £	Art and Design £	Sports £
Overhead					
Student hours					
Recovery rate per student hour					

Task 46.2

Refer to the memo from Susan Woodhouse below.

Having read the memo prepare the schedule of overhead under or over recovered in the period ended 31 March 20X1, in the space provided below.

MEMORANDUM

To: Paul Goodenough
From: Susan Woodhouse
Date: 3 April 20X1
Subject: School overhead period ended 31 March

I list below the actual overhead incurred by the teaching units for the quarter ended 31 March 20X1, together with student hours per cost centre for the period.

Cost Centre	Actual overhead	Student hours
	£	
Maths and Science	61,500	27,500
Business Studies	54,200	29,250
Humanities	59,500	32,100
Art and Design	51,500	30,750
Sports	71,100	34,500
	297,800	154,100

Could you please complete the overhead report for the quarter, showing, per cost centre and in total:

- actual overhead
- overhead recovered
- under- or over-recovery.

Please prepare this by tomorrow morning as I want to complete my management accounting reports for the headmaster by the end of the week.

Many thanks.
Susan.

TEACHING UNITS

Overhead report quarter ended 31 March 20X1

Cost centre	Actual overhead	Overhead recovered	(Under)/over-recovered
	£	£	£
Maths and Science			
Business Studies			
Humanities			
Art and Design			
Sports			

Task 46.3

Write a memo to Susan Woodhouse explaining, in outline only, why the overall recovery of overhead showed a favourable position for the period.

Chapter 6
Job and batch costing systems

▷ ACTIVITY 47

Jetprint Limited

Jetprint Limited specialises in printing advertising leaflets and is in the process of preparing its price list. The most popular requirement is for a folded leaflet made from a single sheet of A4 paper. From past records and budgeted figures, the following data have been estimated for a typical batch of 10,000 leaflets:

Artwork (fixed cost)	£65
Machine setting (fixed cost)	4 hours @ £22 per hour
Paper	£12.50 per 1,000 sheets
Ink and consumables	£40 per 10,000 leaflets
Printers' wages	4 hours @ £8 per hour per 10,000 leaflets

General fixed overheads are £15,000 per period during which a total of 600 printers' labour hours are expected to be worked (not all, of course, on the leaflet). The overheads are recovered only on printers hours.

The firm wishes to achieve 30% profit on sales.

Task

Calculate the selling prices (to the nearest pound) per thousand leaflets for quantities of 10,000 and 20,000 leaflets.

Chapter 7
Process costing

▷ ACTIVITY 48

Mike Everett Ltd produce animal feeds. 'Calfextra' is one of its products. The product is produced in a single process.

The following information relates to week ended 10 February 20X1.

Inputs:	Direct material	2,000 tonnes at £60 per tonne.
	Direct labour	80 labour hours at £8 per hour.
	Overhead	£5.20 per direct labour hour.

Normal loss is based on an allowance of 4% of input and waste has a saleable value of £10 per tonne.

Output for the period was 1,900 tonnes.

Prepare the process account for the period.

▷ ACTIVITY 49

Mike Everett Ltd produces animal feeds. A further product is 'Pigextra' and this is produced in a single process.

For the week ended 10 March 20X1 the following information was available and related to 'Pigextra' production.

Inputs:	Direct material	3,000 tonnes at £70 per tonne.
	Direct labour	95 hours at £8 per hour.
	Overhead	£5.20 per direct labour hour.

Normal loss allowance is 4% of input and waste is saleable at £12 per tonne.

Output for the period was 2,890 tonnes.

Prepare the process account.

▷ ACTIVITY 50

Blake Ltd produces a soft drink in a single process. The following information relates to period 1.

Direct material	1,000 kg at £3.80 per kg
Direct labour	50 hours at £9.60 per hour
Overhead recovery rate	£5 per hour

Normal loss allowance is 10% of input, which can be sold for £0.50 per kg

Finished output	950 kg

There was no opening or closing work in progress

Prepare a process account for the above process.

▷ ACTIVITY 51

Maston Ltd produces a special oil in a single process. The oil is made by introducing 10,000 litres of liquid into a process at a cost of £5 per litre.

The normal loss is 500 litres which can be sold for £1 per litre.

Each process requires £4,000 of labour. The overhead is recovered at 150% of labour.

If there are no abnormal losses or gains, produce the process account for the above.

▷ ACTIVITY 52

Maston Ltd produces a special oil in a single process. The oil is made by introducing 10,000 litres of liquid into a process at a cost of £5 per litre.

The normal loss is 500 litres which can be sold for £1 per litre.

Each process requires £4,000 of labour. The overhead is recovered at 150% of labour.

The output of process 7 is 9,300 litres.

(a) Produce the process account for process 7.
(b) Show clearly your working for the cost of good production and the cost of the abnormal loss for process 7.

▷ ACTIVITY 53

Egton Farm Supplies Ltd produce fertilisers and chemicals. One of its products 'Eg3' is produced in a single process.

The following information relates to period 5, 20X1.

Inputs:	Direct material	1,000 tonnes of 'X' at £70/tonne.
	Direct labour	40 hours at £8/hour.
	Overhead recovery rate	£4/hour.

Completed output: 800 tonnes

Closing work-in-progress: 200 tonnes

There were no losses in the process.

Work-in-progress degree of completion

Material	100%
Labour	80%
Overhead	80%

Prepare the process account for period 5, together with a schedule showing clearly the valuation of the work-in-progress.

▷ ACTIVITY 54

Taylor

Taylor Ltd makes a product using a number of processes. Details for process 1 during a particular period are as follows:

Inputs	5,000 kilo at £2.47 per kilo
Labour	£4,398
Overheads	150% of labour

Normal losses are expected to be 4.7% of input.

All losses can be sold for a scrap value of £1.67 per kilo.

During the period 4,750 kilos were transferred to Process 2. There was no opening or closing work-in-progress.

Task

Prepare the process 1 account for the period.

▷ ACTIVITY 55

Rogo Ltd manufactures plastic containers for use in the soft-drinks industry. The manufacture consists of a number of processes. Amongst these are processes Alpha and Omega which are independent of each other.

Details for Process Alpha in May are as follows:

Materials input	5,000 kilos at a total cost of £14,378
Labour worked	1,200 hours at a total cost of £7,500
Normal loss	5.7% of input
Output	4,679 kilos

There was no opening or closing work in progress.

Task 55.1

Prepare the Process Alpha account for May.

Task 55.2

Details for Process Omega in June are as follows:

Materials input	10,000 kilo at a cost of £2.68 per kilo
Labour worked	1,200 hours at a rate of £4.67 per hour
Machine time	4,800 hours
Normal loss	2.3% of input
Output	9,867 kilos

There was no opening or closing work in progress. Production overheads are absorbed at a rate of £4.20 per machine hour.

A company has approached Rogo Ltd and offered to purchase any scrap material for £2.13 per kilo. Prepare the Process Omega account for June assuming that the scrap is sold.

▷ ACTIVITY 56

Task 56.1

Explain what is meant by an abnormal gain and how it should be treated in the accounts for a company (calculations are NOT required).

Task 56.2

Lewin Ltd operates a manufacturing process. Details for the last period were as follows:

Input material	10,000 kilos @ £1.20 per kilo
Normal losses	20% of input
Labour	400 hours @ £6 per hour
Overheads are absorbed at	£15 per labour hour
Output	7,720 units

All lost units have a scrap value of £0.80 per kilo

Prepare the process account for the period.

Chapter 8
Cost bookkeeping

We only include one question in this section – a fairly straightforward question dealing with the main accounts that are typically tested.

Questions on writing up the various accounts occur throughout the workbook in the material, labour and overheads sections, and it is more beneficial to the students to deal with those questions in their normal context rather than segregate them into a separate chapter.

▷ ACTIVITY 57

XYZ plc provides engineering services to a number of small businesses in Wyetown.

Its services comprise milling, turning and grinding, each of which is a separate cost centre within XYZ plc. The company prepares its accounts annually to 31 October and extracted the following balances from its trial balance on 30 September 20X9:

	Dr £000	Cr £000
Work-in-progress	22	
Production overhead		12
Finished goods	3	
Selling and administration costs	48	

XYZ plc operates an absorption costing system using the following machine hour absorption rates:

Milling	£7.50
Turning	£8.00
Grinding	£9.00

During October 20X9 XYZ plc had the following transactions:

Incurred costs:	£000
Direct materials	40
Indirect materials	8
Direct labour	60
Indirect labour	12
Indirect production expenses	24

The valuation of work-in-progress and finished goods stock on 31 October 20X9 was:

	£000
Work-in-progress	20
Finished goods	4

The number of machine hours during October 20X9 were:

Milling	2,400 hours
Turning	1,800 hours
Grinding	1,600 hours

Task

Fill in the numbers indicated by a letter in the following accounts.

Work-in-progress account

	£000		£000
b/fwd	22.0	Finished goods control	**B**
Stores control	40.0	c/fwd	20.0
Wages control	60.0		
Production overhead control	**A**		
	____		____
	____		____

Production overhead account

	£000		£000
Stores control	8.0	b/fwd	12.0
Wages control	**C**	WIP control	**F**
Expense creditors	**D**		
Profit and loss – over-absorption	**E**		
	____		____
	____		____

Finished goods account

	£000		£000
b/fwd	3.0	Cost of sales	**G**
WIP control		c/fwd	4.0
	____		____
	____		____

Chapter 9
Absorption and marginal costing

▷ ACTIVITY 58

Voliti Limited

Voliti Limited has produced the following budgeted figures for a new product it hopes to launch.

Direct material	£10 per unit
Direct labour	£5 per unit
Variable production overheads	£8 per unit
Fixed production costs	£19,500 per month
Budgeted output	6,500 units per month
Sales price	£30 per unit

	Month 1
Production	6,500
Sales	5,000

Task

Prepare a profit statement for month 1 on each of the following bases, and reconcile the resulting profit figures:

(i) marginal costing

(ii) absorption costing.

▷ ACTIVITY 59

Alpha and Gamma

A company produces and sells two products, Alpha and Gamma, and uses an absorption costing system. Fixed costs are absorbed at a rate of £9.00 per machine hour based upon normal levels of production.

Estimates for the following period include:

	Product Alpha	Product Gamma
Sales (units)	31,600	52,600
Selling price (£/unit)	1.15	2.40
Production (units)	30,600	52,800
Variable cost of production (£)	15,300	64,944
Machine hours	2,040	4,400
Opening stock (units)	3,880	3,740

Fixed production overheads are expected to be £56,700 for the following period, and selling and administrative overheads are expected to be £19,160. Any under- or over-absorbed overheads are transferred to the profit and loss account for the period.

Task

Determine the net profit for the period under absorption costing.

Chapter 10
CVP analysis and limiting factors

▷ ACTIVITY 60

Triproduct Limited makes and sells three types of electronic security systems for which the following information is available.

Expected cost and selling prices per unit

Product	Day scan	Night scan	Omni scan
	£	£	£
Materials	70	110	155
Manufacturing labour	40	55	70
Installation labour	24	32	44
Variable overheads	16	20	28
Selling price	250	320	460

Fixed costs for the period are £450,000 and the installation labour, which is highly skilled, is available for 25,000 hours only in a period and is paid £8 per hour.

Both manufacturing and installation labour are variable costs.

The maximum demand for the products is:

Day scan	Night scan	Omni scan
2,000 units	3,000 units	1,800 units

Task 60.1

Calculate the shortfall (if any) in hours of installation labour.

Task 60.2

Determine the best production plan, assuming that Triproduct Limited wishes to maximise profit.

Task 60.3

Calculate the maximum profit that could be achieved from the plan in Task 60.2 above.

▷ ACTIVITY 61

Burma Limited manufactures two products: A and B. Details about the products are as follows.

Sales price and costs per unit	A	B
Sales price	£16.20	£22.80
Direct materials	£4.00	£6.00
Direct labour	£2.00	£4.00

Fixed production overheads per unit based on labour hour	£3.00	£6.00
Variable selling costs	£0.50	£0.50
Maximum sales units	10,000 units	15,000 units

Direct materials cost £2 per kilo, and direct labour costs £10 per hour.

Task 61.1

In the coming year it is expected that the supply of labour will be limited to 4,000 hours. State how many units of each product Burma Limited should produce in order to maximise profit.

Task 61.2

Fixed production overhead rates have been calculated using the maximum expected number of labour hours available in the coming period. Prepare a marginal costing profit and loss statement giving the maximum profit Burma Limited could make for the year.

▷ ACTIVITY 62

Naturo Limited can synthesise a natural plant extract called Ipethin into one of three products. Ipethin is in short supply and the company at present is able to obtain only 1,000 kgs per period at a cost of £25 per kg.

The budgeted costs and other data for a typical period are as follows:

	Product A	Product B	Product C
Kgs of Ipethin per unit	1.4	0.96	2.6
Labour hours per unit (£8 per hour)	3	8	4
Selling price per unit	£110	£150	£180
Maximum demand (units)	200	400	300

Fixed costs are £25,000 per period.

Task

Determine the preferred order of manufacture in order to maximise profit.

▷ ACTIVITY 63

PDR plc manufactures four products using the same machinery. The following details relate to its products:

	Product A £ per unit	Product B £ per unit	Product C £ per unit	Product D £ per unit
Selling price	28	30	45	42
Direct material	5	6	8	6

Direct labour	4	4	8	8
Variable overhead	3	3	6	6
Fixed overhead*	8	8	16	16
Profit	8	9	7	6
	Hours	Hours	Hours	Hours
Labour hours	1	1	2	2
Machine hours	4	3	4	5
	Units	Units	Units	Units
Maximum demand per week	200	180	250	100

*Absorbed based on budgeted labour hours of 1,000 per week.

There is a maximum of 2,000 machine hours available per week.

Task

Determine the production plan which will maximise the weekly profit of PDR plc and prepare a profit statement showing the profit your plan will yield.

▷ ACTIVITY 64

Task 64.1

Z plc operates a single retail outlet selling direct to the public. The gross profits for August and September 20X6 are as follows:

	August	September
	£	£
Sales	80,000	90,000
Cost of sales	50,000	55,000
Gross profit	30,000	35,000

Use the high and low points technique to identify the fixed cost element in the cost of sales.

Task 64.2

A plc has the following budgeted profit and loss account for the month of June 20X3.

	£
Sales (8,000 units)	80,000
Variable cost	48,000
Gross profit	32,000
Fixed cost	25,000
Profit	7,000

Draw a contribution breakeven chart and identify the monthly breakeven sales volume.

▷ ACTIVITY 65

DH is considering the purchase of a bar/restaurant which is available for £130,000. He has estimated that the weekly fixed costs will be as follows:

	£
Business rates	125
Electricity	75
Insurances	60
Gas	45
Depreciation	125
Telephone	50
Advertising	40
Postage and stationery	20
Motor expenses	20
Cleaning	10

He has estimated that his average weekly sales of drinks will amount to £1,500 and that these will have a contribution to sales ratio of 60%.

He expects to serve 40 customers per week in the restaurant, with each customer spending an average of £20. This excludes the value of any drinks which are included in the weekly estimate of drinks sales above. It is expected that the contribution to sales ratio in the restaurant will be 60%.

There are no specific fixed costs attributable to the sale of drinks or customer sales.

Task

(a) Calculate the weekly breakeven sales value of the business.

(b) Prepare a statement showing the annual profit based on the above cost and revenue estimates. Use a marginal costing format and assume that the business operates for 50 weeks per year and incurs fixed costs for 50 weeks per year..

Chapter 11
Investment appraisal

▷ ACTIVITY 66

Highscore Ltd manufacture cricket bats. They are considering investing £30,000 in a new delivery vehicle which will generate savings compared with sub-contracting out the delivery service. The vehicle will have a life of six years, with zero scrap value.

The accounting technician and the transport manager have prepared the following estimates relating to the savings.

The cash flows from the project are:

		£
Year	1	9,000
	2	11,000
	3	10,000

4	10,500
5	10,200
6	10,100

The business cost of capital is 15%.

Required

Prepare an appraisal of the project using the discounted cash flow (NPV method) technique.

The relevant present value factors are:

	Year 1	Year 2	Year 3	Year 4	Year 5	Year 6
15%	0.870	0.756	0.658	0.572	0.497	0.432

▷ ACTIVITY 67 

Whitby Engineering Factors are considering an investment in a new machine tool with an estimated useful life of five years.

The investment will require capital expenditure of £50,000 and the accounting technician has prepared the following estimates of cash flow over the five-year period:

		£
Year	1	18,000
	2	20,000
	3	21,000
	4	22,000
	5	18,000

The firm's cost of capital is considered to be 12% and it uses this rate to appraise any future projects.

Required

- Prepare an appraisal of the project using the discounted cash flow (NPV method) technique.
- State with reasons whether you would accept or reject the project.

The relevant present value factors are:

	Year 1	Year 2	Year 3	Year 4	Year 5
12%	0.893	0797	0.712	0.636	0.567

▷ ACTIVITY 68

An investment project has the following expected cash flows over its three-year life span.

Year	Cash flow
	£
0	(285,400)
1	102,000
2	124,000
3	146,000

Task

(a) Calculate the net present value of the project at discount rates of 0%, 10% and 20% respectively.

(b) Draw a graph of the project NPVs.

(c) Estimate the IRR from the graph (you won't be asked to do this in the exam, but it reinforces an important point).

The relevant present value factors are:

	Year 1	Year 2	Year 3
0%	1	1	1
10%	0.909	0.826	0.751
20%	0.833	0.694	0.579

▷ ACTIVITY 69

Martinez Limited makes a single product, the Angel.

Martinez Limited has a long-term contract to supply a group of customers with 10,000 units of Angel a year for the next three years.

Martinez is considering investing in a new machine to manufacture the Angel. This machine will produce 10,000 units a year, which have a profit of £8 per unit. The machine will cost £220,000 and will last for the duration of the contract. At the end of the contract the machine will be scrapped with no resale value.

Task

(a) Calculate the present value of the machine ignoring the time value of money, i.e. using a 0% discount rate.

(b) Calculate the present value of the machine project if a 10% discount rate is used.

The relevant present value factors are:

	Year 1	Year 2	Year 3
0%	1	1	1
10%	0.909	0.826	0.751

▷ ACTIVITY 70

Loamshire County Council operates a library service.

In order to reduce operating expenses over the next four or five years, there is a proposal to introduce a major upgrade to the computer system used by the library service. Two alternative projects are under examination with different initial outlays and different estimated savings over time. The computer manager has prepared the following schedule:

	Project A	Project B
	£	£
Initial outlay	75,000	100,000
Annual cash savings		
1st year	20,000	30,000
2nd year	30,000	45,000
3rd year	30,000	45,000
4th year	25,000	40,000
5th year	20,000	–

Assume that the cash savings occur at the end of the year, even though in practice they would be spread over the year. From a technical point of view, both systems meet the librarian's specification. It is assumed that there will be no further savings after year 5. The county uses the net present value method for evaluating projects at a 10% discount rate.

Task

Prepare key points for a report to the County Librarian with your recommendations. Include the relevant calculations in your report. She is not familiar with DCF calculations and has asked you to explain why the authority uses a DCF technique in preference to the 'payback' method of appraising capital projects.

Note: Present value of £1 at a discount rate of 10%.

Number of years from the present	Discount factor
1	0.909
2	0.826
3	0.751
4	0.683
5	0.621
6	0.564

▷ ACTIVITY 71

A transport company is considering purchasing an automatic vehicle-cleansing machine. At present, all vehicles are cleaned by hand.

The machine will cost £80,000 to purchase and install in year 0 and it will have a useful life of four years with no residual value.

The company uses a discount rate of 10% to appraise all capital projects.

The cash savings from the machine will be:

Year	£
0	–
1	29,600
2	29,200
3	28,780
4	28,339

Task

As assistant management accountant, you are asked to carry out an appraisal of the proposal to purchase the machine and prepare a report to the general manager of the company. Your report should contain the following information:

(1) the net present value of the cash flows from the project

(2) the payback period of the proposal

(3) a recommendation as to whether or not the proposal should be accepted.

In your calculations, you should assume that all cash flows occur at the end of the year.

Note: The present value of £1 at a discount rate of 10% is as follows:

Number of years from the present	£
1	0.909
2	0.826
3	0.751
4	0.683

▷ ACTIVITY 72

A company is considering setting up a small in-house printing facility.

Machines costing £14,400 will be purchased in year 0. They will last for four years and will have no value at the end of this time.

The cash savings associated with the machines will be:

Year	£
0	–
1	6,920
2	6,920

3	6,920
4	6,920

Task

(a) Calculate the net present value of the cash flows from the proposal, using a 12% discount rate over four years.

Assume that all cash flows occur at the end of the year.

Note: The present value of £1 at a discount rate of 12% is as follows:

Number of years from the present	DF
1	0.893
2	0.797
3	0.712
4	0.636

(b) Calculate the payback period for the proposal assuming that cash flows occur evenly through the year, and explain the advantages and disadvantages of using this appraisal method.

▷ ACTIVITY 73

Data

RBG plc is a large quoted company using a 25% rate of interest for appraising capital projects. One of its divisional directors has put forward plans to make a new product, the AI. This will involve buying a machine specifically for that task. The machine will cost £600,000 and have a life of 5 years. However, because of the nature of the product, the machine will have no residual value at any time.

The annual cash flow will be as follows:

	£
Turnover per annum	380,000
Material	(90,000)
Labour	(30,000)
Overheads	(20,000)
Annual cash inflow	£240,000

Task

You are asked to write a report to the divisional accountant:

(a) appraising the divisional director's proposal using the net present value method of evaluating discounted cash flows and interpreting the result

(b) calculating the payback period and explaining its possible use. (For this part assume that cash flows occur evenly throughout the year.)

For the calculation of the net present value, it can be assumed that cash flows occur at the end of each year. The present value of £1 at a discount rate of 25% is as follows:

End of year	£	End of year	£
1	0.800	4	0.410
2	0.640	5	0.328
3	0.512	6	0.262

MOCK SIMULATION QUESTIONS

Data and tasks

Instructions

This mock simulation is designed to test your ability to record cost information.

The situation and tasks to be completed are set out on the following pages.

This booklet also contains data that you will need to complete the tasks. You should read the whole mock simulation before commencing work so as to gain an overall picture of what is required.

Your answers should be set out in the answer booklet provided. If you require additional answer pages, ask the person in charge.

You are allowed four hours to complete your work.

A high level of accuracy is required. Check your work carefully before handing it in.

Correcting fluid may be used but it should be used in moderation. Errors should be crossed out neatly and clearly. You should write in black ink, not pencil.

You are reminded that you should not bring any unauthorised material, such as books or notes, into the mock simulation. If you have any such material in your possession, you should surrender it to the assessor immediately.

The situation

Your name is Terry Wallis and you work as the accounts assistant for Executive Shirts Limited. The company is a subsidiary of a dry cleaning company. Its accounting year ends on 30 June.

The cost centres involved in the mock simulation

Customers' shirts are washed, ironed and packaged in cellophane ready for collection by customers.

Washing/drying department

The shirts are washed with detergent and fabric conditioner, then dried.

Ironing/pressing department

The shirts are ironed or pressed. Spray starch is used to obtain a crisp finish.

Packing department

The laundered shirt is wrapped in cellophane.

Stores

This department maintains stocks of materials (direct and indirect).

Canteen
Hot and cold meals are prepared on the premises for serving to the staff.

Executive Shirts employs three full-time laundry operatives who are employed in washing/drying or in ironing/pressing according to demand. There is also a team of part-time laundry operatives that are called upon to respond to peaks in activity. A full-time packing operative is also assisted by a team of part-time packers who work flexible hours.

Personnel involved in the mock simulation

Accounts Assistant, yourself, Terry Wallis.
Administration Manager, Sue Baker.
Supervisor, Washing/Drying, Sheila Barlow.
Supervisor, Ironing/Pressing, Kay Winderman.
Supervisor, Packing, Wayne Peacock.
Canteen Manager, Janet Greaves.

Production activities, overhead absorption and variance analysis

Shirts are laundered in batches of 20. Executive Shirts Limited operates a batch costing system.

Overheads are absorbed on a departmental basis using a predetermined standard rate per batch of 20 shirts. Under-absorption or over-absorption is identified monthly for each department as the total overhead variance and transferred to the profit and loss account.

You are required to perform calculations during the mock simulation.

Tasks to be completed

Transactions in April 20X8

TASK 1

Refer to the stores ledger accounts and materials requisitions at the start of the answer booklet. You are required to complete the stores ledger accounts as far as the information available will allow. Show the stock balance for each item after the last recorded transaction. Note that all materials issues are priced using the same stock valuation method, which is to be inferred from the information already recorded on the stores ledger accounts.

TASK 2

Refer to the materials requisitions at the start of the answer booklet and to the extracts from the company's accounts code list in the data immediately following the tasks. You are required to complete the columns on the requisitions headed 'Cost office only'. Show the total value of each issue and the account number to be charged for each of the transactions referred to by the requisitions.

TASK 3

Refer to your completed stores ledger accounts in the answer booklet. You are required to check whether the company's stock control practices have been followed correctly for these items during April 20X8 and to report your conclusions to the administration manager using the memo form provided in the answer booklet. Your memo should highlight any unusual matters concerning the stock control practices and the stock levels of these items during April, and should suggest possible actions to prevent their recurrence. Date your memo 23 April 20X8.

TASK 4

Refer to the timesheet analysis, the internal policy document and the productivity bonus announcement in the data below. You are required to use this information to complete the calculation of gross wages for full-time laundry and packing operatives for week 42. The working paper for this task is provided in the answer booklet and you will see that your colleague has already begun the task in respect of the first employee.

TASK 5

Refer to the clock records in the data below. Use this information to complete the analysis of gross wages payable to part-time employees for week 42. You will also need to refer again to the internal policy document and the productivity bonus announcement in the data below. Insert your answers in the space provided in the answer booklet.

TASK 6

Refer to the cost ledger data entry sheet provided in the answer booklet and the accounts code list in the data below. You are required to use your gross wages calculations to complete the cost ledger data entry sheet, showing the charges to be made to the cost centres for the wages of these employees. You will also need to refer again to the internal policy document in the data below.

TASK 7

Refer to the clock records of the full-time laundry operatives in the data below (employee numbers 649, 653, 658 and 663). You are required to reconcile these hours with those shown on the timesheet analysis earlier in the data below. Make a note of any discrepancies that you will need to report to the administration manager. Use the space provided in the answer booklet to set out your answer.

TASK 8

Refer to the invoices reproduced in the answer booklet and to the accounts code list in the data below. You are required to complete the boxes at the foot of each invoice to show the amount and the code numbers to which the invoice is to be charged. If you need more information to identify the correct code number, the item should be coded to the suspense account. Note that any VAT on these invoices is fully recoverable by the company and is not to be recorded in the cost accounts.

TASK 9

Prepare a memo to the administration manager, Sue Baker, giving details of any invoices which you were obliged to code to the suspense account. In your memo you should explain what information you need to complete the coding exercise. Use the memo form provided in the answer booklet and date your memo 5 May 20X8.

TASK 10

Refer to the first memo in the data below. Use the information provided to produce an analysis of overheads for 20X8/X9 and to calculate the overhead absorption rates requested by Sue. The overhead analysis sheet to be completed is provided in the answer booklet.

TASK 11

Refer to the second memo in the data below. You are required to reply to this memo, using the memo form provided in the answer booklet. Date your memo 21 May 20X8.

TASK 12

The main dry cleaning company produces a special fabric conditioner which it sells to all its subsidiaries. The conditioner passes through two separate processes before completion. Refer to the details of the processes provided in the data that follows and prepare the following.

(a) Process account for process 1.
(b) Process account for process 2.

Write your answer in the answer booklet.

TASK 13

The main dry cleaning company makes and sells a shirt called a 'Royal' in an overseas location. These shirts are sold through all the subsidiary outlets for £21 each. Refer to the production details in the data from below and prepare profit statements for the period using the proformas in the answer booklet using:
(a) marginal costing
(b) absorption costing.

and reconcile the resulting profits.

TASK 14

Executive Shirts Ltd is considering investing in a new machine. The machine will cost £1,250,000 and will be paid for in two instalments, £1,000,000 now and £250,000 in one years time.

The company will use the machine to speed up the ironing process. It is expected that it will generate an increase in cash contribution of £350,000 for each of the next five years.

At the end of year 5 the machine will be sold for scrap proceeds of £10,000.
(a) Calculate the net present value of the project using discount rates of 10% and 20%.
(b) The internal rate of return of the project is 14%. Explain what this means.

Use the proforma in the answer booklet for your answer.

Data

Accounts code list (extract)

Cost centre codes

100	Washing/drying
200	Ironing/pressing
300	Packing
400	Stores
500	Canteen
900	Suspense account

Expenditure codes

100	Direct materials
200	Indirect materials
300	Direct labour
600	Overtime premium
650	Bonus payments
660	Other indirect wages
710	Equipment repairs
840	Canteen expenses
900	Suspense account

Summary report: timesheet analysis week 42
Full-time laundry and packing operatives

	Monday Hours	Tuesday Hours	Wednesday Hours	Thursday Hours	Friday Hours	Total Hours
Employee number: 649 **Name:** A Bedford **Grade:** 3						
Washing/drying	–	4	2	2	–	8
Ironing/pressing	8	3	5	7	–	23
Other	–	–	–	–	7AL	7
Employee number: 653 **Name:** B Guildford **Grade:** 4						
Washing/drying	–	1	–	6	2	9
Ironing/pressing	–	7	8	2	7	24
Other	7AL	–	–	–	–	7
Employee number: 658 **Name:** C Yarmouth **Grade:** 4						
Washing/drying	2	1	–	–	2	5
Ironing/pressing	7	6	–	–	5	18
Other	–	–	7SS	7SS	–	14
Employee number: 663 **Name:** D Ashurst **Grade:** 3						
Packing	5	8	7	7	8	35
Other	3TR	–	–	–	–	3

Key: AL = annual leave, SS = sick leave, TR = training on premises.

INTERNAL POLICY DOCUMENT

Document number: **17**

Subject: **Wages and duties of laundry operatives and packers**

Issued: **January 20X8**

Wage rates to be paid

Employee grade	£ per hour
3	6.00
4	8.00

Full-time employees work a seven-hour day. They may work overtime as required.

Overtime hours (hours worked in excess of seven hours per day) are paid at the basic rate plus 50%.

A productivity bonus is calculated each week and announced via a written memo pinned to the staff notice board. The total amount of the bonus for full-time employees will be shared in proportion to their gross wages for the week excluding bonus payments.

Full-time employees are paid seven hours at their basic rate for any days when they are sick or on holiday.

Time spent in training is paid at the employee's basic rate.

Part-time employees are all grade 3 employees.

All part time wages (excluding the bonus) are chargeable to packing.

Discrepancies on timesheets

The company wishes to facilitate the prompt payment of wages and early reporting of labour costs to management. Full-time employees will be paid according to the analysis shown on their timesheets. Any discrepancy revealed by a reconciliation with clock times will be adjusted in the following week's pay.

Analysis of wages

Payments made to full-time operatives in respect of holidays, sick leave or training are classified as 'other indirect wages' chargeable to the ironing/pressing cost centre.

Overtime premiums and bonus payments are chargeable to the ironing/pressing cost centre.

PRODUCTIVITY BONUS FOR WEEK 42

The management is pleased to announce that the following productivity bonuses will be paid in respect of week 42.

Full-time employees: £75 total bonus payment to be shared among full-time employees in the usual way.

Part-time employees: £0.22 per hour bonus will be paid.

Congratulations and thank you to everybody!!

CLOCK RECORDS – HOURS SPENT ON PREMISES, WEEK 42
LAUNDRY OPERATIVES AND PACKERS

Full-time employees

Employee number	Clock hours
649	31
653	33
658	25
663	38

Part-time employees

	Clock hours	Analysis of clock hours		
Employee number		Washing/ drying	Ironing/ pressing	Packing
1678	12	2	10	–
1687	8	–	–	8
1691	10	3	6	1
1694	11	5	–	6
1697	9	2	7	–

MEMORANDUM

To: Terry Wallis, Accounts Assistant
From: Sue Baker, Administration Manager
Date: 1 May 20X8
Subject: Overhead absorption rates for 20X8/X9

As we discussed earlier this week, it is time to get started on the job of calculating the overhead absorption rates for next year, 20X8/X9. I have spent some time gathering the information that you requested, as below. Could you please use this information to calculate departmental absorption rates for a batch of 20 shirts. We will need absorption rates for each of the three 'production' departments: washing/drying, ironing/pressing, packing.

1 Budgeted output for 20X8/X9, in all three departments: 9,000 batches of 20 shirts.
2 The three supervisors will be paid annual salaries as follows: washing/drying supervisor £12,750, ironing/pressing supervisor £16,500, packing supervisor £12,750.
3 The storekeeper's salary will be £13,000 for the year.
4 Canteen expenses are forecast to be £8,510.
5 Electricity costs will amount to £1,855. We usually apportion this cost based on the floor area occupied by each of the five departments.
6 Total depreciation cost for the equipment will be £2,140.
7 Administration costs will be £2,400. Use the number of equivalent full-time personnel as an apportionment basis for these costs.
8 Other overhead costs of £1,500 should be apportioned evenly over the five departments.

As for the reapportionment of the stores and canteen, we usually do the following:

- First, reapportion the canteen costs to the other four cost centres based on the number of equivalent full-time personnel.
- Second, reapportion the stores cost to the remaining three cost centres. No charge is made to the canteen for stores costs.

Please complete all apportionments to the nearest £ and calculate the absorption rates to the nearest penny per batch.

Other information you might need is given below:

	Washing/ drying	Ironing/ pressing	Packing	Stores	Canteen
Floor area in square metres	130	170	90	60	80
Full-time equivalent employees	4	7	2	2	1
Cost of equipment	£4,000	£2,800	£1,200	£1,800	£900
Number of materials requisitions	200	160	360	–	100

I hope this gives you all you need. Good luck!

MEMORANDUM

To: Terry Wallis, Accounts Assistant
From: Sue Baker, Administration Manager
Date: 15 May 20X8
Subject: Overhead absorption rates for 20X8/X9

Thank you for all the work that you have done to calculate the overhead absorption rates for next year.

I have been looking at the information you provided and thinking about the bases that we use to apportion overheads. I think that we might achieve better cost control if we apportioned some of the costs more accurately. In particular, I am concerned about the electricity costs.

The nature of our operations means that electricity costs are not incurred equally in all the departments, but is floor area the best way to apportion the cost? Can you think of a fairer basis and, if so, what information would be need?

Thanks for your help.

Details of fabric conditioner process – Task 12

The following data relates to their most recent period when 200,000 units were input to process 1

	Process 1	Process 2
Basic raw material cost(£)	288,013	(From Process 1)
Materials added in Process (£)	–	151,965
Direct labour costs (£)	94,208	68,674
Production overhead as a % of direct labour cost	125	108
Normal loss (% of input units)	4.1	3.0
Scrap value per unit of process losses (£)	0.72	1.04
Output (units)	191,450	185,968

There was no opening or closing work in progress.

Production details of shirts – Task 13

The cost card for one unit of Royal is shown below.

Direct materials	£3
Direct labour	£6
Variable production overhead	£2
Fixed production overhead	£4

Budgeted fixed overheads are based on budgeted production of 5,000 units.There was no stock of finished goods at the start of the period. However, there was stock of 4,000 units by the end of the period.During the period 3,000 units were sold and actual fixed production overheads were £28,000.

MOCK SIMULATION ANSWER BOOKLET

TASKS 1 AND 2

STORES LEDGER ACCOUNT

Material description: Detergent powder: 20-kg boxes
Code number: DP70

Maximum quantity 64
Minimum quantity 20
Reorder level 32
Reorder quantity 35

Date	Receipts			Issues			Stock balance		
	Quantity	Price £ per box	Total £	Quantity	Price £ per box	Total £	Quantity	Price £ per box	Total £
April 6									
							22	26.50	583.00
							35	26.80	938.00
							57		1,521.00
April 8									
				22	26.50	583.00			
				8	26.80	214.40			
				30		797.40	27	26.80	723.60
April 13									
	35	26.85	939.75						

STORES LEDGER ACCOUNT

Material description: Fabric conditioner: 6-litre bottles
Code number: FC45

Maximum quantity 16
Minimum quantity 4
Reorder level 11
Reorder quantity 7

Date	Receipts			Issues			Stock balance		
	Quantity	Price £ per bottle	Total £	Quantity	Price £ per bottle	Total £	Quantity	Price £ per bottle	Total £
April 6							5	3.15	15.75
							7	3.20	22.40
							12		38.15
April 7	7	3.22	22.54				5	3.15	15.75
							7	3.20	22.40
							7	3.22	22.54
							19		60.69

STORES LEDGER ACCOUNT

Material description: Cellophane packaging: 100-metre rolls
Code number: CP09

Maximum quantity 56
Minimum quantity 16
Reorder level 30
Reorder quantity 28

Date	Receipts			Issues			Stock balance		
	Quantity	Price £ per roll	Total £	Quantity	Price £ per roll	Total £	Quantity	Price £ per roll	Total £
April 6							24	2.10	50.40
April 7				4	2.10	8.40	20	2.10	42.00
April 8	22	2.00	44.00						

MATERIAL REQUISITION

Raised by: Sheila Barlow Serial number: 864

Issue to cost centre: Washing/drying Date: 14 April

Code number	Description	Quantity	Cost office only	
			Total value of issue £	Account number to be charged
FC45	Fabric conditioner	7 bottles		

Authorised by: S Barlow Received by: SB

MATERIAL REQUISITION

Raised by: Sheila Barlow Serial number: 867

Issue to cost centre: Washing/drying Date: 14 April

Code number	Description	Quantity	Cost office only	
			Total value of issue £	Account number to be charged
DP70	Detergent powder	20 boxes		

Authorised by: S Barlow Received by: SB

MATERIAL REQUISITION

Raised by: Wayne Peacock Serial number: 869

Issue to cost centre: Packing Date: 14 April

Code number	Description	Quantity	Cost office only	
			Total value of issue £	Account number to be charged
CP09	Packaging	8 rolls		

Authorised by: Wayne Received by: WP

MATERIAL REQUISITION

Raised by: Janet Greaves Serial number: 872

Issue to cost centre: Canteen Date: 15 April

Code number	Description	Quantity	Cost office only	
			Total value of issue £	Account number to be charged
DP70	Detergent powder	2 boxes - for use in washing tea towels, etc		

Authorised by: J Greaves Received by: JG

TASK 3

MEMORANDUM

To:
From:
Date:
Subject:

TASK 4

Calculation of gross wages for week 42 – full-time laundry and packing operatives

	Washing/ drying			*Ironing/ pressing*			*Packing*			*Other*			*Overtime premium*			*Total gross wages excluding bonus*
	Hrs	rate	£	Hrs	rate	£	Hrs	rate	£	Hrs	rate	£	Hrs	rate	£	£
Employee number: 649 grade: 3 hours	8	6	48	23	6	138			–	7	6	42	3	3	9	237
Employee number: grade: hours																
Employee number: grade: hours																
Employee number: grade: hours																
Totals																

Apportionment of productivity bonus for the week

Employee number	Total gross wages excluding bonus £	Bonus apportioned pro rata £	Total gross wages for the week £
649	237.00		

TASK 5

Calculation of part-time employees' gross wages – week 42

Washing/drying:

Workings:

Answer: part-time wages payable (excluding bonus) =

Ironing/pressing:

Workings:

Answer: part-time wages payable (excluding bonus) =

Packing:

Workings:

Answer: part-time wages payable (excluding bonus) =

Bonus payment, all part-time employees:

Workings:

Answer: part-time bonus payable =

Total part-time gross wages (including bonus) =

(**Note**: You are not required to calculate the wages due to any individual part-time employee.)

TASK 6

COST LEDGER DATA ENTRY SHEET

Week number:

Debit accounts:

Cost centre code	Expenditure code	Amount to be debited £
100	300	
200	300	
200	600	
200	650	
200	660	
300	300	

Check total: total wages for week,
laundry operatives and packing, full-time and part-time

Workings

TASK 7

FULL TIME EMPLOYEES: RECONCILIATION OF CLOCK HOURS

Note of any discrepancies to be referred to Administration Manager

TASK 8

MARSDEN OILS

98 Street Lane
Swinbury
Chopshire SR3 7WR
Telephone: 01845 350162 Fax: 01845 350163

Executive Shirts Limited
87 High Street
Swinbury
Chopshire SR7 3PL

VAT registration: 435 8720 76

Date/tax point: 15 April 20X8

INVOICE

	£
Lubricating oils for washing machine Three cases	21.00
VAT @ 17.5%	3.67
Invoice total	**24.67**

Charge to account code number:

£

Terms: 30 days from date of invoice

MULTIPARTS LIMITED

52 Fairway Industrial Estate
Swinbury
Chopshire SR3 3UK
Telephone: 01845 938264 Fax: 01845 938265

Executive Shirts Limited
87 High Street
Swinbury
Chopshire SR7 3PL

VAT registration: 435 7175 98

Date/tax point: 17 April 20X8

INVOICE

	£
Supply of machine part – urgent order, your ref 'Sue'	76.90
VAT @ 17.5%	13.45
Invoice total	**90.35**

Charge to account code number:

£

Terms: 30 days from date of invoice

THE RAPID REPAIR COMPANY

24 Leazdon Lane
Swinbury
Chopshire SR3 6HT
Telephone: 01845 350162 Fax: 01845 350163

Executive Shirts Limited
87 High Street
Swinbury
Chopshire SR7 3PL

VAT registration: 928 33350 65

Date/tax point: 7 April 20X8

INVOICE

	£
Repair to industrial ironing machine	34.00
VAT @ 17.5%	5.95
Invoice total	**39.95**

Charge to account code number:

£

Terms: 30 days from date of invoice
0.5% discount for payment within 15 days

THE QUALITY CATERING COMPANY

Fairway Industrial Estate
Swinbury
Chopshire SR3 7GJ
Telephone: 01845 938264 Fax: 01845 938265

Executive Shirts Limited
87 High Street
Swinbury
Chopshire SR7 3PL

VAT registration: 465 9242 14

Date/tax point: 17 April 20X8

INVOICE

	£
12 cases of paper napkins, delivered to canteen	60.00
VAT @ 17.5%	10.50
Invoice total	**70.50**

Charge to account code number:

£

Terms: 30 days from date of invoice

TASK 9

MEMORANDUM

To:
From:
Date:
Subject:

TASK 10

OVERHEAD ANALYSIS SHEET: 20X8/X9

Overhead expense: primary apportionments and allocations	Basis of allocation/ apportionment	Total £	Washing/ drying £	Ironing/ pressing £	Packing £	Stores £	Canteen £

	Total	Washing/ drying	Ironing/ pressing	Packing	Stores	Canteen
Total of primary allocations	______	______	______	______	______	______
Reapportion canteen		______	______	______	______	(______)
Reapportion stores		______	______	______	(______)	
Total production cost centre overhead	______	______	______	______		
Number of batches						
Overhead absorption rate per batch for 20X8/X9		______	______	______		

TASK 11

MEMORANDUM

To:
From:
Date:
Subject:

TASK 12

TASK 13

(i) *Marginal costing*

	£	£
Sales		
Cost of sales		
Opening stock		
Production		
Closing stock		
Contribution from production		
Less actual fixed overheads		
Profit for the period		

(ii) *Absorption costing*

	£	£
Sales		
Cost of sales		
Opening stock		
Production		
Closing stock		
Profit for the period		

TASK 14

(a)

Time	Cost	Contribution	Scrap	Net cash flow	DF 10%	PV 10%	DF 20%	PV 20%
	£000	£000	£000	£000	£000	£000	£000	£000
0					1		1	
1					0.909		0.833	
2					0.826		0.694	
3					0.751		0.579	
4					0.683		0.482	
5					0.621		0.402	

(b)

MOCK EXAMINATION 1 QUESTIONS

This mock examination is in TWO sections. You are reminded that competence must be achieved in BOTH sections. You should therefore attempt and aim to complete EVERY task in BOTH sections.

Note: ALL essential workings should be included within your answers, where appropriate.

You are advised to spend approximately 1 hour and 30 minutes on each section.

DATA

You are employed as an accounting technician with Ray Ltd, a company that manufactures and sells a range of products for the British electrical goods market.

You report to the Management Accountant, who has asked you to carry out the following tasks.

SECTION 1

You should spend about 90 minutes on this section.

Task 1.1

Complete the stock record card shown below for steel component M, for the month of May 2005.

The company uses the First In, First Out (FIFO) method of stock valuation.

STOCK RECORD CARD FOR STEEL COMPONENT M								
	Receipts			Issues			Balance	
Date 2005	Quantity kg	Cost per kg (£)	Total cost (£)	Quantity kg	Cost per kg (£)	Total cost (£)	Quantity kg	£
Balance as at 1 May							25,000	50,000
9 May	30,000	2.30	69,000					
12 May				40,000				
18 May	20,000	2.50	50,000					
27 May				10,000				

ADDITIONAL INFORMATION

The issue of component M on 12 May was for the production of product A, whilst that on the 27 May was for the production of product B.

The following cost accounting codes are used:

Code	Description
306	Stocks of component M
401	Work-in-progress – Product A
402	Work-in-progress – Product B
500	Creditors Control

Task 1.2

Complete the journal below to record separately the FOUR cost accounting entries in respect of the two receipts and two issues during the month of May 2005.

JOURNAL

Date 2005	Code	Dr £	Cr £
9 May			
9 May			
12 May			
12 May			
18 May			
18 May			
27 May			
27 May			

ADDITIONAL INFORMATION

The following information relates to direct labour costs incurred in producing product C during May 2005:

Normal time hours worked	8,000 hours
Overtime at time and a half worked	1,500 hours
Overtime at double time worked	1,000 hours
Total hours worked	10,500 hours
Normal time hourly rate	£7 per hour

Task 1.3

Overtime premiums paid are included as part of direct labour costs.

Calculate the total cost of direct labour for product C for the month of May 2005.

ADDITIONAL INFORMATION

Ray Ltd has the following four production departments:

- Machining 1
- Machining 2
- Assembly
- Packaging

The budgeted fixed overheads relating to the four production departments for Quarter 3 2005 are:

	£	£
Depreciation		80,000
Rent and rates		120,000
Indirect labour costs:		
Machining 1	40,500	
Machining 2	18,300	
Assembly	12,400	
Packaging	26,700	
Total		97,900
Direct assembly costs		15,600
Total fixed overheads		313,500

Fixed overheads are allocated or apportioned to the production departments on the most appropriate basis.

The following information is also available:

Department	Net book value of fixed assets (£000)	Square metres occupied	Number of employees
Machining 1	1,280	625	8
Machining 2	320	250	4
Assembly	960	500	3
Packaging	640	1,125	7
Total	3,200	2,500	22

Task 1.4

Use the table below to allocate or apportion the fixed overheads between the four production departments, using the most appropriate basis.

Fixed overhead	Basis of allocation or apportionment	Total cost £	Machining 1 £	Machining 2 £	Assembly £	Packaging £
Depreciation		80,000				
Rent and rates		120,000				
Indirect labour costs		97,900				
Direct assembly costs		15,600				
Totals		313,500				

ADDITIONAL INFORMATION

You have consulted the manager of a separate production division, who tells you that this division is highly automated, and operates with expensive machinery which is run wherever possible on a 24-hour a day, seven days a week basis.

The following information relates to this division for July 2005:

Total departmental overheads	£400,000
Total budgeted direct labour hours	3,000
Total budgeted machine hours	10,000
Total actual direct labour hours	2,500
Total actual machine hours	9,000

Task 1.5

Calculate the budgeted fixed overhead absorption rate for the division for July 2005, using the most appropriate basis of absorption.

ADDITIONAL INFORMATION

The following information relates to the manufacture of product D during the month of April 2005:

Direct materials per unit	£10.60
Direct labour per unit	£16.40
Total variable overheads	£60,000
Total fixed overheads	£80,000
Number of units produced	10,000

Task 1.6

Calculate the cost per unit of product D under:

(a) (i) **Variable (marginal) costing**

(ii) **Full absorption costing**

(b) **Explain how it is possible to UNDER-recover fixed overheads.**

Explanation of fixed overhead under-recovery:

SECTION 2

You should spend about 90 minutes on this section.

ADDITIONAL DATA

Ray Ltd also manufactures and sells three other products: Alpha, Beta and Gamma. The following information has been provided by the Finance Director.

Estimates of revenues and costs for January 2005

	Alpha	Beta	Gamma
Sales and production in units	1,000	200	500
Selling price per unit	£50	£120	£80
Direct materials per unit	£10	£24	£16
Direct labour hours per unit – Centre A	2	4	3
Direct labour hours per unit – Centre B	0.5	4	1
Direct labour rate per hour – Centre A	£5	£5	£5
Direct labour rate per hour – Centre B	£6	£6	£6

Direct material and direct labour costs are considered wholly variable. The total expected monthly fixed overheads are £52,000.

Task 2.1

Complete the table below to calculate the total forecast contribution and profit for January.

Product	Alpha £	Beta £	Gamma £	Total £
Sales revenue				
Less Variable costs				
Direct materials				
Direct labour – Centre A				
Direct labour – Centre B				
Total contribution				
Fixed overheads				
Profit				

Task 2.2

Calculate the forecast contribution per unit for the Alpha, Beta and Gamma ranges.

ADDITIONAL DATA

The Production Director believes there will be a shortage of direct labour hours in Centre B in January. He estimates there will be a maximum availability of 1,400 direct labour hours which includes any overtime working. The maximum unit sales for January of Alpha are 1,000 units, Beta 200 units and Gamma 500 units.

Task 2.3

Calculate the number of units of each product range that Ray Ltd should make and sell to maximise its profits for January.

ADDITIONAL DATA

The Sales Manager believes the company should adopt a policy to only sell the high value Beta range.

Task 2.4

(a) **If the company only manufactures the Beta range, calculate the number of units it would need to sell each month to break even.**

(b) **Give TWO reasons for NOT recommending this policy.**

ADDITIONAL DATA

The Board of Directors is considering an investment of £50,000 to buy new machinery for Centre B. The Board has been given the following data relating to this purchase:

Payback period	3 years
Internal Rate of Return	12%
Net Present Value	£4,800

Task 2.5

Write a memo to the Board of Directors dated 1 January 2005 to:

(a) **explain the meaning of the terms 'payback', 'Internal Rate of Return' and 'Net Present Value'**

(b) **explain how these methods are used to assess investment proposals**

(c) **give a recommendation, together with reasons, on whether to proceed with the investment.**

MEMORANDUM

To: **BOARD OF DIRECTORS**
From:
Date:
Subject:

MOCK EXAMINATION 2 QUESTIONS

This mock examination is in TWO sections. You are reminded that competence must be achieved in BOTH sections. You should therefore attempt and aim to complete EVERY task in BOTH sections.

Note: ALL essential workings should be included within your answers where appropriate.

You are advised to spend approximately 1 hour 30 minutes on each section.

SECTION 1

You are advised to approximately 1 hour and 30 minutes on this section.

DATA

Fardo plc manufactures and sells ceramic products made from clay. You work as an accounting technician at Fardo plc, reporting to the Finance Director.

The company operates an integrated absorption costing system. Stocks are valued on a last in first out (LIFO) basis.

The Finance Director has given you the following tasks.

Task 1.1

Complete the following stock card for clay using the LIFO method for valuing issues to production and stocks of materials.

STOCK CARD									
Product:	**Clay**								
	Receipts			**Issues**			**Balance**		
Date	Quantity kg	Cost per kg (£)	Total cost (£)	Quantity kg	Cost per kg (£)	Total cost (£)	Quantity kg	Cost per kg (£)	Total cost (£)
B/f at 1 Nov							15,000	0.50	7,500
8 Nov	60,000	0.45							
9 Nov				45,000					
16 Nov	40,000	0.55							
17 Nov				50,000					

ADDITIONAL DATA

The company's production budget requires 25,000 kgs of clay to be used each week. The company plans to maintain a buffer stock of clay equivalent to one week's budgeted production. It takes between one and two weeks for delivery of clay from the date the order is placed with the supplier.

Task 1.2

Calculate the reorder level for clay.

___

___

___

ADDITIONAL DATA

During November, gross direct labour costs of £33,000 were incurred as follows:

	£
Net wages	20,500
Income tax deductions	7,400
Employees' national insurance contributions	2,100
Employer's national insurance contributions	3,000

The accounting codes used to record direct labour costs are as follows:

Code number	*Description*
1000	Work-in-progress
7000	Income tax payable
7001	National Insurance contributions payable
9001	Net wages control account

Task 1.3

Complete the table below to record the direct labour costs for November.

Code	Dr £	Cr £
1000		
7000		
7001		
9001		

ADDITIONAL DATA

The manufacturing department has two production centres and two service centres as follows:

Production centres

- Moulding
- Glazing

Service centres

- Maintenance
- Canteen

The budgeted fixed production overheads for the manufacturing department for November were as follows:

	£
Indirect glazing materials	1,140
Rent and other property overheads	15,000
Power costs	5,040
Indirect staff costs	8,910
Machine depreciation	8,310
Total budgeted fixed overheads	38,400

The following information is also relevant:

Centres

	Moulding	*Glazing*	*Maintenance*	*Canteen*
Floor space (sq m)	3,000	1,000	500	500
Power costs	£1,200	£3,290	£250	£300
Indirect staff costs	£1,100	£2,010	£3,800	£2,000
Machine depreciation	£1,710	£6,600		
Number of employees	26	8	4	

Overheads are allocated and apportioned between centres on the most appropriate basis. The total canteen overheads are reapportioned to the other three centres based on the number of employees. Maintenance centre overheads are then reapportioned to the moulding and glazing centres. The maintenance records show that 20% of time is spent in the moulding centre and 80% in the glazing centre.

Task 1.4

Complete the following table showing the allocation and apportionment of budgeted fixed overheads between the four centres.

Fixed overheads for November	Total £	Moulding £	Glazing £	Maintenance £	Canteen £
Indirect glazing materials	1,140				
Rent and other property overheads	15,000				
Power costs	5,040				
Indirect staff costs	8,910				
Machine depreciation	8,310				
	38,400				
Canteen					( )
Maintenance				( )	
	38,400				

ADDITIONAL DATA

Moulding centre fixed overheads are absorbed on the basis of direct labour hours. Glazing department fixed overheads are absorbed on the basis of machine hours. The following information relates to the moulding and glazing centres for November:

	Moulding centre	*Glazing centre*
Budgeted labour hours	4,000	
Budgeted machine hours		6,000
Actual labour hours worked	4,200	
Actual machine hours worked		5,600
Actual fixed overheads	£17,200	£20,850

Task 1.5

(a) **Calculate the budgeted overhead absorption rate for November for:**

(i) **the moulding centre**

(ii) **the glazing centre**

Task 1.5, continued

(b) **Calculate the under- or over-absorbed production overheads for November, showing clearly whether the overheads are under- or over-absorbed for:**

(i) **the moulding centre**

(ii) **the glazing centre**

Task 1.6

Explain how an increase in budgeted activity in the moulding and glazing centres would affect the overhead cost to be charged to an individual product.

SECTION 2

Candidates should spend about 90 minutes on this section.

Fardo plc has a subsidiary company, Delta Ltd. Delta Ltd manufacturers and sells jewellery products.

Task 2.1

Delta Ltd has produced three forecasts of activity levels for the next year for Product A. The original budget was to produce only 1,000,000 units, but production levels of 1,500,000 units and 2,000,000 units are also feasible.

(a) **Complete the table below, in order to estimate the production cost per unit of Product A at the different activity levels.**

Units made	*1,000,000*	*1,500,000*	*2,000,000*
Costs:	£	£	£
Variable costs:			
· **direct materials**	5,000,000		
· **direct labour**	4,600,000		
· **overheads**	3,200,000		
Fixed costs:			
· **indirect labour**	2,500,000		
· **overheads**	6,300,000		
Total cost	21,600,000		
Cost per unit	21.60		

(b) **Briefly explain how and why the costs per unit of Product A change as the level of activity increases.**

____

____

____

____

____

____

____

____

(c) The cost schedule above assumes that all production costs are either variable or fixed.

Briefly explain whether this is realistic. Give ONE example of another way that costs can behave, and provide an example of a type of cost that may behave in this way.

Task 2.2

Products B and C have the following budgeted annual sales and cost information:

Product	*B*	*C*
Units made and sold	500,000	750,000
Machine hours required	1,000,000	3,750,000
Sales revenue (£)	5,000,000	9,000,000
Direct materials (£)	1,000,000	2,250,000
Direct labour (£)	1,250,000	2,625,000
Variable overheads (£)	1,500,000	1,500,000

Complete the table below to show the budgeted contribution per unit of B and C sold, and the company's budgeted profit or loss for the year from these two products. Total fixed costs attributable to B and C are budgeted to be £3,450,000.

	B (£)	*C* (£)	*Total* (£)
Unit selling price			
Less unit variable costs			
Direct materials			
Direct labour			
Variable overheads			
Contribution per unit			
Sales volume (units)			
Total contribution			
Less: fixed costs			
Budgeted profit or loss			

Task 2.3

A special exercise has now been carried out to split the £3,450,000 of attributable fixed costs between Products B and C. £1,000,000 was found to relate to Product B and £2,450,000 to Product C.

The latest sales forecast is that 480,000 units of Product B and 910,000 units of Product C will be sold during the year.

(a) On the basis of this new information you are required to complete the table below to:

(i) calculate the budgeted breakeven sales, in units, for each of the two products

(ii) calculate the margin of safety (in units) for each of the two products, by comparing the level of sales currently forecast with the breakeven level

(iii) calculate the margin of safety as a percentage (to two decimal places).

Product	B	C
Fixed costs (£)		
Unit contribution (£)		
Breakeven sales (units)		
Forecast sales (units)		
Margin of safety (units)		
Margin of safety (%)		

(b) **Explain the meaning of the term 'percentage margin of safety', using your calculations of this figure for Products B and C to illustrate your answer.**

Task 2.4

Due to unforeseen circumstances the number of available machine hours is now found to be limited to 3,500,000 during the year.

Using the information, and your calculations, from Task 2.2, complete the table below to recommend how many units of Products B and C should be made in order to maximise the profits or minimise the loss, taking account of the machine hours available.

Product	*B*	*C*	*Total*
Contribution/unit (£)			
Machine hours/unit			
Contribution/machine hr (£)			
Product ranking			
Machine hours available			
Machine hours allocated to: Product Product			
Total contribution earned (£)			
Less: fixed costs (£)			3,450,000
Profit/loss made (£)			

Task 2.5

Delta Ltd is considering introducing a new product, D, for which the following capital expenditure, sales and cost estimates have been produced for its planned three-year product life:

	Year 0 *£000*	*Year 1* *£000*	*Year 2* *£000*	*Year 3* *£000*
Capital expenditure	1,500			
Other cash flows:				
Sales income		700	800	1,000
Operating costs		200	250	300

The company's cost of capital is 12%.

Present value (P/V) factors for a 12% discount rate are:

	Year 0 *£000*	*Year 1* *£000*	*Year 2* *£000*	*Year 3* *£000*
P/V factor	1.0000	0.8929	0.7972	0.7118

You are required to calculate both the net present value and the payback period for the proposed new Product D.

(a) **The Net Present Value**

	Year 0 *£000*	*Year 1* *£000*	*Year 2* *£000*	*Year 3* *£000*
Capital expenditure				
Sales income				
Operating costs				
Net cash flows				
P/V factors				
Discounted cash flows				
Net Present Value				

Task 2.5, continued

(b) **The payback period**

Task 2.6

Based on the information given in Task 2.5 and your calculations for this task, write a report to the Management Accountant in which you:

(a) **recommend, on the basis of both the Net Present Value and the payback period, whether the proposed new Product D should be introduced**

(b) **identify ONE other method of investment appraisal which might also have been used to assess this proposal**

(c) **identify TWO commercial factors that are also relevant to this decision.**

Use the report stationery on the following page.

REPORT

To: The Management Accountant

From:

Subject:

Date:

KEY TECHNIQUES ANSWERS

Chapter 1
Principles of cost accounting

ACTIVITY 1

Cost accounting has been defined as 'the establishment of budgets, standard costs and actual costs of operations, processes, activities or products, and the analysis of variances, profitability or the social use of funds'.

The benefits of cost accounting arise from the information which is generated. This information can:

- disclose which activities are profitable or unprofitable
- highlight waste and inefficiency
- be used to determine the basis for selling prices
- be used as a basis for stock valuation
- be used as a basis for setting budgets and standards for control purposes
- help evaluate the cost-effectiveness of management decisions.

ACTIVITY 2

Management accounting has been defined as 'An integral part of management concerned with identifying, presenting and interpreting information used for:

- formulating strategies
- planning and controlling activities
- decision taking
- optimising the use of resources
- disclosure to shareholders and others external to the entity
- disclosure to employees
- safeguarding assets.'

It assists management in:

- formulating plans to meet objectives – long-term planning
- formulating short-term plans i.e. budgets
- acquisition of finance
- communication of financial and operating information
- taking corrective action to bring plans and results into line – control
- reviewing and reporting on operations, activities and processes.

ACTIVITY 3

Cost and management information must possess the following attributes:

- relevant to the end-user
- timely
- accurate
- complete.

Relevant to the end-user

A periodic report to the production manager would comprise those areas specific to his or her responsibility. The report should contain information from which decisions could be taken to make the production function more cost effective.

Timely

Reports should always be issued on time and meet the agreed time interval schedule.

Reports which are late are ineffective, as it may be too late to take corrective action on an area of inefficiency.

Accurate

The information must be accurate, since effective decision making may be hampered by a lack of correct information.

A lack of accuracy may also lead to management doubting future reports from the same source, and having little confidence in those supplying the information.

Complete

Information must be complete, as reports which are incomplete prevent timely and effective management decisions being made.

ACTIVITY 4

A cost unit is defined as a 'unit of product or service in relation to which costs are ascertained'.

Business activity	***Cost unit***
Accountancy practice	Chargeable hour
Brewery	Barrel of beer
Steel works	Tonne of steel
Cereal farmer	Tonne of cereal harvested
University	Student
Railway company	Passenger mile
Airline company	Passengers carried
Restaurant	Meals served
Motor manufacturer	Vehicles produced
Hospital	Patients treated

ACTIVITY 5

The following cost centres could be identified in an hotel:

- Bar
- Restaurant
- Sport/leisure area
- Housekeeping – cleaners etc
- Administration
- Reception

ACTIVITY 6

· Prime cost (210,000 + 102,000 + 5,250)	£317,250
· Cost of production (317,250 + 40,400)	£357,650
· Cost of admin, sales and distribution and financial overhead (16,500 + 52,300 + 2,100)	£70,900
· Total cost (357,650 + 70,900)	£428,550
· Prime cost per tonne (£317,250 ÷ 2,500)	£126.90
· Production cost per tonne (£357,650 ÷ 2,500)	£143.06
· Total cost per tonne (£428,550 ÷ 2,500)	£171.42

ACTIVITY 7

Sales invoices:

· Whitwell High School	100/200
· White Swan Hotel	100/210
· Worcester Royal Hospital	120/220
· Dudley Council	120/230
· Brown's Hotel	120/210
· Eskdale School	110/200
· Royal Victoria Hotel	110/210
· Dunn and Musgrove	110/230
· Rother Valley Hospital	100/220

ACTIVITY 8

A fixed cost is unaffected by a change in the activity level. A variable cost varies as the activity level changes.

Cost	*Fixed*	*Variable*
Direct materials		✓
Direct labour		✓
Heat and light	✓	
Power		✓
Consumables		✓
Accounts department salaries	✓	
Insurance sales cars	✓	
Depreciation workshop	✓	
Insurance machinery	✓	
Training costs	✓	
Stores department salaries	✓	
Agents sales commission		✓
Audit fees	✓	
Petrol managers car	✓	
Advertising	✓	

ACTIVITY 9

Direct costs	*Production overhead*	*Administration overhead*	*Sales and distribution overhead*
Direct materials Direct labour	Heat and light Power Consumables Depreciation (workshop) Insurance of machinery Training costs Stores department salaries	Accounts department salaries Audit fees Petrol for managers car	Insurance sales cars Agents commission Advertising

Chapter 2
Material costs

ACTIVITY 10

The point at which a purchase requisition should be raised is when the balance of the stock level equals or falls below the predetermined reorder level.

ACTIVITY 11

The purchase requisition is an official request from the stores department or other department requiring goods or services, to the purchasing department, for them to raise an order per the requisition.

The requisition should be signed by the person requesting the goods or services and authorised by a departmental or cost/expense centre manager – this is a measure of internal control.

ACTIVITY 12

When goods are received they can be checked against the details on the copy purchase order and the details entered on a goods received note, a GRN.

A copy of the goods received note will remain with the goods when they are checked for quality, prior to entering the stores.

Other copies of the GRN should include: one for the purchasing department, one for the accounts department and one for the area originally requesting the goods.

ACTIVITY 13

Using FIFO

Issues:

		£
15 Jan	30 pairs @ £2	60
29 Jan	35 pairs @ £2	70
Value of issues		130

Closing stock valuation:

		£
(150 – 65)	85 pairs @ £2	170
	40 pairs @ £1.90	76
	125 pairs	246

ACTIVITY 14

Using FIFO

Issues:

		£
Week ending	7 Dec 400 units	
	200 @ £0.90	180
	200 @ £1.00	200
Week ending	14 Dec 350 units	
	350 @ £1.00	350
Week ending	21 Dec 410 units	
	250 @ £1.00	250
	160 @ £0.95	152
Week ending	28 Dec 475 units	
	475 @ £0.95	451
		1,583
Closing stock		
	565 units @ £0.95	£537

Using LIFO

Issues:

		£
Week ending	7 Dec 400 units	
	400 @ £1.00	400
Week ending	14 Dec 350 units	
	350 @ £1.00	350
Week ending	21 Dec 410 units	
	410 @ £0.95	390
Week ending	28 Dec 475 units	
	475 @ £0.95	451
		1,591

Closing stock valuation			£
	565 units		
Comprises:			
	200	units @ £0.90	180
	50	units @ £1.00	50
	315	units @ £0.95	299
			529

△ ACTIVITY 15

Maximum stock level:
The highest level to which stock should normally be allowed to rise, otherwise too much working capital is tied up, thus sacrificing liquidity; and there is a risk of loss through deterioration or obsolescence. It takes account of the reorder level, the reorder quantity and the minimum consumption in the minimum delivery period.

Minimum stock level:
The lowest level to which stock should normally be allowed to fall, and is held as a buffer stock to be made available in situations such as non-delivery by a supplier. It takes into account the reorder level and average consumption in the average delivery period.

Re-order level:
This is the stock level at which an order for replenishment would normally be sent to a supplier.

It takes into account the maximum usage in the maximum delivery period.

Reorder quantity or economic order quantity:
This is the stock replenishment order size which is most economical to order as it minimises the costs of ordering and the carrying costs such as storage, insurance and interest on capital.

△ ACTIVITY 16

Six factors to consider when setting stock levels would include:

- working capital available and the cost of capital
- forecast consumption or production requirement
- the reorder period – the period between placing an order and receiving delivery
- storage space available
- market conditions
- economic order quantity.

Others could be included from:

- possibility of loss through deterioration or obsolescence
- cost of ordering, receiving, inspecting and accounting for goods.

ACTIVITY 17

	Receipts			Issues			Stock		
	Units	Cost	£	Units	Cost	£	Units	Cost	£
1 Sept							75	40.00	3,000
1 Sept	100	40.00	4,000				175	40.00	7,000
10 Sept	75	42.00	3,150				250	*40.60	10,150
15 Sept				60	40.60	2,436	190		7,714
20 Sept				55	40.60	2,233	135		5,481
23 Sept	45	42.00	1,890				180	*40.95	7,371
30 Sept				50	40.95	2,048	130	40.95	5,323

Value of issues:£6,717

Stock valuation: £5,323

*Weighted average price = $^{10,150}/_{250}$ = £40.60

*£7,371/180 = £40.95

ACTIVITY 18

Ravenscar Engineering

Component XZ7

Reorder level:
Maximum usage per period x maximum delivery period
600 x 6 = 3,600 units

Maximum stock level:
Reorder level + Reorder quantity – (minimum usage in minimum delivery period)
= 3,600 + 2,500 – (400 x 4)
= 4,500 units

Minimum stock level:
Reorder level – (average usage in average reorder period)
= 3,600 – (500 x 5)
= 1,100 units

Average stock level:
This is defined as (maximum + minimum) divided by 2

$$\frac{4,500 + 1,100}{2} = 2,800 \text{ units}$$

The average level would represent around five weeks based on maximum consumption.

ACTIVITY 19

Answer Task 19.1

STORES LEDGER CARD

Material: Sugar **Month:** November 1998

Date	Receipts			Issues			Balance		
	Quantity (kilos) 000s	Cost (per kilo) £	Value £	Quantity (kilos) 000s	Cost (per kilo) £	Value £	Quantity (kilos) 000s	Cost (per kilo) £	Value £
Balance b/f Nov 1							50	0.175	8,750
Nov 4	34	0.180	6,120				84	50,000 x 0.175 34,000 x 0.180	14,870
Nov 10				46	0.175	8,050	38	4,000 x 0.175 34,000 x 0.180	6,820
Nov 15	29	0.200	5,800				67	4,000 x 0.175 34,000 x 0.180 29,000 x 0.200	12,620
Nov 19	16	0.240	3,840				83	4,000 x 0.175 34,000 x 0.180 29,000 x 0.200 16,000 x 0.240	16,460
Nov 22				52	4,000 x 0.175 34,000 x 0.180 14,000 x 0.200	9,620	31	15,000 x 0.200 16,000 x 0.240	6,840
Nov 26	32	0.220	7,040				63	15,000 x 0.200 16,000 x 0.240 32,000 x 0.220	13,880
Nov 28				39	15,000 x 0.200 16,000 x 0.240 8,000 x 0.220	8,600	24	24,000 x 0.220	5,280

Answer Task 19.2

	Quantity (kilos)
Buffer stock	35,000
Re-order level	70,000

Answer Task 19.3

(a) FIFO does not meet the objective as issues from stores to production are based upon the oldest prices rather than the most recent.

(b) The reorder level is the level at which a new order should be placed and will consist of the material consumed in the lead-time and buffer stock. The buffer stock is the reserve to avoid the risk of stock-out.

ACTIVITY 20

Answer Task 20.1

STORES LEDGER CARD

Material: Sugar **Month:** May 20X8

	Receipts			Issues			Balance		
Date	Quantity	Price £	Total £	Quantity	Price £	Total £	Quantity	Price £	Total £
1/5 Balance							2,420	5.200	12,584
7/5	2,950	5.500	16,226				5,370	5.365	28,810
11/5	3,200	5.700	18,239				8,570	5.490	47,049
14/5				4,105	5.490	22,536	4,465	5.490	24,513
21/5	1,535	5.400	8,289				6,000	5.467	32,802
27/5				1,800	5.467	9,841	4,200	5.467	22,961
30/5				2,600	5.467	14,214	1,600	5.467	8,747

Answer Task 20.2

MEMORANDUM

To: Warehouse and Transport Manager
From: Accounting Technician
Date: 16 May 20X8
Subject: Weighted Average Method

The weighted average method for costing issues from stores and valuing stock is based upon taking the weighted average for all the stock in store prior to an issue. Issues are then costed at this weighted average and the remaining stock in store also uses this figure for valuation. Whenever there is a new receipt of stock before a further issue the weighted average is recomputed. The strength of this method is that it evens out fluctuations in price of the stock over the period and is simpler as stock balances do not have to be identified.

There are fluctuations in purchase price of the item under review and the weighted average will not give an issue price or stock valuation that is based upon an actual price. It might be better to use a method that more accurately reflects issue price or stock valuation.

Answer Task 20.3

(a) Due to rising prices and the large and homogeneous nature of stock each individual item of stock cannot be identified. It is therefore necessary to have a system that can account in a systematic manner for all units of stock.

(b) (i) Last-In-First-Out
(ii) First-In-First-Out

ACTIVITY 21

Answer Task 21.1

STORES LEDGER ACCOUNT

Material description:
Cotton lining material
50 metre rolls

Code: C310

Control levels:

Maximum	200
Minimum	60
Reorder level	90
Reorder quantity	100

	Receipts			Issues			Stock Balance		
Date	Quantity	Unit price £	Total £	Quantity	Unit price £	Total £	Quantity	Unit price £	Total £
1 Mar							80	87.00	6,960.00
2 Mar	100	87.00	8,700.00				180	87.00	15,660.00
5 Mar				100	87.00	8,700.00	80	87.00	6,960.00
9 Mar	75	90.00	6,750.00				155 { 80	87.00	13,710.00
							75	90.00	
12 Mar				100 { 80	87.00	6,960.00	55	90.00	4,950.00
				20	90.00	1,800.00			
16 Mar	80	90.00	7,200.00				135	90.00	12,150.00
19 Mar				80	90.00	7,200.00	55	90.00	4,950.00
23 Mar	100	87.00	8,700.00				155 { 55	90.00	13,650.00
							100	87.00	

STORES LEDGER ACCOUNT

Material description:
Cotton red
50 metre rolls

Code: C322

Control levels:
Maximum 150
Minimum 45
Reorder level 80
Reorder quantity 50

	Receipts			Issues			Stock Balance		
Date	Quantity	Unit price £	Total £	Quantity	Unit price £	Total £	Quantity	Unit price £	Total £
1 Mar							75.00	100.00	7,500.00
9 Mar	50	102.00	5,100.00				125 { 75	100.00	12,600.00
							50	102.00	
10 Mar				60	100.00	6,000.00	65 { 15	100.00	6,600.00
							50	102.00	
16 Mar	50	102.00	5,100.00				115 { 15	100.00	11,700.00
							100	102.00	
20 Mar				60 { 15	100.00	6,090.00	55	102.00	5,610.00
				45	102.00				
27 Mar				10	102.00	1,020.00	45	102.00	4,590.00

Answer Task 21.2

MEMORANDUM

To: Neil Barker
From: Jan Calvert
Date: 5 April 20X1
Subject: Stock levels, raw materials

I refer to the stores ledger account for the 50-metre rolls of material C310 cotton lining, and wish to make the following observations:

- The deliveries on the 9 March and the 16 March were 75 and 80 rolls respectively which are both short of the predetermined reorder quantity of 100 rolls.

  These predetermined quantities are based on the economic order quantity model and should be adhered to.

- The lower quantities ordered have increased the purchase price by £3 per roll, probably due to quantity discount no longer being available.

- On the 12 March and 19 March the stock level fell below the predetermined minimum level of 60 rolls to a level of 55 rolls of stock.

  This could, in the event of a late delivery by the supplier, cause short-term production flow problems.

If we had maintained the normal order quantity, this problem with the minimum level referred to above would have been avoided.

We need to bring these issues to the attention of the staff responsible for raising the purchase requisition and subsequently the purchase order.

ACTIVITY 22

Answer Task 22.1

STORES LEDGER ACCOUNT

Material 100 page A4 notebooks

Code 4.100

Stock levels

Maximum	1,200
Minimum	50
Re-order level	300
Re-order quantity	1,000

	Receipts			Issues			Stock Balance		
Date	Units	Unit price £	Value £	Units	Unit price £	Value £	Units	Unit price £	Value £
1 Jan							250	0.80	200.00
15 Jan				200	0.80	160.00	50	0.80	40.00
30 Jan	1,000	0.82	820.00						
							50	0.80	40.00
							1,000	0.82	820.00
							1,050		860.00
				50	0.80	40.00			
2 Feb				450	0.82	369.00	550	0.82	451.00
15 Feb				400	0.82	328.00	150	0.82	123.00
28 Feb	1,000	0.80	800.00						
							150	0.82	123.00
							1,000	0.80	800.00
							1,150		923.00

	Receipts			Issues			Stock Balance		
Date	Units	Unit price £	Value £	Units	Unit price £	Value £	Units	Unit price £	Value £
4 Mar				150	0.82	123.00			
				200	0.80	160.00	800	0.80	640.00
21 Mar				500	0.80	400.00	300	0.80	240.00
31 Mar	1,000	0.81	810.00						
							300	0.80	240.00
							1,000	0.81	810.00
							1,300		1,050.00

Answer Task 22.2

COST SCHEDULE

Issues of A4 notebooks for the quarter ended 31 March 20X1

Cost Centre and expense code	*Cost of issues* £
200.100	160.00
210.100	328.00
220.100	409.00
230.100	400.00
240.100	283.00
250.100	–
	£1,580.00

Chapter 3
Labour costs

ACTIVITY 23

(a) A timesheet is filled out by every employee at regular time intervals to record the time worked. It is an important document in the costing system as it can be used to:

- reconcile hours worked with an analysis of these hours to cost centre, cost unit, job, process or activity
- form a basis for the labour charge to a cost centre, cost unit, job, process or activity
- calculate each employee's gross pay (as it is a record of total hours worked by each employee).

(b) An organisation would wish to record its hourly paid employees' hours of work as these would be required so that the employees' gross pay can be calculated.

ACTIVITY 24

Client job number		£
701		
L Astbury	13 hours @ £8	104
S White	4 hours @ £12	48
P Dunn	3 hours @ £25	75
		227
704		
L Astbury	6.5 hours @ £8	52
S White	4.5 hours @ £12	54
		106
706		
L Astbury	2.5 hours @ £8	20
707		
L Astbury	6 hours @ £8	48
708		
L Astbury	6 hours @ £8	48
709		
L Astbury	6 hours @ £8	48
P Dunn	4 hours @ £25	100
		148
710		
S White	8 hours @ £12	96
711		
S White	14 hours @ £12	168
J Musgrove	5 hours @ £25	125
		293
712		
S White	9.5 hours @ £12	114
J Musgrove	4 hours @ £25	100
		214

ACTIVITY 25

Gross wages	*Carter*	*Noble*
Basic pay	37 ½ hrs @ £4 £150.00	37 ½ hrs @ £4 £150.00
Overtime	3 hrs @ £6 £18	3 ½ hrs @ £6 £21

Productivity bonus	Good production	Good production
	164 x 97%	180 x 97 ½ %
	= 159 shorts	= 175 shorts
	= 159 ÷ 15 batches	175 ÷ 15 batches
	10 batches	11 batches
	@ £4	@ £4
	£40.00	£44.00
	£208.00	£215.00

△ ACTIVITY 26

Advantages include:

- possibility of higher wages for the employee
- may motivate employees
- possibility of a greater level of output for the benefit of the employer
- may lead to lower cost per unit of output.

△ ACTIVITY 27

	Cost centre			£
130	Hairdressing salon	2.5 hours	@ £8.50	21.25
140	Swimming pool/gym	10.0 hours	@ £8.50	85.00
150	Bedrooms	5.0 hours	@ £8.50	42.50
160	Exterior building maintenance	8.00 hours	@ £8.50	68.00
170	Car park	3.00 hours	@ £8.50	25.50
180	External grounds	11.50 hours	@ £8.50	97.75
				340.00

△ ACTIVITY 28

Gross wage:

Basic pay	40 hrs @ £6	£240.00
Overtime	5 hrs @ £9	£45.00

Bonus:

25 doors x 2 hours = 50 hours allowed
Time taken 45 hours

Time saved – 5 hours x £3

	£15.00
	£300.00

△ ACTIVITY 29

Answer Task 29.1

TIMESHEET

Week ending 23 March 20X1

Employee name: John Collinson Employee No: 157

Cost centre: Cutting

Activity	*Monday output*	*Tuesday output*	*Wednesday output*	*Thursday output*	*Friday output*	*Total output*
Cutting am	–	–	12	10	10	32
Cutting pm	–	–	12	12	10	34
Total output	–	–	24	22	20	66
Hours on production	–	–	8	8	8	24
Training	–	–	–	–	–	–
Sick pay	–	–	–	–	–	–
Holiday	8	8	–	–	–	16
Total hours	8	8	8	8	8	40
Reject units			2	1	1	4
Gross pay:						
Piecework earnings	–	–	26.40	25.20	22.80	74.40
Training	–	–	–	–	–	–
Sick pay	–	–	–	–	–	–
Holiday	38.00	38.00	–	–	–	76.00
	38.00	38.00	26.40	25.20	22.80	150.40

Guaranteed pay: £ 25.00

Gross pay: £ 152.60

TIMESHEET

Week ending 23 March 20X1

Employee name: June Mullhen Employee No: 158

Cost centre: Cutting

Activity	*Monday output*	*Tuesday output*	*Wednesday output*	*Thursday output*	*Friday output*	*Total output*
Cutting am	13	12	–	12	10	47
Cutting pm	14	13	–	12	10	49
Total output	(28) ← ERROR	25		24	20	97
Hours on production	8	8	–	8	6	30
Training	–	–	–	–	2	2
Sick pay	–	–	8	–	–	8
Holiday	–	–	–	–	–	–
Total hours	8	8	8	8	8	40
Reject units	–	2		1	1	4
Gross pay:						
Piecework earnings	33.60	27.60	–	27.60	22.80	111.60
Training	–	–	–	–	9.50	9.50
Sick pay	–	–	38.00	–	–	38.00
Holiday	–	–	–	–	–	–
	33.60	27.60	38.00	27.60	32.30	159.10

Guaranteed pay: £25 per day has been earned

Gross pay: £159.10

Wages analysis week ending 23 March 20X1

	Employee 157	*Employee 158*	*Total*
	£	£	£
Direct labour	76.60	111.60	188.20
Indirect labour:			
Training	–	9.50	9.50
Holiday	76.00	–	76.00
Sick pay	–	38.00	38.00
	£152.60	£159.10	£311.70

Direct labour cost per unit of output:

$$\frac{\text{Total direct labour}}{\text{Total good production}} = \frac{£188.20}{155} = £1.21$$

COST LEDGER DATA ENTRY SHEET

Week ending:

Debit accounts:

Cost Centre Codes	*Expenditure Code*	£
100	220	188.20
	230	123.50
110	220	
	230	
120	220	
	230	
130	220	
	230	
140	220	
	230	
		£ 311.70

Answer Task 29.2

MEMORANDUM

To: Karl Meyer
From: Jan Calvert
Date: 23 March 20X1
Subject: Timesheet discrepancies
Cutting Cost Centre – employee no: 158

I refer to June Mullhen's timesheet for the week ending 23 March.

The detail showing output in units for Monday includes 13 in the morning and 14 in the afternoon, however the total output is shown as 28 units.

Could you please check from your production records the actual output for the day, so that I can amend the timesheet.

I have based June's pay on the 28 units shown, however if this is found to be incorrect I will adjust the gross pay and the analysis of direct labour next week.

I look forward to your response to my query.

Answer Task 29.3

Direct labour cost per unit of output for the week ended 23 March 20X1

$$\frac{\text{Total direct labour}}{\text{Total good production}} = \frac{£188.20}{155} = £1.21$$

Alternative – consolidated rate per hour

	Employee 157	Employee 158	Total (hours)
Direct labour hours	24	30	54

Total hours x Rate per hour = 54 x £5 = £270.00

Direct labour cost per unit of output based on alternative

$$\frac{\text{Direct labour cost}}{\text{Total good units}} = \frac{£270.00}{155} = £1.74$$

ACTIVITY 30

PART TIME STAFF
TIMESHEET – TEACHING

Cost Centre: Sports
Cost Centre Code: 240
Expense Code: 110
Date: Week ended 28 March 20X1
Name: Raymond Staniland

Please ✓ each completed am/pm session

	am	pm
Monday	✓	✓
Tuesday	–	–
Wednesday	✓	–
Thursday	✓	✓
Friday	–	–

Gross pay: 2 ½ days x £ 125 per day
= £312.50

Authorised by: *S Woodhouse*

PART TIME STAFF
TIMESHEET – TEACHING

Cost Centre: Art and Design
Cost Centre Code: 230
Expense Code: 110
Date: Week ended 28 March 20X1
Name: James Parker

Please ✓ each completed am/pm session

	am	pm
Monday	✓	✓
Tuesday	–	–
Wednesday	–	–
Thursday	–	–
Friday	✓	✓

Gross pay: 2 days x £120 per day
= £240

Authorised by: *S Woodhouse*

PART TIME STAFF
TIMESHEET – TEACHING

Cost Centre: Business Studies
Cost Centre Code: 210
Expense Code: 110
Date: Week ended 28 March 20X1
Name: Elizabeth Jones

Please ✓ each completed am/pm session

	am	pm
Monday	✓	–
Tuesday	✓	✓
Wednesday	✓	–
Thursday	–	–
Friday	✓	✓

Gross pay: 3 days x £135 per day
= £405

Authorised by: *S Woodhouse*

PART TIME STAFF
TIMESHEET – TEACHING

Cost Centre: Maths and Science
Cost Centre Code: 200
Expense Code: 110
Date: Week ended 28 March 20X1
Name: John Brewster

Please ✓ each completed am/pm session

	am	pm
Monday	✓	–
Tuesday	✓	–
Wednesday	✓	–
Thursday	✓	–
Friday	✓	–

Gross pay: 2 ½ days x £135 per day
= £337.50

Authorised by: *S Woodhouse*

PART TIME STAFF
TIMESHEET – ESTATES AND CATERING

Cost Centre: Catering
Cost Centre Code: 270
Expense Code: 120
Date: Week ended 28 March 20X1
Name: Carol Heyes

	am	pm	Total hours
Sunday	4	5	9
Monday	4	3	7
Tuesday	4	3	7
Wednesday	4	6	10
Thursday	4	6	10
Friday	4	3	7
Saturday	4	4	8
	28	30	58

Basic time	49 hours x £5	= £	245.00
Overtime	9 hours x £7.50	= £	67.50
Gross pay		£	312.50

Authorised by: S Woodhouse

PART TIME STAFF
TIMESHEET – ESTATES AND CATERING

Cost Centre: Estates
Cost Centre Code: 260
Expense Code: 130
Date: Week ended 28 March 20X1
Name: Simon Jones

	am	pm	Total hours
Sunday	–	–	–
Monday	4	3	7
Tuesday	–	–	–
Wednesday	4	4	8
Thursday	–	–	–
Friday	4	5	9
Saturday	–	–	–
	12	12	24

Basic time	21 hours x £5.25	= £	110.25
Overtime	3 hours x £7.875	= £	23.63
Gross pay		£	133.88

Authorised by: S Woodhouse

Chapters 4 and 5
Expenses and accounting for overheads

ACTIVITY 31

Capital expenditure is expenditure incurred in:

- the acquisition of fixed assets required for use in the business and not for resale, or
- the alteration or improvement of fixed assets for the purpose of increasing their revenue earning capacity.

Revenue expenditure is expenditure incurred in:

- the acquisition of goods or services acquired for conversion into cash (ie goods for resale), or
- costs relating to manufacturing, selling and distribution of goods and the day to day administration of business, or
- the maintenance of the revenue earning capacity of fixed assets (i.e. maintenance and repair).

ACTIVITY 32

The items classified as capital expenditure would be:

- purchase of delivery vehicle
- painting and sign-writing of new vehicle in firm's livery and colours
- cost of own labour in building workshop extension
- installation of air conditioning unit in workshop
- installation and setting up of new machinery.

ACTIVITY 33

Overhead allocation is the allotment of whole items of cost to cost centres or cost units.

Overhead apportionment is the allotment of proportions of items of cost to cost centres or cost units.

Overhead absorption is the charging of overhead to cost units, by the use of overhead recovery rates.

ACTIVITY 34

Bases of apportionment

- Plant value
- Kilowatt hours of power used
- Floor area
- Floor area
- Plant value
- Floor area
- Number of employees
- Stores requisitions
- Number of employees or direct labour hours
- Direct labour hours
- Direct labour hours
- Direct labour hours

ACTIVITY 35

Answer Task 35.1

OVERHEAD ANALYSIS SHEET (TASK 35.1)

R Noble Agricultural Engineers Budget Period End 31 March 20X1

Overhead Item	Total	Basis	Machining	Fabrication	Fitting	Outside work	Canteen	Stores	Maintenance
	£		£	£	£	£	£	£	£
Indirect labour	7,250	Allocated					1,375	2,750	3,125
Indirect materials	5,025	Allocated	1,625	1,125	275	150	188	287	1,375
Vehicle costs	1,950	Allocated				1,950			
Depreciation m/c	5,000	m/c value	2,000	950	500	1,000	50	125	375
Insurance m/c	2,100	m/c value	840	399	210	420	21	53	157
Insurance buildings	1,500	Build value	375	437	313	–	94	125	156
Heat and light	800	Area	200	233	167	–	50	67	83
Power	1,750	KWH ratio	700	525	280	–	35	35	175
Rent and rates	2,250	Area	563	656	469	–	141	187	234
Shop floor admin	500	No of emp	250	167	83				
Consumable tools	900	DL hrs	337	225	113	225			
Consumable mats	410	DL hrs	152	102	51	105			
Supervision sals	4,000	No of emp	1,200	800	400	800	–	400	400
	£33,435		8,242	5,619	2,861	4,650	1,954	4,029	6,080
Reapportionment:									
Canteen		No of emp	586	391	196	391	(1,954)	195	195
							–	4,224	
Stores		No of material req	1,077	828	663	1,104		(4,224)	552
									6,827
Maintenance		DL hours	2,536	1,691	856	1,744			(6,827)
			£12,441	£8,529	£4,576	£7,889			–

Answer Task 35.2

Overhead recovery rates:

$$\frac{\text{Cost centre overhead}}{\text{Direct labour hours}}$$

Machining $\frac{£12,441}{1,600}$ = £7.77 per DL hour

Fabrication $\frac{£8,529}{1,067}$ = £7.99 per DL hour

Fitting $\frac{£4,576}{540}$ = £8.47 per DL hour

Outside work $\frac{£7,889}{1,100}$ = £7.17 per DL hour

ACTIVITY 36

R Noble and Sons

Cost centre		*Overhead recovered*	*Actual incurred*	*(Under)/Over-recovered*
		£	£	£
Machining	500 hrs @ £7.77	3,885	4,150	(265)
Fabrication	350 hrs @ £7.99	2,797	2,600	197
Fitting shop	180 hrs @ £8.47	1,525	1,450	75
Outside work	400 hrs @ £7.18	2,872	2,950	(78)
		11,079	11,150	(71)

ACTIVITY 37

Replacement doors for grain drier

	£
Direct materials	3,500
Direct labour:	
28 hours @ £7.50	210
Overhead:	
Machining 15 hrs @ £7.77	117 *
Fabrication 8 hrs @ £7.99	64
Fitting shop 5 hrs @ £8.47	42
Production cost	£3,933

*overhead to nearest £.

ACTIVITY 38

Overhead control account

	£		£
May Creditors	11,600	May WIP Control	11,290
		May Under-recovery Costing P/L	310
	11,600		11,600

ACTIVITY 39

(a)

BUDGETED COST SCHEDULE		YEAR 1999		
		ACTIVITY (Packets)		
		175,000	200,000	225,000
Description	**Cost**	**£**	**£**	**£**
Direct material	8p per packet	14,000	16,000	18,000
Direct labour	6p per packet	10,500	12,000	13,500
Packing costs	1p per packet	1,750	2,000	2,250
Depreciation costs	£12,000	12,000	12,000	12,000
Rent and rates	£26,000	26,000	26,000	26,000
Supervisory costs	£12,000	12,000	12,000	12,000
Administration costs	£8,000	8,000	8,000	8,000

(b)

	ACTIVITY (Packets)		
	175,000	200,000	225,000
COST	**£**	**£**	**£**
Total variable cost	26,250	30,000	33,750
Total fixed cost	58,000	58,000	58,000
Total cost	84,250	88,000	91,750
Cost per packet	0.481	0.440	0.408

ACTIVITY 40

(a) The cost per packet moved from 48.1p per packet at 175,000 units of production to 40.8p per packet at 225,000 units of production.

(b) The reason for this is that fixed costs remained constant and are therefore recovered over a larger volume and fall on a unit basis.

ACTIVITY 41

(a)

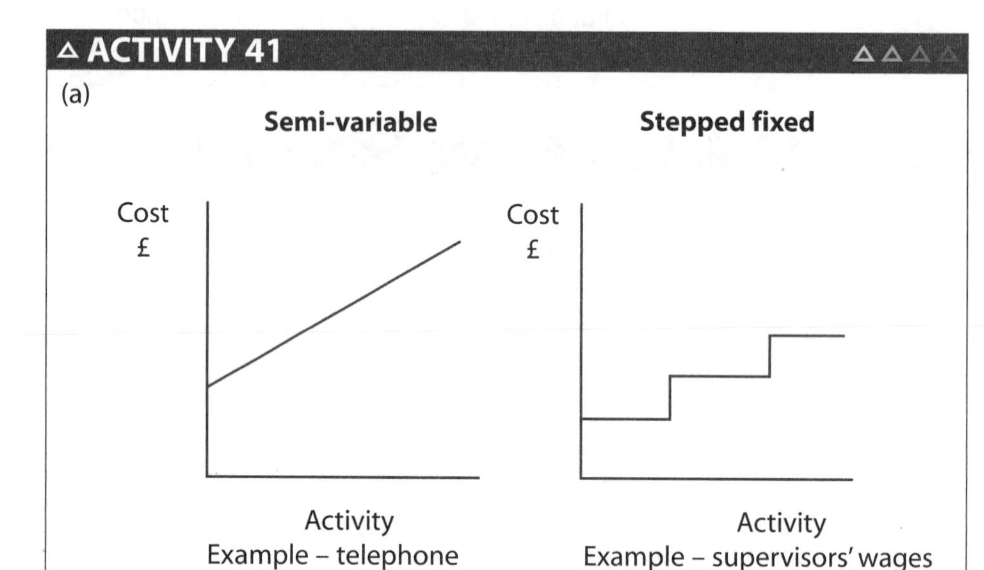

(b) The rental cost of a telephone remains fixed whatever the usage whilst the call charges are based on usage. Supervisors' wages will remain constant until the pool of workers increases to such a size that another supervisor has to be employed.

ACTIVITY 42

Answer Task 42.1

	Mixing £	Baking £	Packing £
Budgeted overhead Absorption rate	£2.50 per £1 direct labour	£14 per machine hour	£12.50 per labour hour

Answer Task 42.2

PRODUCTION OVERHEAD SCHEDULE
Month: November 1998

	Mixing £	Baking £	Packing £
Budgeted overheads	164,000	228,900	215,000
Actual overheads	171,500	224,000	229,000
Overhead absorbed	159,250	225,400	200,000

Answer Task 42.3

	Mixing £	Baking £	Packing £
Over-absorbed overheads		1,400	
Under-absorbed overheads	12,250		29,000

Answer Task 42.4

(a) A stores overhead absorption rate is not calculated as it is a service cost centre and the cost unit does not travel through it so that costs can be absorbed.

(b) Stores overheads are reapportioned to the production cost centres on some equitable basis related to the service provided.

Answer Task 42.5

A time-based method of absorption is more appropriate as time reflects more accurately the occurrence of overheads than value-based methods.

ACTIVITY 43

Answer Task 43.1

BUDGETED DEPARTMENT OVERHEAD SCHEDULE
YEAR ENDED 31 MAY 20X9

	Electrical £	House-hold £	Clothing £	Food £	Buying £	Admin £	Ware-house and trans £	Total £
Allocated overhead	224,600	213,200	203,000	194,600	42,200	102,300	51,300	1,031,200
Rent and rates	71,100	73,800	97,500	48,000	4,500	7,500	78,000	380,400
Canteen services	20,400	20,800	21,600	16,400	2,400	8,400	4,800	94,800
Total	316,100	307,800	322,100	259,000	49,100	118,200	134,100	1,506,400

Answer Task 43.2

NOTES TO CHIEF ACCOUNTANT

The departments that will need to have their overheads reapportioned are the buying, administration and warehouse and transport departments.
The departments that will need to have overheads reapportioned to them are the sales departments.

The reason for the reapportionment is that the buying, administration and warehouse and transport departments are service departments to the sales departments and in order to fully reflect the costs of the sales departments their share of the service cost centres needs to be included.

Answer Task 43.3

(a) (i) Identify unique items/Avoid ambiguity
(ii) Aid processing/Reduce data storage(Any two will be acceptable)

(b)

	£
Cost	20,000
Depreciation May 20X7	4,000
Reduced balance	16,000
Depreciation May 20X8	3,200

(c)

	Dr	Cr
	£	£
Warehouse and transport overhead a/c	3,200	
Fixed asset control a/c		3,200

ACTIVITY 44

Answer Task 44.1

The actual level of activity for the quarter ended 31 March 20X1 was:

Cost centre	*Cutting*	*Finishing*	*Packing*
Machine hours	5,450		
Direct labour hours		4,390	3,870
Actual cost (overheads)	£52,000	£36,500	£27,750

Overhead recovered

Cost centre:

Cutting	Actual machine hours	x	Overhead recovery rate	
	5,450	x	£9.50	= £51,775
Finishing	Actual direct labour hours	x	Overhead recovery rate	
	4,390	x	£8.50	= £37,315
Packing	Actual direct labour hours	x	Overhead recovery rate	
	3,870	x	£7.25	= £28,058

Under or over recovery of overhead for the quarter ended 31 March 20X1

Cost centre	*Overhead recovered*	*Actual cost*	*(Under)/ Over-recovered*
	£	£	£
Cutting	51,775	52,000	(225)
Finishing	37,315	36,500	815
Packing	28,058	27,750	308
	£117,148	£116,250	£898

Answer Task 44.2

Production Overhead Control Account

31 Mar	£	*31 Mar* WIP	£
Creditors and wages control (i.e. overheads)		Cutting	51,775
Cutting	52,000	Finishing	37,315
Finishing	36,500	Packing	28,058
Packing	27,750	(overhead recovered)	
Profit and loss a/c (over-recovery)	898		
	£117,148		£117,148

ACTIVITY 45

Answer Task 45.1

OVERHEAD ANALYSIS SHEET

Overhead	Total	Basis	Motor Repairs	Valeting	Tow Bars	Stores
	£		£	£	£	£
Depreciation	18,000	Plant value	10,000	3,500	4,300	200
Rent and rates	30,000	Area	18,000	6,000	4,500	1,500
Heat and light	2,100	Area	1,260	420	315	105
Power	3,100	Consumption ratio	1,240	620	930	310
Workshop manager's salary	21,000	No of employees	10,500	5,250	2,625	2,625
Stores salary	12,500	Allocated				12,500
Consumables	1,850	Dir lab hours	1,057	529	264	
Insurance plant	2,500	Plant value	1,389	486	597	28
Insurance buildings	4,100	Area	2,460	820	615	205
	95,150		45,906	17,625	14,146	17,473
Reapportionment of stores		Material requisitions	9,707	4,854	2,912	(17,473)
			£55,613	£22,479	£17,058	
Direct labour hours			8,000	4,000	2,000	
Recovery rate per DL hour			£6.9516	£5.6198	£8.5290	

Answer Task 45.2

OVERHEAD SCHEDULE FOR THE QUARTER ENDED 31 MARCH 20X1

Profit centre	*Overhead recovered*	*Actual overhead*	*(Under)/Over-recovered*
	£	£	£
Motor repairs	57,003	57,100	(97)
Valeting	22,760	23,400	(640)
Tow Bars	17,271	17,750	(479)
	£97,034	£98,250	£ (1,216)

Working

Overhead recovered		£
Motor repairs	8,200 standard hours x £6.9516	57,003
Valeting	4,050 standard hours x £5.6198	22,760
Tow Bars	2,025 standard hours x £8.5290	17,271

△ ACTIVITY 46

Answer Task 46.1

ESK VALLEY SCHOOL – OVERHEAD SCHEDULE

Overhead	Total	Basis	Maths and Science	Business Studies	Human -ities	Art and Design	Sports	Admin	Estates	Catering
	£	£	£	£	£	£	£	£	£	£
Wages and salaries	691,000	Allocated	155,000	130,000	141,000	125,000	140,000			
Pension costs	41,460	% of salaries	9,300	7,800	8,460	7,500	8,400			
Employer's NI	55,280	% of salaries	12,400	10,400	11,280	10,000	11,200			
Consumables	71,400	Allocated	15,000	12,000	14,500	11,900	18,000			
Buildings insurance	12,500	Estates							12,500	
Heat and light	23,500	Estates							23,500	
Equipment insurance	4,750	Estates							4,750	
Estate costs	131,500	Allocated							131,500	
Catering	85,000	Allocated								85,000
Admin-istration	72,400	Allocated						72,400		
	1,188,790		191,700	160,200	175,240	154,400	177,600	72,400	172,250	85,000

Reapportionment: Catering		Student hours	14,875	16,292	17,708	17,142	18,983			(85,000)
										–
Estates		Ratio area	25,838	20,670	17,225	17,225	67,177	24,115	(172,250)	
									–	
Administration		Student hours	16,890	18,499	20,107	19,464	21,555	(96,515)		
	1,188,790		249,303	215,661	230,280	208,231	285,315	–		

OVERHEAD RECOVERY RATES

Teaching Cost Centres	Maths and Science £	Business Studies £	Humanities £	Art and Design £	Sports £
Overhead	249,303	215,661	230,280	208,231	285,315
Student hours	105,000	115,000	125,000	121,000	134,000
Recovery rate per student hour	£2.37	£1.88	£1.84	£1.72	£2.13

Answer Task 46.2

TEACHING UNITS

Overhead report quarter ended 31 March 20X1

Cost centre	Actual overhead £	Overhead recovered £	(Under)/over-recovered £
Maths and Science	61,500	65,175	3,675
Business Studies	54,200	54,990	790
Humanities	59,500	59,064	(436)
Art and Design	51,500	52,890	1,390
Sports	71,100	73,485	2,385
	£297,800	£305,604	£7,804

Answer Task 46.3

MEMORANDUM

To: Susan Woodhouse
From: Paul Goodenough
Date: 4 April 20X1
Subject: Over-recovery of overhead quarter ended 31 March

The total over-recovery for the period was £7,804.

The main reason for this was additional volume in student hours for the period.

The expected student hours for the period were 600,000/4 = 150,000, whereas the actual hours were 154,100 i.e. an extra 2.7%.

Forecast overhead was £1,188,790/4 = £297,197, whereas actual expenditure was £297,800. This showed a marginal overspend of £603, the bulk of the over-recovery thus being due to volume.

Regards,
Paul

Chapter 6
Job and batch costing

ACTIVITY 47

Jetprint Limited

	Cost of batch 10,000 leaflets	Cost of batch 20,000 leaflets
	£	£
Artwork	65.00	65.00
Machine setting	88.00	88.00
Paper	125.00	250.00
Ink and consumables	40.00	80.00
Printers' wages	32.00	64.00
	350.00	547.00
General fixed overheads (W1)	100.00	200.00
Total cost	450.00	747.00
Profit	192.86	320.14
Sales revenue required	(W2) 642.86	(W3) 1,067.14
Selling price per 1,000	64.00	53.00

Do not forget to calculate the selling price per 1,000 leaflets as this is what the requirement is and if you omit this you will have lost marks.

Workings

(W1) $\text{OAR} = \frac{£15,000}{600} = £25 \text{ per hour}$

(W2) Sales revenue required:

$\frac{£450}{0.7} = £642.86$

Therefore profit = £642.86 – £450 = £192.86

(W3) $\frac{£747}{0.7} = £1,067.14$

Therefore profit = £1,067.14 – £747 = £320.14

Chapter 7
Process costing

ACTIVITY 48

Mike Everett Ltd – 'Calfextra'

Determination of losses/gains:

	Tonnes
Input	2,000
Normal loss 4% of input	80
Normal output	1,920
Actual output	1,900
Difference = abnormal loss	20

Process account

Date		Units	£	Date		Units	£
10 Feb	Direct material	2,000	120,000	10 Feb	Normal loss	80	800
	Direct labour		640		Output	1,900	119,003
	Overhead		416		Abnormal loss	20	1,253
		2,000	121,056			2,000	121,056

Normal cost of normal production:

$$\frac{£121,056 - £800}{2,000 - 80} = \frac{£120,256}{1,920}$$

= £62.63333 per tonne

Output 1,900 x £62.63333 = £119,003

Abnormal loss 20 x £62.63333 = £1,253

ACTIVITY 49

Mike Everett Ltd – 'Pigextra'

Determination of losses/gains:

	Tonnes
Input	3,000
Normal loss 4% of input	120
Normal output	2,880
Actual output	2,890
Difference = abnormal gain	10

Process account

Date		*Units*	£	*Date*		*Units*	£
10 Mar	Direct material	3,000	210,000	10 Mar	Normal loss	120	1,440
	Direct labour		760		Output	2,890	210,542
	Overhead		494				
	Abnormal gain	10	728				
		3,010	211,982			3,010	211,982

Normal cost of normal production:

$$\frac{£211{,}254 - £1{,}440}{3{,}000 - 120} = \frac{£209{,}814}{2{,}880}$$

= £72.85208 per tonne

Output	2,890 x £72.85208	= £210,542
Abnormal gain	10 tonnes x £72.85208	= £728

ACTIVITY 50

Process account

	Kg	£			*Kg*	£	
Direct material	1,000	3,800		Normal loss	100	50	
Director labour (50 x £9.60)		480		Output	950	4,729	(W1)
Overhead (50 x £5)		250					
Abnormal gain	50	249	(W2)				
	1,050	4,779			1,050	4,779	

(W1) Normal cost of normal output $\frac{(3{,}800 + 480 + 250) - 50}{(1{,}000 - 100)} =$

= £4.98 per Kg

Cost of output = 950 x £4.98 = £4,729

(W2) Cost of abnormal gain = 50 x £4.98 = 249

△ ACTIVITY 51

Process account

	Litre	£		Litre	£
Direct material	10,000	50,000	Normal loss	500	500
Direct labour		4,000	Output	9,500	59,500
Overhead		6,000			
	10,000	60,000		10,000	60,000

△ ACTIVITY 52

Process account

	Litre	£		Litre	£
Direct material	10,000	50,000	Normal loss	500	500
Direct labour		4,000	Abnormal loss	200	1,253 (W)
Overhead		6,000	Output	9,300	58,247 (W)
	10,000	60,000		10,000	60,000

Working

Normal cost of normal output $= \frac{59,500}{9,500}$ = £6.2631 per litre.

Therefore, output and the abnormal loss are both costed at £6.2631 per litre.

△ ACTIVITY 53

Egton Farm Supplies Ltd

Process account

Date		*Units*	£	*Date*		*Units*	£
Period 5	Direct material	1,000	70,000	Period 5	Output	800	56,400
	Direct labour		320		Work-in-progress	200	14,080
	Overhead		160				
		1,000	70,480			1,000	70,480

Work-in-progress valuation

Statement of equivalent units and statement of cost

Element of cost	Comp output	WIP	% completion	Equivalent units	Cost £	Cost per unit
Direct materials	800	200	100	1,000	70,000	70.0000
Direct labour	800	200	80	960	320	0.3333
Overhead	800	200	80	960	160	0.1666
						£70.4999

Valuation of output and work-in-progress

		£
Completed output	800 tonnes x £70.4999	56,400

Work-in-progress

Direct materials	200 tonnes x £70.00	14,000
Direct labour	160 tonnes x £0.3333	53
Overhead	160 tonnes x £0.1666	27
		14,080

ACTIVITY 54

Taylor

Flow of units

Input = Good output + Losses

5,000 = 4,750 + 250 (to balance)

Process 1 account

	Units	£		Units	£
Materials *@£2.47 per kilo*	5000	12,350	Normal loss *4.7% x 5,000*	235 *@ £1.67 per kilo*	392
Labour		4,398	Abnormal loss *Balancing figure*	15 *@ £4.817 per kilo*	72
Overheads *150% of labour*		6,597			
			Output	4,750 *@ £4.817 per kilo*	22,881
Total	5000	23,345	Total	5000	23,345

Value of output and abnormal loss = $\frac{£23,345 - £392}{5,000 - 235} = \frac{£22,953}{4,765} = £4.817$

ACTIVITY 55

Answer Task 55.1

Process Alpha – May account

	Units	£		*Units*	£
Materials	5,000	14,378	Output	4,679 @ *£4.64*	21,711
Labour	–	7,500	Normal loss	285	Nil
			Abnormal loss (bal fig)	36 @ *£4.64*	167
	5,000	21,878		5,000	21,878

Value of output = £21,878/(5,000 – 285) = £4.64 per unit

Answer Task 55.2

Process Omega – June account

	Units	£		*Units*	£
Materials	10,000	26,800	Output	9,867 @ *£5.33*	£52,591
Labour	–	5,604			
Overheads	–	20,160			
	10,000	52,564	Normal loss	230 @ *£2.13*	£490
Abnormal gain (bal fig)	97 @ *£5.33*	517			
	10,097	53,081		10,097	53,081

Value of output = (£52,564 – £490) / (10,000-230) = £5.33 per unit

ACTIVITY 56

Answer Task 56.1

The phrase 'abnormal gain' is a slightly misleading since it does not mean that the process has 'gained' any units (this would mean there was more output than input which is impossible).

An abnormal gain refers to when less units are lost than normal. For example, if 1,000 units are put into a process and 50 are normally lost, then 950 units should be output. If actual output is 980 units, only 20 have been lost, the abnormal gain is therefore the additional 30 (50 – 20) that have been output.

The net costs attributed to an abnormal gain are treated as a credit to the profit and loss account.

Answer Task 56.2

Process account

	Units	£		*Units*		£
Input materials	10,000	12,000	Normal loss			
Labour (W)	–	2,400	20% x10,000	= 2,000	@ £0.80 =	1,600
Overheads (W)	–	6,000	Output	7,720	@ £2.35 (W) =	18,142
			Abnormal loss (bal fig)	280	@ £2.35 =	658
	10,000	20,400		10,000		20,400

Workings

Labour = 400 hours @ £6 = £2,400
Overheads = 400 hours @ £15 = £6,000

Value per unit for output and abnormal loss $= \frac{£20,400 - £1,600}{10,000 - 2,000}$

$= £2.35$ per unit

Chapter 8
Cost bookkeeping

ACTIVITY 57

A £46,800

B £148,800

C £12,000

D £24,000

E £14,800

F £46,800

G £147,800

Work-in-progress account

	£000		£000
b/fwd	22.0	Finished goods control	148.8
Stores control	40.0	c/fwd	20.0
Wages control	60.0		
Production overhead control	46.8		
	168.8		168.8

Production overhead account

	£000		£000
Stores control	8.0	b/fwd	12.0
Wages control	12.0	WIP control	46.8
Expense creditors	24.0		
Profit and loss – over-absorption	14.8		
	58.8		58.8

Finished goods account

	£000		£000
b/fwd	3.0	Cost of sales	147.8
WIP control	148.8	c/fwd	4.0
	151.8		151.8

Workings

(W1) Production overheads absorbed

		£
Milling	£7.50 x 2,400	18,000
Turning	£8.00 x 1,800	14,400
Grinding	£9.00 x 1,600	14,400
		46,800

Chapter 9
Absorption and marginal costing

ACTIVITY 58

Voliti Limited

(i) *Marginal costing*

		Month 1	
	Units	£	£
Sales £30 pu	5,000		150,000
Opening stock	–	Nil	
Cost of production £10 + £5 + £8 = £23	6,500	149,500	
	6,500	149,500	
Closing stock £23 each	(1,500)	(34,500)	
Variable cost of sales	5,000		(115,000)
Contribution			35,000
Fixed costs			(19,500)
Profit			15,500

(ii) *Absorption costing*

		Month 1	
	Units	£	£
Sales £30	5,000		150,000
Opening stock	–	Nil	
Cost of production (Working) £10 + £5 + £8 + £3 = £26	6,500	169,000	
	6,500	169,000	
Closing stock £26 each	(1,500)	(39,000)	
Fully absorbed cost of sales	5,000		(130,000)
Profit			20,000

Working

Fixed overheads absorbed at $\frac{£19,500}{6,500 \text{ units}}$ = £3 per unit

Reconciliation of profits

	£
Profit under marginal costing	15,500
Add: fixed costs c/f in stock (1,500 x £3)	4,500
Profit under absorption costing	20,000

ACTIVITY 59

Alpha and Gamma

Absorption costing

	Product Alpha			Product Gamma		Total
	£	£		£	£	£
Sales						
31,600 x £1.15		36,340	52,600 x £2.40		126,240	
Opening stock (W1/W3)						
3,880 x £1.10	4,268		3,740 x £1.98	7,405		
Production						
30,600 x £1.10	33,660		52,800 x £1.98	104,544		
Closing stock (W2/W4)						
(2,880 x £1.10)	(3,168)		(3,940 x £1.98)	(7,801)		
		(34,760)			(104,148)	
Gross profit		1,580			22,092	23,672
Over-absorption (W5)						1,260
Sales and administration						(19,160)
Net profit						5,772

Workings

(W1) *Cost per unit of Alpha*

Variable cost per unit + Fixed cost per unit

Variable cost per unit = Total variable cost/units produced in period

$$= \frac{£15,300}{30,600}$$

$$= £0.50 \text{ per unit}$$

Fixed costs are absorbed at a rate of £9.00 per machine hour (given in the question).

Production of 30,600 units required 2,040 hours. This means that each unit of Alpha took $\frac{2,040}{30,600}$ = 0.067 hours. At £9.00 per hour this means each unit absorbs 0.067 x £9.00 = £0.60.

Production cost per unit of Alpha = £0.50 + £0.60 = £1.10

(W2) Closing stock of Alpha = 3,880 + 30,600 – 31,600 = 2,880 units

(W3) Cost per unit of Gamma

Variable cost per unit $= \frac{£64,944}{52,800} = £1.23$ per unit

Fixed cost $= £9.00 \times \frac{4,400}{52,800}$ (rate per machine hour x machine hours per unit)

$=$ £0.75 per unit

Total cost per unit = £1.23 + £0.75 = £1.98 per unit

(W4) Closing stock of Gamma = 3,740 + 52,800 – 52,600 = 3,940

(W5) Over/under absorption

Total overheads absorbed (actual machine hours x £9.00 per machine hour)

= (2,040 x £9.00) + (4,400 x £9.00) = £57,960

Total expenditure = £56,700

Over absorption = £1,260

Chapter 10
CVP analysis and limiting factors

ACTIVITY 60

Approach to limiting factor questions

Step 1 Identify the limiting factor, this will either be given in the question or you may need to calculate it.

Step 2 Calculate the contribution per unit for each product/service competing for the limiting factor.

Step 3 Calculate the contribution per limiting factor per unit for each product/service competing for the limiting factor.

Step 4 Rank the products/services in the order which maximises the contribution per limiting factor per unit.

Step 5 Allocate the limiting factor and devise the optimum production plan.

Answer Task 60.1

Hours of installation labour required to satisfy maximum demand

		Hours
Day scan:	2,000 units x 3 hours/unit (£24/£8)	6,000
Night scan:	3,000 units x 4 hours/unit (£32/£8)	12,000
Omni scan:	1,800 units x 5.5 hours/unit (£44/£8)	9,900
		27,900
Available hours		25,000
Shortfall		2,900

Answer Task 60.2

	Day scan	Night scan	Omni scan
	£	£	£
Selling price	250	320	460
Variable costs			
Materials	(70)	(110)	(155)
Manufacturing labour	(40)	(55)	(70)
Installation labour	(24)	(32)	(44)
Variable overheads	(16)	(20)	(28)
Contribution per unit	100	103	163
Installation hours required	3	4	5.5
Contribution per installation hour	£33.33	£25.75	£29.64
Production priority	1st	3rd	2nd

Best production plan

	Units	Hours used
Day scan to maximum demand	2,000 (x 3)	6,000
Omni scan to maximum demand	1,800 (x 5.5)	9,900

This leaves (25,000 – 6,000 – 9,900) = 9,100 installation labour hours for Night scan

Therefore production of Night scan = $\frac{9,100}{4}$ = 2,275 units

Answer Task 60.3

Maximum profit achievable

	Day scan	Omni scan	Night scan	Total
Units	2,000	1,800	2,275	
	£	£	£	£
Contribution	200,000	293,400	234,325	727,725
Fixed costs				(450,000)
Maximum profit				277,725

△ ACTIVITY 61

		A		B
		£		£
Sales price per unit		16.20		22.80
Variable costs per unit	4.00 + 2.00 + 0.50 =	6.50	6.00 + 4.00 + 0.50 =	10.50
Contribution per unit		9.70		12.30
Labour hours per unit	(£2/£10)	0.2	(£4/£10)	0.4
Contribution per labour hour		£48.50		£30.75

Conclusion: manufacture as many units of A as possible.

This requires 10,000 x 0.2 = 2,000 hours

The remaining 4,000 – 2,000 = 2,000 hours can be used to produce units of B

This allows 5,000 units of B to be made.

We therefore produce 10,000 units of A and 5,000 units of B.

Answer Task 61.2

	A	B	Total
	£	£	£
Sales (10,000 units, 5,000 units)	162,000	114,000	276,000
Variable costs (£6.50, £10.50)	(65,000)	(52,500)	(117,500)
Contribution	97,000	61,500	158,500
Fixed costs (W1)			(60,000)
Profit			98,500

Working

(W1) *Fixed production overheads*

Using (say) product A: fixed overheads per unit = £3; Labour hours per unit = 0.2.

Thus fixed overheads per hour = £3/0.2 = £15.

Maximum hours available = 4,000.

Fixed production overheads budgeted at 4,000 x £15 = £60,000.

△ ACTIVITY 62

	Product		
	A	*B*	*C*
	£	£	£
Selling price	110	150	180
Ipethin	(35)	(24)	(65)
Labour	(24)	(64)	(32)
Contribution	51	62	83
Limiting factor (kg of Ipethin)	1.4	0.96	2.6
Contribution per unit of limiting factor	£36.43	£64.58	£31.92
Preferred order of manufacture	2	1	3

ACTIVITY 63

	A	*B*	*C*	*D*
		Product		
Contribution (W1)	£16	£17	£23	£22
Unit machine hours	4	3	4	5
Contribution per machine hour	£4	£5.67	£5.75	£4.40
Ranking	4	2	1	3

Product		Quantity Units	Machine Hours	Contribution £
C		250	1,000	5,750
B		180	540	3,060
D	(to balance)	92	460	2,024
			2,000	10,834
	Fixed costs			8,000 *
	Profit			2,834

* Fixed OAR = £8 per hour
1,000 labour hours x £8.00 per hour = £8,000

Workings

(W1) Contribution per unit

		A	*B*	*C*	*D*
		£	£	£	£
Selling price		28	30	45	42
Less:	Direct material	5	6	8	6
	Direct labour	4	4	8	8
	Variable overhead	3	3	6	6
Contribution/Unit		16	17	23	22

ACTIVITY 64

Answer Task 64.1

Steps to follow:

Step 1 Identify the highest and lowest activity levels and their costs.

Step 2 Subtract the cost at the lowest activity level from the cost at the highest activity level. If there is a difference this represents variable cost. If there is no difference then the cost must be fixed and no further steps are required.

Step 3 Calculate the variable cost per unit by dividing the difference in cost by the difference in activity.

Step 4 Calculate the total variable cost at the highest or lowest activity level and identify any difference between variable and total costs. If there is no difference all of the cost must be variable, if there is a difference this must be the fixed cost element.

Note: Usually activity is measured in units (sales or production). However here we only have information about sales value Assuming the same selling price in August and September, this will directly relate to sales units and can be used in a similar way to extract the fixed and variable cost of sales elements.

	Cost of sales	Sales
Highest	£55,000	£90,000
Lowest	£50,000	£80,000
Difference	£5,000	£10,000

Variable cost per £1 of sales = $\frac{£5,000}{£10,000}$ = £0.50 (or 50% of sales)

Substitute into highest (say)

Total cost	=	£55,000
Variable cost = £90,000 Sales x 50p/£	=	£45,000
Fixed cost = Difference		£10,000

Answer Task 64.2

Fixed costs £25,000

Contribution per unit £32,000/8,000 =£4

Breakeven sales $\frac{£25,000}{£4}$ = 6,250 units

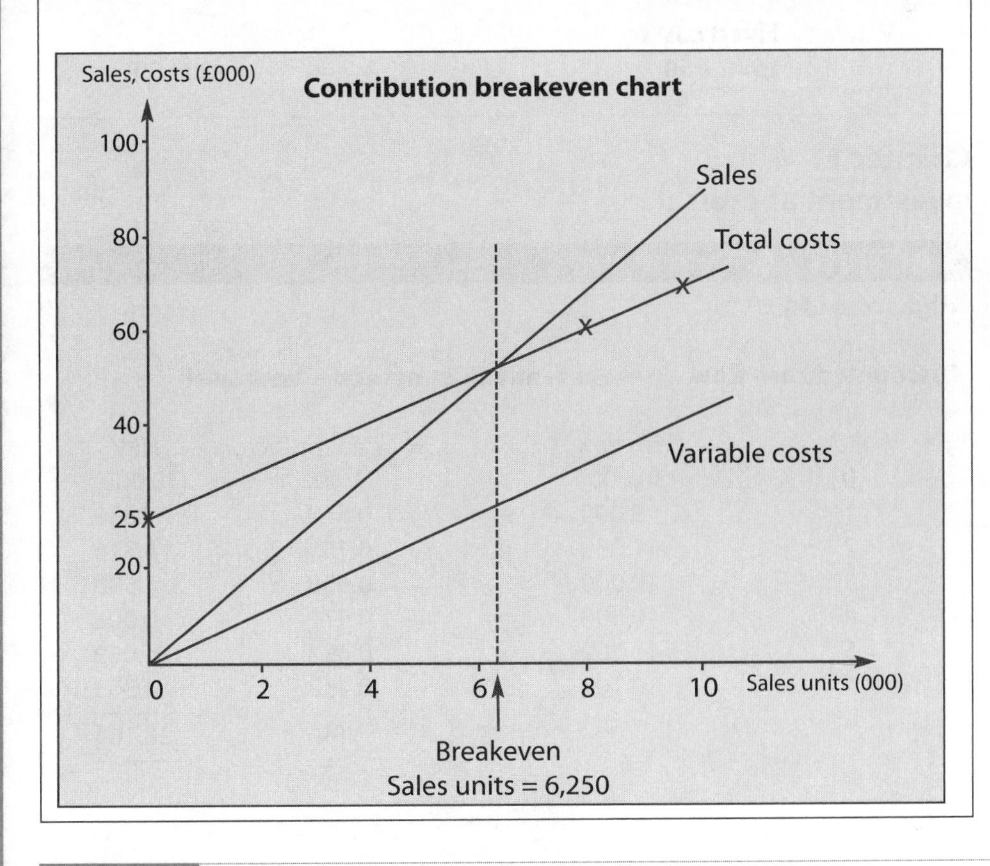

ACTIVITY 65

(a) Weekly fixed costs are £570; C/S ratio is 0.6
Weekly breakeven sales £570/0.6 = £950

(b)

	Bar	Restaurant	Total
	£	£	£
Sales (W1)	75,000	40,000	115,000
Variable costs (W2)	30,000	16,000	46,000
Contribution	45,000	24,000	69,000
Fixed costs (W3)			28,500
Profit			40,500

Workings

(W1) **Sales**

Restaurant sales (40 x £20) x 50	=	£40,000
Bar sales £1,500 x 50	=	£75,000

(W2) **Variable cost**

If contribution is 60% of Bar Sales/Restaurant then variable cost must be 40%.

Bar = £75,000 x 40%	=	£30,000
Restaurant = £40,000 x 40%	=	£16,000
Total variable cost	=	£46,000

(W3) **Fixed costs**

£570 x 50	=	£28,500

Chapter 11
Investment appraisal

ACTIVITY 66

Highscore Ltd

Discounted cash flow – Net Present Value method – appraisal

Year	*Cash flow*	*15% discount factor*	*NPV*
0	(30,000)	1.00	(30,000)
1	9,000	0.870	7,830
2	11,000	0.756	8,316
3	10,000	0.658	6,580
4	10,500	0.572	6,006
5	10,200	0.497	5,069
6	10,100	0.432	4,363
		NPV	£8,164

ACTIVITY 67

Whitby Engineering Factors

Discounted cash flow (NPV method)

Year	*Cash flow*	*12% discount factor*	*NPV*
0	(50,000)	1.00	(50,000)
1	18,000	0.893	16,074
2	20,000	0.797	15,940
3	21,000	0.712	14,952
4	22,000	0.636	13,992
5	18,000	0.567	10,206
		NPV	£21,164

As the NPV is positive, the project is achieving a rate of return in excess of 12% - the business' cost of capital.

The business should therefore accept the project.

ACTIVITY 68

(a)

Discount factors

Time	Cash flow £	0%	PV 0%	10%	PV 10%	20%	PV 20%
0	(285,400)	1.000	(285,400)	1.000	(285,400)	1.000	(285,400)
1	102,000	1.000	102,000	0.909	92,718	0.833	84,966
2	124,000	1.000	124,000	0.826	102,424	0.694	86,056
3	146,000	1.000	146,000	0.751	109,646	0.579	84,534
Net present value			£86,600		£19,388		(£29,844)

(b)

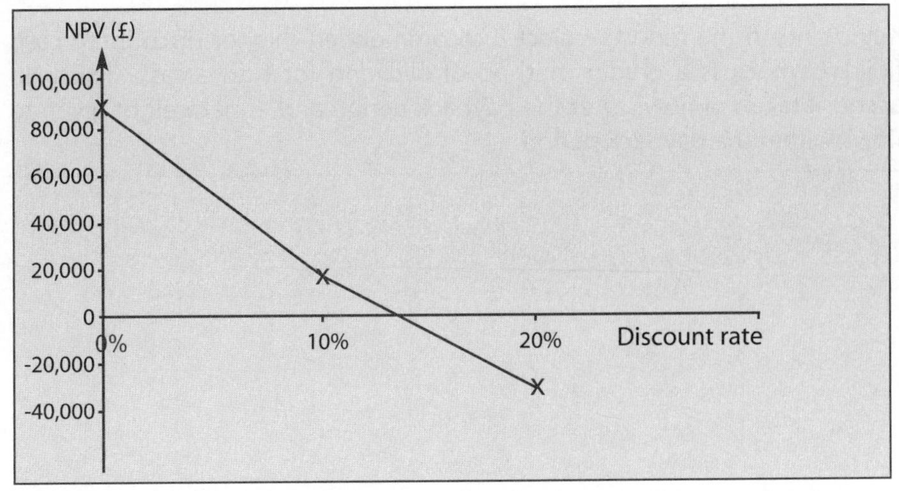

(c) The IRR is approximately 14.5%.

ACTIVITY 69

(a)

	£
Cost of machine	(220,000)
Three years of cash profits (3 x 10,000 x £8)	240,000
Present value at 0%	20,000

(b)

	Cost of machine	Cash from sales	Net cash flow	10% discount factor	PV
	£	£	£		£
Time 0	(220,000)		(220,000)	1.000	(220,000)
Time 1		80,000	80,000	0.909	72,720
Time 2		80,000	80,000	0.826	66,080
Time 3		80,000	80,000	0.751	60,080
Net present value					(21,120)

ACTIVITY 70

		Project A		Project B	
	10% discount factor	Cash flow	DCF	Cash	DCF
		£	£	£	£
Initial outlay	1.000	(75,000)	(75,000)	(100,000)	(100,000)
Annual cash savings					
1st year	0.909	20,000	18,180	30,000	27,270
2nd year	0.826	30,000	24,780	45,000	37,170
3rd year	0.751	30,000	22,530	45,000	33,795
4th year	0.683	25,000	17,075	40,000	27,320
5th year	0.621	20,000	12,420	–	–
			19,985		25,555

Key points in the report: Project B recommended (higher discounted cash flow). Payback is a cruder method of allowing for future cash flows. No account taken of flows after the payback period and equal weight given to flows within the payback period.

ACTIVITY 71

Transport company

MEMORANDUM

To: General Manager
From: Assistant management accountant
Date: 13 June 20X4
Subject: Report on proposal to purchase vehicle cleansing machine

(1, 2) The results of the investment appraisal

I have carried out an appraisal of this proposal using the net present value method and the payback method. The results of my calculations are shown in the Appendix.

The cash flows from the project are forecast to pay back the initial outlay in approximately 2.7 years, which is a long payback period for a project with a life of only four years.

However, the project generates a positive net present value of £11,995. This means that the wealth of the company would be increased by this amount if the project is undertaken.

(3) A recommendation concerning the proposal

Since the proposal is forecast to result in a positive net present value, I recommend that it should be accepted.

If I can be of any further assistance in this matter, please do not hesitate to contact me.

Appendix: appraisal calculations

The net present value of the cashflows from the project

Year	*Total cash flow*	*Discount factor*	*Present value*
	£		£
0	(80,000)	1.000	(80,000)
1	29,600	0.909	26,906
2	29,200	0.826	24,119
3	28,780	0.751	21,614
4	28,339	0.683	19,356
		Net present value	11,995

Payback period

Year	*Cumulative cash flow*
	£
0	(80,000)
1	(50,400)
2	(21,200)
3	7,580

Payback period = 2 + (21,200/28,780) years = 2.7 years approx, assuming even cash flows.

△ ACTIVITY 72

Printing company

(a)

Time	Cash	P/V factor	P/V
	£	12%	
0	(14,400)	1	(14,400)
1	6,920	0.893	6,180
2	6,920	0.797	5,515
3	6,920	0.712	4,927
4	6,920	0.636	4,401
		Net Present Value	6,623

(b) Payback period $\frac{£14,400}{£6,920}$ = 2.1 years, assuming even cash flows:

The advantages of the payback method include the following:

(1) It is simple to calculate and understand.

(2) It helps to preserve an organisation's liquidity, by focusing on early cash flows.

(3) It helps to reduce risk, since it places less emphasis on later cash flows, which can be difficult to forecast with any certainty.

The disadvantages include the following:

(1) It ignores cash flows after the payback period. These may be substantial and potentially large profits may be forgone.

(2) It does not help to distinguish between proposals which have the same or similar payback periods.

(3) It does not quantify the time value of money, i.e. the fact that cash received earlier can be reinvested by the organisation.

ACTIVITY 73

MEMORANDUM

To: The divisional accountant
From: Assistant management accountant
Date: 7 December 20X5
Subject: Capital appraisal of new machine

As a result of using discounted cash flow, the net present value of the project is £45,600 and so the proposal appears to be worthwhile. This amount represents the gain to the company in the equivalent of pounds today from carrying out the proposal.

Taking risk into account brings in greater complexities. Although not always so, risk often increases with time. The further into the future are the cash flows, the more uncertain they tend to become. Because of this, many organisations supplement the net present appraisal with the payback period. The proposal has a payback of 2½ years. Should it be terminated within that period, it will not have added any value to the company. The payback period on its own, however, is inadequate as it ignores the value of any possible positive cash flows beyond the period.

Recommendation

Given that the proposal has a positive Net Present Value at 25 per cent, it meets the company's requirements for investment proposals. Before finally deciding whether or not to go ahead with the project, further consideration should be given to any risk inherent in such a long payback period.

Appendix 1 Investment appraisal (£)

End of year	*Cash flow £*	*Discount factor*	*Discounted cash flow*
0	(600,000)	1.000	(600,000)
1	240,000	0.800	192,000
2	240,000	0.640	153,600
3	240,000	0.512	122,880
4	240,000	0.410	98,400
5	240,000	0.328	78,720
		Net Present Value	45,600

Appendix 2 Payback period

Payback period = $\frac{£600{,}000}{£240{,}000}$ = 2½ years (assuming even cash flows).

MOCK SIMULATION ANSWERS

TASKS 1 AND 2

STORES LEDGER ACCOUNT

Material description: Detergent powder: 20-kg boxes
Code number: DP70

Maximum quantity 64
Minimum quantity 20
Reorder level 32
Reorder quantity 35

Date	Receipts			Issues			Stock balance		
	Quantity	Price £ per box	Total £	Quantity	Price £ per box	Total £	Quantity	Price £ per box	Total £
April 6									
							22	26.50	583.00
							35	26.80	938.00
							57		1,521.00
April 8									
				22	26.50	583.00			
				8	26.80	214.40			
				30		797.40	27	26.80	723.60
April 13									
	35	26.85	939.75				27	26.80	723.60
							35	26.85	939.75
							62		1,663.35
April 14									
				20	26.80	536.00	7	26.80	187.60
							35	26.85	939.75
							42		1,127.35
April 15				2	26.80	53.60	5	26.80	134.00
							35	26.85	939.75
							40		1,073.75

STORES LEDGER ACCOUNT

Material description: Fabric conditioner: 6-litre bottles
Code number: FC45

Maximum quantity 16
Minimum quantity 4
Reorder level 11
Reorder quantity 7

Date	Receipts			Issues			Stock balance		
	Quantity	Price £ per bottle	Total £	Quantity	Price £ per bottle	Total £	Quantity	Price £ per bottle	Total £
April 6							5	3.15	15.75
							7	3.20	22.40
							12		38.15
April 7	7	3.22	22.54				5	3.15	15.75
							7	3.20	22.40
							7	3.22	22.54
							19		60.69
April 14				5	3.15	15.75	5	3.20	16.00
				2	3.20	6.40	7	3.22	22.54
				7		22.15	12		38.54

STORES LEDGER ACCOUNT

Material description: Cellophane packaging: 100-metre rolls
Code number: CP09

Maximum quantity 56
Minimum quantity 16
Reorder level 30
Reorder quantity 28

Date	Receipts			Issues			Stock balance		
	Quantity	Price £ per roll	Total £	Quantity	Price £ per roll	Total £	Quantity	Price £ per roll	Total £
April 6							24	2.10	50.40
April 7				4	2.10	8.40	20	2.10	42.00
April 8	22	2.00	44.00				20	2.10	42.00
							22	2.00	44.00
							42		86.00
April 14				8	2.10	16.80	12	2.10	25.20
							22	2.00	44.00
							34		69.20

MATERIAL REQUISITION

Raised by: Sheila Barlow   Serial number: 864

Issue to cost centre: Washing/drying   Date: 14 April

Code number	Description	Quantity	Cost office only	
			Total value of issue £	Account number to be charged
FC45	Fabric conditioner	7 bottles	22.15	100/100

Authorised by: S Barlow   Received by: SB

MATERIAL REQUISITION

Raised by: Sheila Barlow   Serial number: 867

Issue to cost centre: Washing/drying   Date: 14 April

Code number	Description	Quantity	Cost office only	
			Total value of issue £	Account number to be charged
DP70	Detergent powder	20 boxes	536.00	100/100

Authorised by: S Barlow   Received by: SB

MATERIAL REQUISITION

Raised by: Wayne Peacock   Serial number: 869

Issue to cost centre: Packing   Date: 14 April

Code number	Description	Quantity	Cost office only	
			Total value of issue £	Account number to be charged
CP09	Packaging	8 rolls	16.80	300/100

Authorised by: Wayne   Received by: WP

MATERIAL REQUISITION

Raised by: Janet Greaves   Serial number: 872

Issue to cost centre: Canteen   Date: 15 April

Code number	Description	Quantity	Cost office only	
			Total value of issue £	Account number to be charged
DP70	Detergent powder	2 boxes - for use in washing tea towels, etc	53.60	500/840

Authorised by: J Greaves   Received by: JG

TASK 3

MEMORANDUM

To: Sue Baker
From: Terry Wallis
Date: 23 April 20X8
Subject: Stock Control Policy

I refer to the stock ledger account for code FC45 fabric conditioner – 6-litre bottles and note that the stock control policy has not been adhered to this period.

The maximum stock level has been set at a quantity of 16, whereas on the 7 April the actual quantity held in stock was 19 units.

It is apparent that this excess stockholding was the result of an order being raised before the reorder level had been reached.

The order had been raised early in the month, whereas the reorder level would not have occurred until an issue on the 14 April. The actual value of the stockholding in this case is not significant, however there are other areas where, if there are similar occurrences, the stockholding is much more in terms of value.

We need to ensure that pre-set policies are adhered to.

It is also noted that the reorder quantity for CP09 cellophane packaging is 28, whereas the delivery received on 8 April was for 22 rolls. We need to check with the person responsible for this order whether the incorrect amount was ordered or if this is a part delivery by the supplier.

TASK 4

Calculation of gross wages for week 42 – full-time laundry and packing operatives

	Washing/ drying			*Ironing/ pressing*			*Packing*			*Other*			*Overtime premium*			*Total gross wages excluding bonus*
	Hrs	rate	£	Hrs	rate	£	Hrs	rate	£	Hrs	rate	£	Hrs	rate	£	£
Employee number: 649 grade: 3 hours	8	6	48	23	6	138				7	6	42	3	3	9	237
Employee number: 653 grade: 4 hours	9	8	72	24	8	192				7	8	56	5	4	20	340
Employee number: 658 grade: 4 hours	5	8	40	18	8	144				14	8	112	2	4	8	304
Employee number: 663 grade: 3 hours							35	6	210	3	6	18	3	3	9	237
Totals			160			474			210			228			46	1,118

Apportionment of productivity bonus for the week

Employee number	Total gross wages excluding bonus £	Bonus apportioned pro rata £	Total gross wages for the week £
649	237.00	15.90	252.90
653	340.00	22.81	362.81
658	304.00	20.39	324.39
663	237.00	15.90	252.90
	1,118.00	75.00	1,193.00

TASK 5

Calculation of part-time employees' gross wages – week 42
Washing/drying:

Workings: 12 hours x £6

Answer: part-time wages payable (excluding bonus) = £72.00

Ironing/pressing:

Workings: 23 hours x £6

Answer: part-time wages payable (excluding bonus) = £138.00

Packing:

Workings: 15 hours x £6

Answer: part-time wages payable (excluding bonus) = £90.00

Bonus payment, all part-time employees:

Workings: 50 hours x £0.22

Answer: part-time bonus payable = £11.00

Total part-time gross wages (including bonus) = £311.00

(**Note**: You are not required to calculate the wages due to any individual part-time employee.)

TASK 6

COST LEDGER DATA ENTRY SHEET

Week number: 42

Debit accounts:

Cost centre code	Expenditure code	Amount to be debited £
100	300	160.00
200	300	474.00
200	600	46.00
200	650	86.00
200	660	228.00
300	300	510.00
Check total: total wages for week, laundry operatives and packing, full-time and part-time		1,504.00

Workings

Code		*Amount to be debited* £
100/300	(from Task 4)	160
200/300	(from Task 4)	474
200/600	(from Task 4)	46
200/650	(£75 + £11)	86
200/660	(from Task 4)	228
300/300	(£210 + £311 – £11 bonus)	510
Check total:	(£1,193 + £311)	1,504

TASK 7

FULL TIME EMPLOYEES: RECONCILIATION OF CLOCK HOURS

Employee number	Clock hours	Timesheet	Difference
649	31	31	–
653	33	33	–
658	25	23	2
663	38	38	–
	127	125	2

Note of any discrepancies to be referred to Administration Manager

Note: There was an under-recording of clock hours to the timesheet by employee 658.

TASK 8

MARSDEN OILS

98 Street Lane
Swinbury
Chopshire SR3 7WR
Telephone: 01845 350162 Fax: 01845 350163

Executive Shirts Limited
87 High Street
Swinbury
Chopshire SR7 3PL

VAT registration: 435 8720 76

Date/tax point: 15 April 20X8

INVOICE

	£
Lubricating oils for washing machine Three cases	21.00
VAT @ 17.5%	3.67
Invoice total	**24.67**

Charge to account code number:
100/200
£21.00

Terms: 30 days from date of invoice

MULTIPARTS LIMITED

52 Fairway Industrial Estate
Swinbury
Chopshire SR3 3UK
Telephone: 01845 938264 Fax: 01845 938265

Executive Shirts Limited
87 High Street
Swinbury
Chopshire SR7 3PL

VAT registration: 435 7175 98

Date/tax point: 17 April 20X8

INVOICE

	£
Supply of machine part – urgent order, your ref 'Sue'	76.90
VAT @ 17.5%	13.45
Invoice total	**90.35**

Charge to account code number:
900/900
£76.90

Terms: 30 days from date of invoice

THE RAPID REPAIR COMPANY

24 Leazdon Lane
Swinbury
Chopshire SR3 6HT
Telephone: 01845 350162 Fax: 01845 350163

Executive Shirts Limited
87 High Street
Swinbury
Chopshire SR7 3PL

VAT registration: 928 33350 65

Date/tax point: 7 April 20X8

INVOICE

	£
Repair to industrial ironing machine	34.00
VAT @ 17.5%	5.95
Invoice total	**39.95**

Charge to account code number:
200/710
£34.00

Terms: 30 days from date of invoice
0.5% discount for payment within 15 days

THE QUALITY CATERING COMPANY

Fairway Industrial Estate
Swinbury
Chopshire SR3 7GJ
Telephone: 01845 930264 Fax: 01845 930265

Executive Shirts Limited
87 High Street
Swinbury
Chopshire SR7 3PL

VAT registration: 465 9242 14

Date/tax point: 17 April 20X8

INVOICE

	£
12 cases of paper napkins, delivered to canteen	60.00
VAT @ 17.5%	10.50
Invoice total	**70.50**

Charge to account code number:
500/840
£60.00

Terms: 30 days from date of invoice

TASK 9

MEMORANDUM

To: Sue Baker
From: Terry Wallis
Date: 5 May 20X8
Subject: Coding of Invoices

I refer to an invoice received from Multiparts Ltd dated 17 April for the supply of a machine part – per our urgent order ref 'Sue'.

I have coded this to suspense as I am unsure from the invoice which cost centre this machine part is for.

Could you please inform me of the location of this machine, so that I can allocate the cost to the relevant centre, by a transfer from suspense.

TASK 10

OVERHEAD ANALYSIS SHEET: 20X8/X9

Overhead expense: primary apportionments and allocations	Basis of allocation/ apportionment	Total £	Washing/ drying £	Ironing/ pressing £	Packing £	Stores £	Canteen £
Supervisory salaries	Allocated	42,000	12,750	16,500	12,750		
Stores salary	Allocated	13,000				13,000	
Canteen expenses	Allocated	8,510					8,510
Electricity	Area	1,855	455	595	315	210	280
Depreciation	Equipment values	2,140	800	560	240	360	180
Admin costs	No of employees	2,400	600	1,050	300	300	150
Other overheads	Apportioned evenly	1,500	300	300	300	300	300
Total of primary allocations		71,405	14,905	19,005	13,905	14,170	9,420
Reapportion canteen			2,512	4,396	1,256	1,256	(9,420)
Reapportion stores			4,285	3,428	7,713	(15,426)	
Total production cost centre overhead		71,405	21,702	26,829	22,874		
Number of batches			9,000	9,000	9,000		
Overhead absorption rate per batch for 20X8/X9			£2.41	£2.98	£2.54		

TASK 11

MEMORANDUM

To: Sue Baker
From: Terry Wallis
Date: 21 May 20X8
Subject: Apportionment of Overhead

I refer to your memo of 15 May regarding the apportionment of overhead and in particular the treatment of electricity costs.

We have used floor area as the basis, but as both the 'washing and drying' cost centre and the 'ironing and pressing' centre are using equipment, it would be more appropriate to estimate the usage by assessing the kilowatt hours for each, based on the operating hours to achieve the planned output of 9,000 batches. The packing cost centre uses little equipment.

We could also accurately estimate the electricity usage in the canteen and stores. We need to discuss this issue further so that we can proceed with the estimate of usage.

TASK 12

(a)

Process 1 account (full)

	Units	£		Units	£
Raw materials	200,000	288,013	Output (W3)	191,450	
Materials added	–	–		@ £2.576	493,175
Labour	–	94,208	Normal loss		
Overheads	–	117,760	(W1) and (W2)	8,200	
				@ £0.72	5,904
			Abnormal loss		
			(W3)	350	
				@ £2.576	902
	200,000	499,981		200,000	499,981

(W1) Normal loss = 4.1% of input = 4.1% x 200,000 = 8,200 units

(W2) Value of normal loss = £0.72 therefore total value = 8,200 x £0.72 = £5,904

(W3) Value per unit of output and abnormal loss

$$= \frac{\text{Total cost} - \text{Scrap value of normal loss}}{\text{Units input} - \text{Normal loss}}$$

$$= \frac{499{,}981 - 5{,}904}{200{,}000 - 8{,}200} = \frac{494{,}077}{191{,}800} = £2.576$$

(b)

Process 2 account (full)

	Units	£		Units	£
Input from			Output (W3)	185,968	
Process 1	191,450	493,175		@ £4.211	783,111
Materials			Normal loss		
added	–	151,965	(W1) and (W2)	5,744	
Labour	–	68,674		@ £1.04	5,974
Overheads					
(=108% x labour)	–	74,168			
Abnormal gain					
(W3)	262				
	@ £4.211	1,103			
	191,712	789,085		191,712	789,085

(W1) Normal loss units = 3.0% of input = 3.0% x 191,450 = 5,744

(W2) Scrap value of normal loss = £1.04 per unit = 5,744 x £1.04 = £5,974

(W3) Value of output and abnormal gain

$$= \frac{£(493{,}175 + 151{,}965 + 68{,}674 + 74{,}168 - 5{,}974}{191{,}450 - 5{,}744} = \frac{£782{,}008}{185{,}706}$$

=£4.211 per unit

TASK 13

(a) *Marginal costing*

		£	£
Sales	3,000 x 21		63,000
Cost of sales			
Opening stock		-	
Production	7,000 x 11	77,000	
Closing stock	(4,000) x 11	(44,000)	
			(33,000)
Contribution from production			30,000
Less actual fixed overheads			(28,000)
Profit for the period			2,000

(b) *Absorption costing*

		£	£
Sales	3,000 x 21		63,000
Cost of sales			
Opening stock		-	
Production	7,000 x 15	105,000	
Closing stock	(4,000) x 15	(60,000)	
			(45,000)
Profit for the period			18,000

Reconciliation of profits

	£
Profit under marginal costing	2,000
Add: fixed overheads in closing stock (4,000 x £4)	16,000
Profit under absorption costing	18,000

TASK 14

(a)

Time	Cost	Contribution	Scrap	Net cash flow (P/V 0%)	DF 10%	PV 10%	DF 20%	PV 20%
	£000	£000	£000	£000	£000	£000	£000	£000
0	(1,000)			(1,000)	1	(1,000)	1	(1,000)
1	(250)	350		100	0.909	90.90	0.833	83.30
2		350		350	0.826	289.10	0.694	242.90
3		350		350	0.751	262.85	0.579	202.65
4		350		350	0.683	239.05	0.482	168.70
5		350	10	360	0.621	223.56	0.402	144.72
				510		105.46		(157.73)

(b) The internal rate of return (IRR) is the discount rate at which the NPV of the project is zero. For the project above it can be seen that the NPV is positive for discount rates at least up to 10%; by the time we get to a discount rate of 20% the NPV has turned negative. The IRR is thus between these two rates – 14% (we are told). The internal rate of return can be thought of as a cut-off point for whether to invest in a project or not. If the company discovers that they can borrow below 14% then they should go ahead with the project; if above 14% then they should not.

MOCK EXAMINATION 1 ANSWERS

SECTION 1

Task 1.1

STOCK RECORD CARD FOR STEEL COMPONENT M								
	Receipts			Issues			Balance	
Date 2005	Quantity kg	Cost per kg (£)	Total cost (£)	Quantity kg	Cost per kg (£)	Total cost (£)	Quantity kg	£
Balance as at 1 May							25,000	50,000
9 May	30,000	2.30	69,000				55,000	119,000
12 May				40,000	25,000 x 2.00 15,000 x 2.30	50,000 34,500 84,500	15,000	34,500
18 May	20,000	2.50	50,000				35,000	84,500
27 May				10,000	10,000 x 2.30	23,000	25,000	61,500

The FIFO method assumes that issues will be made from the oldest stock available, leaving the latest purchases in stock.

Therefore, the issue of 40,000 kg on 12 May is valued as follows:

(1)	25,000 kg @ £2 per kg	=	£50,000
(2)	15,000 kg @ £2.30 per kg	=	£34,500
			£84,500

Note that (1) is made up of the oldest stock items (in stock on 1 May) and (2) is made up of the next oldest stock items (purchased on 9 May).

Task 1.2

JOURNAL

Date 2005	Code	Dr £	Cr £
9 May	306	69,000	
9 May	500		69,000
12 May	401	84,500	
12 May	306		84,500
18 May	306	50,000	
18 May	500		50,000
27 May	402	23,000	
27 May	306		23,000

In cost bookkeeping, remember that stock received is debited to the stocks of component M account, and when stock is used in production the stock value used is credited from the stocks of component M account and debited to the relevant work-in-progress account.

Task 1.3

Total hours worked	=	8,000 + 1,500 + 1,000	=	10,500
				£
Normal hours worked – cost	=	10,500 hours x £7	=	73,500
Overtime (time and a half)	=	1,500 hours x £7 x 0.5	=	5,250
Overtime (double time)	=	1,000 hours x £7	=	7,000
Total cost of direct labour – Product C				85,750

Task 1.4

Fixed overhead	Basis of allocation or apportionment	Total £	Machining 1 £	Machining 2 £	Assembly £	Packaging £
Depreciation	Net book value (W1)	80,000	32,000	8,000	24,000	16,000
Rent and rates	Square metres occupied (W2)	120,000	30,000	12,000	24,000	54,000
Indirect labour costs	Allocated	97,900	40,500	18,300	12,400	26,700
Direct assembly costs	Allocated	15,600			15,600	
Totals		313,500	102,500	38,300	76,000	96,700

Workings

(W1) Depreciation is commonly apportioned on the basis of net book values.

Total depreciation cost = £80,000

Total net book value of fixed assets = £3,200,000

Depreciation apportioned to Machining 1 = $\frac{\text{NBV of fixed assets in Machining 1}}{\text{Total NBV of fixed assets}}$ x Total depreciation

= $\frac{1,280,000}{3,200,000}$ x £80,000

= £32,000

Depreciation apportioned to Machining 2 = $\frac{320,000}{3,200,000}$ x £80,000

= £8,000

Depreciation apportioned to Assembly = $\frac{960,000}{3,200,000}$ x £80,000

= £24,000

Depreciation apportioned to Packaging = $\frac{640,000}{3,200,000}$ x £80,000

= £16,000

(W2) Rent and rates are commonly apportioned on the basis of square metres occupied.

Total rent and rates = £120,000

Total square metres occupied = 2,500

Rent and rates apportioned to Machining 1 = $\frac{\text{Square metres occupied by Maching 1}}{\text{Total square metres occupied}}$ x £120.000

= $\frac{625}{2,500}$ x £120,000

= £30,000

Rent and rates apportioned to Machining 2 = $\frac{250}{2,500}$ x £120,000

= £12,000

Rent and rates apportioned to Assembly = $\frac{500}{2,500}$ x £120,000

= £24,000

Rent and rates apportioned to Packaging = $\frac{1,125}{2,500}$ x £120,000

= £54,000

Note: Indirect labour costs are directly allocated to each department as are the direct assembly costs.

Task 1.5

$$\text{Budgeted fixed overhead absorption rate} = \frac{\text{Total dept overheads}}{\text{Total budgeted machine hours}}$$

$$= \frac{£400,000}{10,000 \text{ machine hours}}$$

$$= £40 \text{ per machine hour}$$

Note: The overhead absorption rate is calculated using total budgeted machine hours because the division concerned is **highly automated**.

Task 1.6

(a) (i) **Total variable costs**

	£ per unit
Direct materials	10.60
Direct labour	16.40
Prime cost	27.00
Variable overhead $\left(\frac{£60,000}{10,000}\right)$	6.00
Variable cost per unit	33.00

(ii) **Full absorption costing**

Full absorption costing includes a fixed overhead cost per unit.

$$\text{Fixed overhead per unit} = \frac{\text{Total fixed overheads}}{\text{Number of units produced}}$$

$$= \frac{£80,000}{10,000 \text{ units}}$$

$$= £8 \text{ per unit}$$

Therefore, £8 per unit must be added to the variable cost per unit of Product D calculated in part (i) above.

Marginal (variable) cost per unit	33
Fixed overhead per unit	8
Full absorption cost per unit	41

(b) **Fixed overhead under-recovery**

The overhead absorption rates calculated at the beginning of an accounting period are based upon **budgeted figures** (budgeted fixed overheads and budgeted output or usage). Overheads are usually recovered on the basis of machine or labour hours. It is unlikely that budgeted overheads and production levels will turn out to be exactly as estimated at the beginning of the accounting period and therefore the use of the pre-determined overhead absorption rate will give rise to an under- or over-recovery of overheads.

Under-recovery of fixed overheads is possible when:

- actual machine or labour hours are less than budgeted
- actual fixed overheads are greater than budgeted fixed overheads.

SECTION 2

Task 2.1

Product	Alpha £	Beta £	Gamma £	Total £
Sales revenue (W1)	50,000	24,000	40,000	114,000
Less Variable costs				
Direct materials (W2)	10,000	4,800	8,000	22,800
Direct labour – Centre A (W3)	10,000	4,000	7,500	21,500
Direct labour – Centre B (W4)	3,000	4,800	3,000	10,800
Total contribution (Sales revenue – variable costs)	27,000	10,400	21,500	58,900
Fixed overheads				52,000
Profit				6,900

Workings

(W1) **Sales revenue**

Sales revenue = sales units x selling price per unit
Alpha = 1,000 units x £50 = £50,000
Beta = 200 units x £120 = £24,000
Gamma = 500 units x £80 = £40,000

(W2) **Direct materials**

Direct materials = production units x direct materials per unit
Alpha = 1,000 units x £10 = £10,000
Beta = 200 units x £24 = £4,800
Gamma = 500 units x £16 = £8,000

(W3) **Direct labour – Centre A**

Direct labour = production units x direct labour hours per unit x rate per hour
Alpha = 1,000 units x 2 hours x £5 = £10,000
Beta = 200 units x 4 hours x £5 = £4,000
Gamma = 500 units x 3 hours x £5 = £7,500

(W4) **Direct labour – Centre B**

Alpha = 1,000 units x 0.5 hours x £6 = £3,000
Beta = 200 units x 4 hours x £6 = £4,800
Gamma = 500 units x 1 hour x £6 = £3,000

Task 2.2

Forecast contribution per unit $= \frac{\text{Total contribution}}{\text{Budgeted production level}}$

Forecast contribution per unit – Alpha $= \frac{£27,000}{1,000 \text{ units}} = £27$ per unit

Forecast contribution per unit – Beta $= \frac{£10,400}{200 \text{ units}} = £52$ per unit

Forecast contribution per unit – Gamma $= \frac{£21,500}{500 \text{ units}} = £43$ per unit

Task 2.3

Profits are maximised when contribution is maximised, i.e. when products are made in order of the contribution earned per unit of limiting factor.

	Alpha	Beta	Gamma
Contribution per unit (Task 2.2)	£27	£52	£43
Centre B hours per unit	0.5 hours	4 hours	1 hour
Contribution per Centre B labour hour*	£54	£13	£43
Rank	1st	3rd	2nd

* The Centre B labour hour is the limiting factor in this situation.

Contribution per Centre B labour hour $= \frac{\text{Contribution per unit}}{\text{Centre B hours per unit}}$

Product Alpha is ranked 1st and therefore Ray Ltd should manufacture and sell 1,000 units. Each unit of Product Alpha requires 0.5 Centre B labour hours per unit = 1,000 units x 0.5 labour hours = 500 labour hours.

Maximum availability = 1,400 direct labour hours

After making 1,000 units of Product Alpha, there will be 900 direct labour hours still available (1,400 hours – 500 hours).

Product Gamma is ranked 2nd and therefore Ray Ltd should aim to make 500 units of this product.

500 units of Product Gamma requires 500 direct labour hours (500 units x 1 labour hour per unit).

After making 500 units of Product Gamma, there will be 400 direct labour hours still available (900 hours – 500 hours).

All 400 direct labour hours should be used to manufacture Product Beta which requires 4 direct labour hours per unit.

$\therefore$ manufacture 100 units of Product Beta $\left(\frac{400 \text{ hours}}{4 \text{ hours per visit}} = 100 \text{ units}\right)$

Summary

Product	*Hours required*	*Units*
Alpha	500	1,000
Gamma	500	500
Beta	400	100
	1,400	1,600

Task 2.4

(a) Breakeven point $= \dfrac{\text{Fixed costs}}{\text{Contribution per unit (Beta)}}$

$= \dfrac{£52{,}000}{£52}$

$=$ 1,000 units

(b) Two reasons for not recommending this policy are as follows:

(i) Estimated sales in January = 200 units of Beta and it is therefore unlikely that the breakeven sales of 1,000 units is achievable.

(ii) Beta requires 4 direct labour hours per unit. Therefore, if 1,000 units needed to be manufactured and sold, this would require 4,000 direct labour hours (1,000 units ´ 4 direct labour hours per unit). Maximum direct labour hours available are limited to 1,400 per month and so it would not be possible to manufacture the 1,000 units of Beta required to breakeven.

Task 2.5

MEMORANDUM

To: Board of Directors
From: Accounting Technician
Date: 1 January 2005
Subject: Investment Appraisal

Payback

Payback period is an investment appraisal technique that involves calculating the amount of time it takes to recover or 'payback' a capital investment. It is not unusual for most organisations to set policies regarding payback periods. For example, if an organisation has a policy whereby investments are accepted if the payback period is less than four years, it will reject any projects where the recovery of the initial capital investment is more than four years. The Board of Directors has stated that the investment of £50,000 will be 'paid back' over three years.

Internal Rate of Return

The Internal Rate of Return (IRR) is defined as the discount rate that causes the cash flow of a project to have a Net Present Value equal to zero. Most organisations will only invest in a project if the IRR of the project is greater than a specified IRR. Depending on the policy of the company, an investment with an IRR of 12% will either be accepted or rejected if 12% is greater than the company's cost of capital.

Net Present Value

The Net Present Value (NPV) of an investment indicates whether an investment should be accepted or rejected. This method involves discounting future cash flows so that they are in today's terms (present values) and adding them up to give an NPV. In general, if the NPV is positive, then the project should be accepted (because the cash inflows are worth more than the outflows). Similarly, if the NPV is negative, then the cash inflows are worth less than the outflows.

Recommendation

It is recommended that the investment in new machinery should go ahead because it results in a positive NPV (£4,800).

MOCK EXAMINATION 2 ANSWERS

Task 1.1

STOCK CARD									
Product: Clay									
	Receipts			**Issues**			**Balance**		
Date	Quantity kg	Cost per kg (£)	Total cost (£)	Quantity kg	Cost per kg (£)	Total cost (£)	Quantity kg	Cost per kg (£)	Total cost (£)
B/f at 1 Nov							15,000	0.50	7,500
8 Nov	60,000	0.45	27,000				75,000		34,500
9 Nov				45,000	0.45	20,250	30,000		14,250
16 Nov	40,000	0.55	22,000				70,000		36,250
17 Nov				50,000	See working	26,500	20,000		9,750

Working

The LIFO method assumes that issues will be made from the newest stock available leaving the earliest purchases in stock.

Therefore, the issue of 50,000 kg on 17 November is valued as follows:
(1) 40,000 kg @ £0.55 per kg = £22,000
(2) 10,000 kg @ £0.45 per kg = £4,500

Note that (1) is made up of the newest stock items (purchased on 16 November) and (2) is made up of the next newest stock items (purchased on 8 November).

Task 1.2

Re-order level = maximum usage x maximum lead time

However, when buffer stocks are to be maintained, the formula for the re-order level is as follows:

Re-order level = Buffer stock + (maximum (budgeted) usage x maximum lead time)
= 25,000 + (25,000 x 2)
= 25,000 + 50,000
= 75,000 kg

(Buffer stock = one week's budgeted production = 25,000 kg)

Task 1.3

Code	Dr £	Cr £
1000	33,000	
7000		7,400
7001		5,100
9001		20,500

Gross direct labour costs are debited to the work-in-progress account where they are analysed further.

Task 1.4

Fixed overheads for November	Total £	Moulding £	Glazing £	Maintenance £	Canteen £
Indirect glazing materials (direct allocation)	1,140		1,140		
Rent and other property overheads (W1)	15,000	9,000	3,000	1,500	1,500
Power costs (direct allocation)	5,040	1,200	3,290	250	300
Indirect staff costs (direct allocation)	8,910	1,100	2,010	3,800	2,000
Machine depreciation (direct allocation)	8,310	1,710	6,600		
	38,400	13,010	16,040	5,550	3,800
Canteen (W2)		2,600	800	400	(3,800)
Maintenance (W3)		1,190	4,760	(5,950)	
	38,400	16,800	21,600		

Workings

(W1) **Rent and other property overheads**

Rent and other property overheads are apportioned on the basis of floor space.
Total rent and other property overheads = £15,000
Total floor space = (3,000 + 1,000 + 500 + 500) square metres
= 5,000 square metres

Overheads apportioned to Moulding centre $= \frac{\text{Moulding centre floor space}}{\text{Total floor space}}$ x Total property overheads

$= \frac{3{,}000}{5{,}000} \times £15{,}000$

$= £9{,}000$

Overheads apportioned to Glazing centre $= \frac{1{,}000}{5{,}000} \times £15{,}000 = £3{,}000$

Overheads apportioned to Maintenance centre $= \frac{500}{5{,}000} \times £15{,}000 = £1{,}500$

Overheads apportioned to Canteen $= \frac{500}{5{,}000} \times £15{,}000 = £1{,}500$

(W2) **Canteen overheads**

Canteen overheads after allocation and apportionment = £3,800

Re-apportioned to Moulding centre $= \frac{\text{Moulding centre employees}}{\text{Total employees}}$ x £3,800

$= \frac{26}{(26 + 8 + 4)} \times £3{,}800$

$= \frac{26}{38} \times £3{,}800$

$= £2{,}600$

Re-apportioned to Glazing centre $= \frac{8}{38} \times £3{,}800 = £800$

Re-apportioned to Maintenance centre $= \frac{4}{38} \times £3{,}800 = £400$

(W3) **Re-apportionment of Maintenance centre overheads**

Total Maintenance centre overheads after Canteen re-apportionment = £5,950
Re-apportioned to Moulding centre = 20% x £5,950 = £1,190
Re-apportioned to Glazing centre = 80% x £5,950 = £4,760

Task 1.5

(a) Budgeted overhead absorption rates $= \frac{\text{Budgeted fixed overheads}}{\text{Budgeted machine or labour hours}}$

(i) **Moulding centre**

Budgeted overhead absorption rate $= \frac{\text{£16,800}}{\text{Budgeted labour hours}}$

$= \frac{\text{£16,800}}{\text{4,000 labour hours}}$

= £4.20 per labour hour

(ii) **Glazing centre**

Budgeted overhead absorption rate $= \frac{\text{£21,600}}{\text{Budgeted machine hours}}$

$= \frac{\text{£21,600}}{\text{6,000 machine hours}}$

= £3.60 per machine hour

(b) (i) **Moulding centre**

	£
Actual overheads	17,200
Overheads absorbed (4,200 hours x £4.20)	17,640
Over-absorbed overheads	440

(ii) **Glazing centre**

	£
Actual overheads	20,850
Overheads absorbed (5,600 hours x £3.60)	20,160
Under-absorbed overheads	690

Task 1.6

Budgeted overhead cost per unit $= \frac{\text{Budgeted overheads}}{\text{Budgeted activity level}}$

If the budgeted activity in the Moulding and Glazing centres is increased, then the overhead cost per unit will fall and less overhead will be charged to an individual product.

SECTION 2

Task 2.1

(a)

Units made	*1,000,000*	*1,500,000*	*2,000,000*
Costs:	£	£	£
Variable costs:			
· **direct materials (W1)**	5,000,000	7,500,000	10,000,000
· **direct labour (W2)**	4,600,000	6,900,000	9,200,000
· **overheads (W3)**	3,200,000	4,800,000	6,400,000
Fixed costs:			
· **indirect labour (W4)**	2,500,000	2,500,000	2,500,000
· **overheads (W5)**	6,300,000	6,300,000	6,300,000
Total cost	21,600,000	28,000,000	34,400,000
Cost per unit $\left(\frac{\text{Total cost}}{\text{Units made}}\right)$	21.60	18.67	17.20

Workings

(W1) **Direct materials**

Direct materials variable cost per unit = $\frac{£5,000,000}{1,000,000 \text{ units}}$

= £5 per unit

Direct materials cost – 1,500,000 units = 1,500,000 units x £5 per unit

= £7,500,000

Direct materials cost – 2,000,000 units = 2,000,000 units x £5 per unit

= £10,000,000

(W2) **Direct labour**

Direct labour variable cost per unit = $\frac{£4,600,000}{1,000,000 \text{ units}}$

= £4.60 per unit

Direct labour cost – 1,500,000 units = 1,500,000 units x £4.60 per unit

= £6,900,000

Direct labour cost – 2,000,000 units = 2,000,000 units x £4.60 per unit

= £9,200,000

(W3) **Overheads**

Overheads variable cost per unit = $\frac{£3,200,000}{1,000,000 \text{ units}}$

= £3.20 per unit

Overheads cost – 1,500,000 units = 1,500,000 units x £3.20 per unit

= £4,800,000

Overheads cost – 2,000,000 units = 2,000,000 x £3.20 per unit
= £6,400,000

(W4) **Indirect labour** is a fixed cost and is therefore unaffected by different levels of activity.

(W5) **Overheads** are also a fixed cost and are therefore unaffected by different levels of activity.

(b) Cost of 1,000,000 units $= \dfrac{£21{,}600{,}000}{1{,}000{,}000 \text{ units}}$

= £21.60 per unit

The *£21,600,000* can be analysed as follows:

Cost	*Total*	*Cost per unit*
	£	£
Variable	12,800,000 (÷ 1,000,000)	12.80
Fixed	8,800,000 (÷ 1,000,000)	8.80
		21.60

Cost of 1,500,000 units $= \dfrac{28{,}000{,}000}{1{,}5000{,}000}$ = £18.67 per unit

The £28,000,000 can be analysed as follows:

Cost	Total	Cost per unit
	£	£
Variable	19,200,000 (÷ 1,500,000)	12.80
Fixed	8,800,000 (÷ 1,500,000)	5.87
		18.67

We can see that the variable cost per unit does not vary with activity; it is constant at £12.80 per unit. The fixed cost per unit (in the short term), however, falls as more units are produced (from £8.80 per unit to £5.87 per unit). It is for this reason that the cost per unit falls as the activity level increases.

(c) It is not very realistic to assume that all production cost are either variable or fixed. Marginal cost accounting, however, identifies costs as being either fixed or variable in order to assist in short-term decision-making problems.

In reality, most costs are semi-variable (mixed) costs, that is to say that they have both fixed and variable elements. An example of another way that costs can behave is therefore semi-variable, for example, telephone charges. Telephone charges include a fixed element (the standing/quarterly charge) and a variable element (based on the cost of an individual call).

Task 2.2

	B (£)	*C* (£)	*Total* (£)
Unit selling price	10	12	
Less unit variable costs			
Direct materials	2.00	3.00	
Direct labour	2.50	3.50	
Variable overheads	3.00	2.00	
Contribution per unit	2.50	3.50	
Sales volume (units)	500,000	750,000	
Total contribution	1,250,000	2,625,000	3,875,000
Less: fixed costs			3,450,000
Budgeted profit or loss			425,000

Workings

(W1) **Unit selling price**

Unit selling price $= \frac{\text{Sales revenue}}{\text{Units made and sold}}$

Product B $= \frac{£5,000,000}{500,000} = £10$ per unit

Product C $= \frac{£9,000,000}{750,000} = £12$ per unit

(W2) **Direct materials**

Direct materials cost per unit $= \frac{\text{Direct materials cost}}{\text{Units made and sold}}$

Product B $= \frac{£1,000,000}{500,000} = £2$ per unit

Product C $= \frac{£2,250,000}{750,000} = £3$ per unit

(W3) **Direct labour**

Direct labour cost per unit $= \frac{\text{Direct labour cost}}{\text{Units made and sold}}$

Product B $= \frac{£1,250,000}{500,000} = £2.50$ per unit

Product C $= \frac{£2,625,000}{750,000} = £3.50$ per unit

(W4) **Variable overheads**

Variable overheads cost per unit $= \frac{\text{Variable overheads cost}}{\text{Units made and sold}}$

Product B $= \dfrac{£1,500,000}{500,000} = £3$ per unit

Product C $= \dfrac{£1,500,000}{750,000} = £2$ per unit

(W5) Contribution per unit = selling price – unit variable costs
Product B = £(10 – 2 – 2.50 – 3) = £2.50
Product C = £(12 – 3 – 3.50 – 2) = £3.50

Task 2.3

(a)

Product	*B*	*C*
Fixed costs (£)	1,000,000	2,450,000
Unit contribution (£)	2.50	3.50
Breakeven sales (units) (W1)	400,000	700,000
Forecast sales (units)	480,000	910,000
Margin of safety (units) (W2)	80,000	210,000
Margin of safety (%) (W3)	16.67%	23.08%

Workings

(W1) Breakeven sales $= \dfrac{\text{Fixed costs}}{\text{Unit contribution}}$

Product B $= \dfrac{£1,000,000}{£2.50} = 400,000$ units

Product C $= \dfrac{£2,450,000}{£3.50} = 700,000$ units

(W2) Margin of safety (in units) = Budgeted sales units – Breakeven sales units
Product B = 480,000 – 400,000 = 80,000
Product C = 910,000 – 700,000 = 210,000

(W3) Margin of safety (%) $= \dfrac{\text{Margin of safety}}{\text{Budgeted sales units}} \times 100\%$

Product B $= \dfrac{80,000}{480,000} \times 100\% = 16.67\%$

Product C $= \dfrac{210,000}{910,000} \times 100\% = 23.08\%$

(b) The term 'percentage margin of safety' shows the amount by which the budgeted (forecast) sales can fall before the business makes a loss. It can be expressed in absolute units or relative percentage terms.

Margin of safety (%) = $\frac{\text{Margin of safety (units)}}{\text{Budgeted sales (units)}}$ x 100%

In this task, the percentage margin of safety shows that sales (in units) of Product B could fall by 16.67% before it would make a loss. Product C, on the other hand, has a percentage margin of safety of 23.08% which means that sales (in units) of this product could fall by 23.08% before Product C would make a loss.

Task 2.4

Product	*B*	*C*	*Total*
Contribution/unit (£)	2.50	3.50	
Machine hours/unit	2.00	5.00	
Contribution/machine hr (£)	1.25	0.70	
Product ranking	1st	2nd	
Machine hours available			3,500,000
Machine hours allocated to: **Product B (W3)** **Product C (W4)**	1,000,000	2,500,000	
Total contribution earned (£)	1,250,000	1,750,000	3,000,000
Less: fixed costs (£)			3,450,000
Profit/loss made (£)			(450,000)

Workings

(W1) Machine hours per unit = $\frac{\text{Machine hours required}}{\text{Units made and sold}}$

Product B = $\frac{1,000,000}{500,000} = 2$

Product C = $\frac{3,750,000}{750,000} = 5$

(W2) Products are ranked according to the amount of contribution earned per unit of limiting factor, i.e. £1.25 is higher than £0.70 so Product B is ranked first.

(W3) The maximum number of units of Product B should be made, i.e. 500,000 units which require 1,000,000 machine hours (therefore leaving 3,500,000 – 1,000,000 = 2,500,000 machine hours available for the production of Product B).

(W4) Machine hours available for production of Product C = 2,500,000. Machine hours per unit of Product C = 5.

$\therefore$ number of units produced with 2,500,000 machine hours = $\frac{2,500,000}{5}$

= 500,000

(W5) Total contribution earned = number of units made and sold ´ contribution per unit
Product B = 500,000 units x £2.50 = £1,250,000
Product C = 500,000 units x £3.50 = £1,750,000

Task 2.5

(a) Net Present Value

	Year 0 *£000*	*Year 1* *£000*	*Year 2* *£000*	*Year 3* *£000*
Capital expenditure	(1,500)			
Sales income		700	800	1,000
Operating costs		(200)	(250)	(300)
Net cash flows	(1,500)	500	550	700
P/V factors	1.0000	0.893	0.797	0.712
Discounted cash flows	(1,500)	446.5	438.35	498.4
Net Present Value	(116.75)			

Net Present Value = –1,500 + 446.5 + 438.35 +498.4
= –116.75

(b) Payback period

Time	*Cash flow*	*Cumulative position*	*Working*
£000	£000		
t = 0	(1,500)	(1,500)	
t = 1	500	(1,000)	(1,500) + 500
t = 2	550	(450)	(1,000) + 550
t = 3	700	250	(450) + 700

The payback period is between two and three years.

The project has repaid all but £450,000 by the end of year 2. This £450,000 will be repaid at the following point in year 3.

$\frac{450,000}{700,000}$ x 12 months = 7.7 months (approximately 8 months)

The profit will be completely repaid after 2 years and 8 months.

Task 2.6

REPORT

To: Management Accountant
From: Accounting Technician
Subject: Investment Appraisal
Date: 1 December 2004

(a) Net Present Value of proposed new product = – £116,830 (negative)
Payback period = 2 years 8 months

On the basis of the negative NPV, the introduction of this product should not be recommended.

On the basis of the payback period, the new product does not appear to be viable since it only has a three-year life. Even though the payback period is less than the life expectancy of the product, this project does not appear to be worthwhile.

(b) The Internal Rate of Return (IRR) is another method of investment appraisal which might also have been used to assess this proposal.

(c) Commercial factors relevant to this decision:

- whether the expected life of Product D could be extended
- other competitors in Product D's market
- risks involved in undertaking this project
- how accurate the predicted future cash flows are
- how the sales of Product D will affect the sales of the other products produced by Delta Ltd.

GLOSSARY

Term	Description
Abnormal gain	The amount by which normal loss exceeds actual loss.
Abnormal loss	The amount by which actual loss exceeds normal loss.
Absorption costing	Stock units are valued at variable cost plus fixed production overheads absorbed using a pre-determined absorption rate.
Batch costing	The costing system used for a business where production is made up of different product batches of identical units.
Bonus scheme	A day rate combined with a bonus based on output achieved.
Breakeven point	The level of activity required to make no profit and no loss.
Buffer stock	Stock held to cover variations in: – lead time, and – demand during the lead time. Sometimes defined as 'stock held in excess of average units demanded in average lead time'.
Capital expenditure	Expenditure on the purchase or improvement of fixed assets, appearing in the balance sheet.
Contribution	Sales revenue less variable cost of sales.
Cost absorption	The charging of overhead costs to cost units.
Cost accounting	The analysis of costs and revenues to provide useful information to assist the management accounting function.
Cost allocation	The charging of overhead costs to the specific cost centre that incurred them.
Cost apportionment	The splitting of shared overhead costs between relevant cost centres using an appropriate basis.
Cost centre	A location, function, activity or item of equipment in respect of which costs are accumulated.
Cost coding	The allocation of a unique code to costs, usually on the source documentation, to allow accurate and detailed analysis.
Cost unit	An individual unit of product or service for which costs can be separately ascertained.
Cost-volume-profit (CVP) analysis	Analysis of the effects of changes of volume on contribution and profit.
Depreciation	An annual internal charge to the profit and loss account that spreads the net cost of a fixed asset over the number of years of its useful life.

Term	Description
Depreciation	An annual internal charge to the profit and loss account that spreads the net cost of a fixed asset over the number of years of its useful life.
Direct costs	Costs that can be related directly to a cost unit.
Direct expenses	Expenses that can be related specifically to a cost centre.
Discounted cash flow	An investment appraisal technique which discounts future cash flows to a present value.
Economic batch quantity (EBQ)	To minimise the total of the inventory costs.
Economic order quantity (EOQ)	The quantity to be ordered/produced.
Equivalent unit	The number of whole units to which a partially completed unit is equivalent (= physical units x percentage completion).
Expenses	Items of expenditure that are not labour or materials related.
FIFO	A method of valuing issues of stock that assumes that issues are made from the oldest stock available (First In First Out).
Financial accounting	The production of an historic record of transactions presented in a standard format for use by parties external to the business.
Fixed costs	Costs that vary with time, not activity level.
Idle time	Paid for, but non-productive, hours.
Integrated bookkeeping system	A bookkeeping system whereby ledger accounts are kept that provide the necessary information for both costing and financial accounting.
Internal rate of return	The rate of interest which will cause the stream of cash flows discounted at that rate of interest to have a nil net present value.
Job costing	The costing system used for a business where production is made up of individual, different, large jobs.
Key factor analysis	The technique of allocating resources between products according to contribution per unit of resource.
Lead time	The time between an order for goods being placed and the receipt of that order.
LIFO	A method of valuing issues of stock that assumes that issues are made from the newest stock available (Last In First Out).
Management accounting	The generation, presentation and interpretation of historic, budgeted and forecast information for management for the purposes of planning, control and decision-making.

Term	Description
Margin of safety	The amount by which the level of activity can fall below budget before a loss is made.
Marginal costing	Stock units are valued at variable production cost; fixed overheads are accounted for as period costs.
Normal loss	The level of expected loss of input from a process.
Over/under absorption (recovery)	Where the amount of overhead absorbed into cost units, using the pre-determined absorption rate, is more/less than the overheads actually incurred.
P/V (C/S) ratio	The ratio of contribution to sales value.
Payback period	The amount of time it takes for an investment project to recover the cash cost of the original investment.
Piecework rates	Where a constant fixed amount is paid per unit of output.
Present value	The value at today's date of an amount of cash received/paid at some time in the future, taking account of the compound interest earned over the relevant period.
Re-order level	The quantity of stock in hand at the time when a new order is placed.
Re-order quantity	The quantity of stock ordered. (Be careful to distinguish between re-order level and re-order quantity.)
Revenue expenditure	Expenditure on goods and services that will be charged to the profit and loss account.
Secondary apportionment	The re-apportionment of service cost centres' overhead costs to production cost centres.
Semi-variable costs	Costs with both a fixed and variable element.
Stock control	The method of ensuring that the right quantity of the right quality of stock is available at the right time and the right place.
Stock control levels	Key stock quantities that assist in stock control, including re-order level, economic order quantity (EOQ), minimum and maximum stock levels.
Stock-outs	Occasions when one or more items of stock are needed but there are none in stock.
Stores record card	A record kept for each stock line, detailing receipts, issues and balance on hand, in terms of both physical quantities and monetary value.
Timesheet	A record of how an employee has spent his/her time, split between jobs/clients and non-productive time.
Usage	The quantity of items required for sale (in the case of goods for resale) or production (in the case of components or raw materials) in a given period.
Variable costs	Costs that vary in direct proportion to the level of activity.

Term	Description
Weighted average cost	A method of valuing issues of stock that takes account of the relative quantities of stock available purchased at different prices.

INDEX

R

S

T

U

V

W